Television Sports Production

TELEVISION SPORTS PRODUCTION

Fourth Edition

by Jim Owens

Asbury College

ELSEVIER

AMSTERDAM • BOSTON • HEIDELBERG • LONDON
NEW YORK • OXFORD • PARIS • SAN DIEGO
SAN FRANCISCO • SINGAPORE • SYDNEY • TOKYO
Focal Press is an imprint of Elsevier

Focal
Press

Acquisitions Editor: Elinor Actipis
Project Manager: Dawnmarie Simpson
Associate Acquisitions Editor: Cara Anderson
Marketing Manager: Christine Degon Veroulis
Cover Design: Eric DeCicco

Focal Press is an imprint of Elsevier
30 Corporate Drive, Suite 400, Burlington, MA 01803, USA
Linacre House, Jordan Hill, Oxford OX2 8DP, UK

Library of Congress Cataloging-in-Publication Data
Owens, Jim, 1957-
     Television sports production / Jim Owens. -- 4th ed.
         p. cm.
     Includes index.
     ISBN-13: 978-0-240-80916-8 (pbk. : alk. paper)
     ISBN-10: 0-240-80916-5 (pbk. : alk. paper) 1. Television broadcasting of sports. 2.
Television--Production and direction. I. Title.
     GV742.3.O84 2007
     070.4'497960973--dc22

                                                         2006026784

British Library Cataloguing-in-Publication Data
A catalogue record for this book is available from the British Library.

ISBN 13: 978-0-240-916-8
ISBN 10: 0-240-80916-5

For information on all Focal Press publications
visit our website at www.books.elsevier.com

08 09 10   10 9 8 7 6 5 4 3 2

Printed in the United States of America

CONTENTS

Football (Soccer)
Motorcycle Road Race
Tennis

Appendix IV   **Microphone Diagrams** 223
Baseball
Basketball
Football (Soccer)
Tennis

Appendix V   **Event Storyboards** 233
Opening Ceremony XIX Olympic Winter Games

Appendix VI   **Intercom Diagrams** 241
Small-scale Production Intercom System
Medium-scale Production Intercom System
Large-scale Production Intercom System

Appendix VII   **Lighting Plan** 245

                Sources and Recommended Readings 255

                Glossary 261

                Index 275

FOREWORD

With a presence in nearly every nation, television broadcasting has become one of the most influential means of communicating to the world at large. Through advancements in remote television production, it has become possible for billions of people around the world to get the "best seat in the house" at the greatest events in the history of sport without leaving the comfort of their own homes. From the kick-off of the World Cup, to the final pitch of the World Series, to the triumphs of Olympic competition, live sport broadcasting captivates viewers and makes them a part of the action.

Many factors can affect the coverage of a remote sport event, including weather, lighting, and natural sound. A successful production relies on extensive planning, taking into account location, budget, technology, and the intricacies of the sport itself. More importantly, the people selected for the production crew have the greatest impact on the overall success of the production.

This publication provides a broad overview of how to successfully plan and implement a remote television production. You will find detailed descriptions of the types of mobile units/OB vans, cameras, audio equipment, and lighting requirements used to produce live or taped coverage of sport events. You will learn about different types of sport action and different techniques used by producers and directors to capture the essence of each sport.

I would like to thank the many contributors to this publication and, as you explore the contents, I hope you will find Television Sports Production to be a useful resource.

Manolo Romero, President
International Sports Broadcasting

ACKNOWLEDGMENTS

Many people generously provided their expertise and support for this project. We would like to thank the following contributors:

Editorial: Hank Levine, Mark Parkman, Linda Parker, and Kathy Bruner

Technical and Production Assistance: James Angio, Larry Auman, Iain Logie Baird, Dennis Baxter, Greg Breckel, Steven Brill, Anna Chrysou, Helen Borobokas-Grinter, Keith Brown, John Bruner, Craig Cornwell, Ron Crockett, Chad Crouch, Darryl Cummings, Thom Curran, Peter Diamond, Pat Dixon, Brian Douglas, Yiannis Exarchos, Mike Edwards, Kent Farnsworth, Pem Farnsworth, Gabriel Fehervari, Steve Fleming, Haik Gazarian, Tom Genova, Marsha Groome, Mike Hampton, Michael Hartman, Mike Hasselbeck, Lytle Hoover, Mike Jakob, Chris Jensen, Kostas Kapatais, Sue Keith, Dimitris Koukoubanis, Joe Kusic, John Lawler, David Lewis, Joseph Maar, Alexander Magoun, Rachael Masters, Dan MacLellan, Bryan McDougal, Steve McVoy, Gary Milkis, Don Mink, Mark Orgera, Maria Persechino-Romero, Jeffrey Phillips, The Poynter Institute, Ed Reitan, Steve Restelli, Scott Rogers, Ursula Romero, Andy Rosenberg, Pedro Rozas, Josep Rubies, Joe Sidoli, Don Slonski, Donald Slouffman, Kristin Spiessens, Ralph Strader, Meg Streeter, David Rodriguez, Dave Schoemaker, Ryan Soucy, Keith Southwick, Sportscliche.com/tv, Matthew Straeb, Curt Wallin, Doug Walker, Mark Wallace, David Warnock, Adam Wilson, WLWT, Dan Wolfe, and David Worley,

Layout and Design: Teri Jarrard

Photographs/Illustrations: ABC News, Alphacam, Asbury College, Audio-Technica, Auman Museum of Radio & Television, Dennis Baxter, John Bruner, Dartfish, Fischer Connectors, Flying Cam, Gyron Systems International, International Olympic Committee, Lemo Connectors, Lighting Design Group, Gary Milkis, Miranda Technologies, Mountain Mobile Television, NBC Olympics Inc., ORAD Hi-Tec Systems Ltd., RF Central, Manolo Romero, Rycote, David Sarnoff Library, Shook Electronics USA, Shure Incorporated, Sportvision, Swe Dish Wahlberg Selin and Vinten Camera Support Systems, Telex Communications, Temple University Archives, and Visage-HD,

Text Illustrations: Lynn Owens, Katie Brandt, and Teri Jarrard

Special thanks to Asbury College

PREFACE

The first live television coverage of a sports event, utilizing electronic cameras, is thought to be the 1936 Berlin Olympics. The monstrous camera, almost 7½ feet (2.3 m) long, was dubbed the "television canon." The camera could be used only when the sun was shining. Since home televisions were not yet popular, eight specially installed television viewing rooms, known as Fernsehstuben, were built around the venue so that people could see the television coverage. The telecast covered four venues, utilized a total of three television cameras, and shot a total of 72 hours of live transmission during the Berlin Games. In addition to the electronic cameras, a special film camera mounted on the top of a van equipped with film developing facilities was used to produce delayed television signals. In this process, known as the "intermediate film" system, scenes were shot on film, and this was immediately developed and scanned. In Berlin, news films of the Games were rushed to the United States by Zeppelin airships.

A History of Television, Broadcasting the Olympics *and*
Television in the Olympic Games: The New Era

The development of television broadcasting has had a major impact on the way sporting events are viewed around the world. While the stadium can host thousands of spectators in the stands, television broadcasts reach millions more who are unable to attend. Television provides a unique perspective unavailable to most spectators in the stands. Using advanced technology, specialty equipment, and production techniques, the television broadcast has become the best seat in the house. The majority of this coverage occurs through remote television productions.

Remote productions, or multi-camera outside broadcasts, occur on a daily basis around the world, from news events to parades, pageants to award programs, and concerts to sports.

In this handbook we will focus on the sports remote production. Concepts important to a

> **Television Quality—1936 Olympic Games**
> *The German television picture with 180 lines and 25 frames per second attains a remarkable picture quality.*
>
> **Television in Germany**, the official program of the 1936 Olympic television coverage

The Beginning of Commercial Olympic Television

Experimentation with television at the 1936 Berlin Games and the release of Leni Riefenstahl's two-part Olympia documentary marked the first intrusion of the moving image into the Olympics. For the next Games in 1948, the London Olympic organizing committee charged the BBC 1500 pounds to telecast the event. But when the 1956 Melbourne organizing committee attempted to sell television rights to the Games, broadcast networks in the United States and Europe boycotted the Games, demanding the same access without charge that radio and newsreels had always enjoyed in covering the Olympics as news not entertainment.

The result was that only six pre-recorded, half-hour programs of features and highlights were presented on a scattering of independent stations in the United States. Following that controversy, the International Olympic Committee (IOC) in 1958 passed a new regulation establishing that the local organizing committee shall sell rights with the approval of the IOC. With that policy, the principle of commercial Olympic television was established, and the Olympics would never again be the same.

Michael Real, Television Quarterly

Olympic Syndrome

Data proves the massive interest of Japanese for the Olympic Games. Even though a lot of competitions were broadcast late at night, all white-collar workers waited in front of their screens to watch them, and were literally sleeping in their offices the day after. This phenomenon was even called the "Olympic Syndrome", with the national productivity going down during the Games."

Hisashi Hieda, CEO, Fuji TV, Japan

Television Sports Failures

If sport is not working on TV, is not attracting an audience, is languishing, the problem lies with the people controlling that sport. They have either failed to keep that sport vital and alive, through laziness or mismanagement, or they have allowed people presenting their sport to the public through television to get away with sloppy, lazy or inattentive production.

David Hill, *Chairman & CEO*
Fox Sports Television

sports remote can be adapted to all other types of remote productions since they all use much the same equipment and personnel. Coverage strategies may differ but the concepts are still the same.

Of all the different types of remotes, why focus on sport? Sporting events are the most popular type of television program. In the United States, historically half of the programs attaining the largest viewing audience are sports programs.

The viewing audience for the 2000 Olympic Games was estimated at nearly 35 billion cumulative people *(Sydney Uplink)*. Dick Pound, International Olympic Committee member, stated that it is calculated that an unprecedented 9 out of 10 individuals on the planet with access to a television watched some part of the [Sydney] Olympics. Viewing of the 2000 Olympic broadcast ranged from an average four hours per viewer in some markets, to more than 37 hours per viewer in Japan and 49 hours per viewer in Australia. David Hill, CEO of Fox Sports, says that "Sport is part of the fabric of society, its the ultimate reality show, and it's the only form of programming guaranteed to attract huge audiences."

Television sports are often broadcast live. If the director misses a lay-up during a basketball game, they can't redo it. Some things, such as commentary, can be reworked in post-production, but the action is live. That means the television broadcast has to be done right the first time, with no retakes, and it has to be done with quality. This live event pressure makes television sport one of the most difficult, if not the most difficult, type of television production.

Sport productions can exist on a very small scale, such as two cameras at a local basketball game shown on cable, as compared to 41 cameras at the Super Bowl or 400 cameras at a multievent Olympic Games.

Throughout this book you will find real-life examples from a variety of events, such as the Olympic Games, World Cup Football, the Super Bowl, the Goodwill Games, the Indianapolis 500, and others, with an emphasis primarily on the larger events. Our hope is that these examples will allow you to adapt the plans outlined to the football game that you are covering with four cameras or any other sporting event.

This is not a stand-alone guide to television production. Our goal was to create a book or text that supplements other existing television production handbooks (see recommended readings). We wanted to provide an overview of the various aspects of the television remote production industry. However, some basic production material has also been covered in an attempt to get everyone to the same level.

A multi-camera remote production is like a symphony. It is not a solo effort. The director is the conductor, juggling the various components, relying on an incredibly talented crew, to create a production that allows the audience to feel as though they are at the event and as though they have participated.

This is a process style manual. It covers the planning, pre-production and set-up, the production and, finally, post-production, and everything that goes with each of those phases. The emphasis has been placed on how the production goes together, not on specific skills or equipment. That means that some information (such as cameras) will be included multiple times throughout the text.

Beyond familiar production terminology, remote productions sometimes have their own language, definitions, and unique equipment. Our goal is to give you an inside view of how a remote production goes together and the role of each participant.

The Host Broadcast of the Olympics

Every Olympic Games has a Host Broadcaster who is responsible for the unbiased radio and television coverage of every sport event, press conference, and other official Olympic event. The Host Broadcaster's coverage is called the international signal or world feed. Rights Holding Broadcasters take the feed and determine if, or how, they will use it. If they believe the event is of national interest, they will fit it into their broadcast schedule. Broadcasters have the right to alter it, add commentary, insert pre-produced interviews or other stories and add graphics. The goal is for the Broadcaster to make it more interesting specifically for the viewers in their countries. Just as taste and styles are different from country to country, so is the interest in sport.

...to say that the televised Olympics—along with the Super Bowl, the Oscars, the World Cup, and other super-events—play a leading role in celebrating and shaping our global culture is to begin to approach a realistic sense of television's complex place in the world of today.

Michael Real, Television Quarterly

PART 1:
Introduction to Remote Production

CHAPTER 1
What Is Remote Production?

Why live? Live events are the core of TV. They are the one thing TV can do that no other medium can match. There are things movies can do better. There are things radio can do better. But no other medium can bring you a visual report of an event as it's happening. TV makes everyone part of history.

Tony Verna, *Director,* 5 Super Bowls and 12 Kentucky Derbys *and*
Live TV: An Inside Look at Directing and Producing

Remote or outside broadcast (OB) production can be defined as a multi-camera production occurring outside of a studio context. Remotes come in all sizes. A small remote may consist of a two-camera production operating out of a small production mini-van. A big remote may include 20 or more cameras including a blimp shot and point-of-view (POV) specialty cameras.

The key to a quality production is to assemble a team that can predict what is going to happen and where it is going to happen. It is important to build a crew that will work well together. The crew must understand how the event will unfold and how best to apply their television-related skills. Key to those predictive skills is the ability to plan for contingencies in case something goes wrong.

The more familiar the crew is with the event, the better they can cover it. Understanding the intricacies of the event allows the director and talent to clearly communicate what is happening on the field of play, allows the audio people to know how to set microphones for the event, and gives camera operators the ability to predict how they should be moving their cameras. Some people are specialists who work only at specific types of events. For instance a producer may specialize in figure skating events.

> **The Remote**
> *The remote broadcast environment challenges you personally and professionally in every which way; mentally, physically, technically, creatively, and in more ways than can be imagined.*
>
> **Peteris Saltans,**
> Audio Broadcast Engineer & Mixer

Today, many events are covered by live remotes. Live events grab the viewers' attention and help them feel as though they are witnessing history as it happens. The crew is also impacted by a live event. With no way to edit their work, there is a palpable need to get it right the first time. The result is a heightened sense of teamwork and concern for quality. Without adequate preparation, "live" can also kill the broadcast production.

Live versus Live-to-Tape

Remote productions can take a number of different forms. Most remote productions utilize a mobile production unit outfitted with live switching gear, recorders, graphics, and space for the crew. However, some sport productions can be covered with multiple electronic news gathering (ENG) cameras. In this case the entire production must be edited in post-production. While live switching is faster, it requires an expensive remote unit, more equipment, longer set-up time, and more crew members. Multiple ENG cameras require an expensive post-production facility and take more time in the post-production process, but in the end are generally less expensive.

Remote versus Studio Production

While the studio can provide the director with the most control over the situation, the advantage to a remote production is the ability to capture the event as it is happening. Producers involved in the event from the beginning may be able to help select the event location so that the best visual background for the event is obtained. At times it is less expensive to shoot in the field than in a studio setting; sometimes it is easier than scheduling studio time.

Weather can be one of the biggest disadvantages to an outside remote because bad weather will often mean cancelling the event.

In the studio you have ultimate control over sound and light, but in the field they can become the biggest problems. On a remote, the production is dependent on people who don't necessarily understand the production process, such as police and venue management/technical personnel.

The mobile unit's size may cause traffic problems, or parking spaces may not be available for the crew who are close to the mobile unit. A portable generator may be required to provide power or even backup power. If the production is occurring far from the home base, management has to be concerned with food, lodging, and transportation for the crew, which can add considerable expense to the production costs.

Often location permits are required for a crew to shoot in remote situations. Obtaining those permits can be a time-consuming process.

When the advantages of a remote production outweigh the disadvantages then you hit the road, with crew and equipment in tow.

CHAPTER 2
Personnel

The producer has the final word on all matters—but don't tell that to the director or talent; most think they do.

Joseph Maar & Rom Rosenblum

Understanding how the remote production goes together requires the understanding of the role of each of the participants, their responsibilities and how they interact. Responsibilities vary with the production company, station, network, and event. People are often required to wear multiple hats in a production.

Additionally, the name of production functions may vary from company to company. While it is difficult to give a definitive description of each position, the following is a brief description of the most common roles within a remote sports crew.

Figure 2.1: The director and producer giving an overview of the production to their crew.

Personnel Descriptions

I've always maintained that with the right crew (producer, director, play-by-play commentator, and analyst) you can make a toenail clipping competition riveting television. With the wrong crew you can make an FA Cup boring.
—David Hill, CEO of Fox Sports Television, Australia

Executive Producer: Responsible for the planning and logistics of one production or a series of productions. Gives overall vision for a production or a series of productions. The Executive Producer's responsibilities generally include finance, scheduling, and sometimes major creative decisions. Negotiating with sport organizations on rights, camera placement, and coverage is often

The Producer
Producers give the sportscast its viewpoint, its flavor. The best producers are master painters, Picassos or Rembrandts. The mechanics of their profession – the hows and whens to use different brush strokes – are second nature to them so they are able to rise to another level, combining the individual strokes to create a masterpiece that interprets the world in a unique way. The best producers have the mechanics down cold so they are free to develop a storyline, using the talents of the broadcast crew as their brushes. Good producers have three common characteristics:
(1) they are organized;
(2) they are cool under pressure; and
(3) they respect and support the broadcast team working with them.

Call of the Game

The Sports Director's Role

Directors must understand the way in which viewers watch television: how they think, feel, and want to be entertained. This means that the director must find ways to capture the viewer's interest. This is best done by doing thorough homework and proper storytelling: the two keys to better coverage.

Homework

By homework we mean not only getting acquainted with the venue, the organizers, and the tools of television production, but also exploring the sport itself. The director's preparation should include in-depth research into the key players: the athletes. Beyond the athlete's names, it is crucial to identify them and their potential. The director must know not only the favorites and the defending champions, but also those athletes with their last shot at a win, recovering from an injury or showing exceptional nerve at a major event.

All of this forms the most important part of production planning, because it hints at, or even reveals, how the event will unfold during the competition. Only then do the start lists begin to make sense. Only then there is solid ground to draft the potential story and decide how to tell it with cameras and microphones.

Storytelling

The viewer expects and demands to be entertained. To do this, we must touch his or her feelings. We must realize that only when a viewer chooses an athlete as a favorite, and identifies with him or her, do the athlete's rivals become a threat.

In his book Poetics*, Aristotle (384–322 B.C.) explained the fundamentals of storytelling. In order to capture the viewer's emotions, he said, a story should contain three parts: the beginning, the middle, and the end. This formula perfectly suits athletics. In athletics the beginning includes the heats of the track events and the qualifications for field event. Here the favorites must be highlighted so that the viewer can recognize them. This is achieved at the cost of other athletes, who appear less in the pictures. This is very important, because, as Aristotle puts it, if we do not know the player, what may happen to him later makes no difference. In the first part of the story, the ingredients are planted in order to evoke expectations. The viewer enjoys the feelings of excitement and suspense that are connected with this anticipation.*

The middle part includes the semifinals and finals of track events and the finals of field events. These are the highlights of the event: the battle for the medals. The competition should be filmed in an intelligible way, without missing any essential incidents. A viewer anywhere in the world must be able to comprehend both the competition itself and the story line. The middle part ends with a climax: as the final of each event concludes, everything becomes clear.

The third section, the end, covers the euphoria of victory and the disappointment of defeat. This part also includes a motivated step back to analyze the race or field event final.

The Viewer's Position

In watching sporting events, particularly athletics, the viewer looks into the depth of the picture. He or she picks out objects of interest from this depth, normally the key athletes of the event. The viewer is reluctant to lose visual contact with his or her favorite. The viewer also participates in the coverage, in effect using the mind as a camera. There is pleasure in mentally zooming, panning, and tilting in the view of a camera shot. The producer and director need to understand this when cutting between cameras. Rapid cutting without any clear motivation irritates the viewer, as visual contact with a favorite competitor may be lost and has to be reestablished. Unnecessary slow-motion replays have the same effect. Furthermore, the filming plan should allocate the viewer the best seats in the stands. These angles should be maintained through the event. The cutting must answer three questions for the viewer. First: where are we or which event? Second: which athlete? Third: how is this athlete doing in relation to his or her rivals?

This approach to directing sports leads to good storytelling, as the reality of the competition becomes entertaining. The target should always be the viewer's mind.

Adapted from
Kalevi Uusivuori & Tapani Parm,
Producer/Directors, YLE television network, Finland

the responsibility of the executive producer. The executive producer may oversee a number of producers or coordinating producers.

Coordinating Producer: Keeps track of budgets, quality control, and logistics for multiple producers. The coordinating producer may also be responsible for the overall look and elements, such as animation and graphics. Reports to the executive producer or the head of production.

Producer: Responsible for planning and logistics before the event. The producer works with the director to implement the overall production plan. Together they are responsible for overseeing all elements of the production of an event. During the production the producer is responsible for coordinating the commercials, calling the replays, and making sure that the needs of the talent are met, in addition to keeping the production within budget and on schedule. Reports to the executive producer, coordinating producer or head of production.

Associate Producer/Assistant Producer (AP): The AP is given specific producing responsibilities by the producer or executive producer. This person often supervises post-production and/or the production of edited video packages and teases that appear within a production. The associate producer may be assigned some of the same responsibilities as the associate director. This person is sometimes called a features producer. Reports to the producer.

Features Producer: See Associate Producer.

Director: Under the guidance of the producer, responsible for the creative and aesthetic portions of the production. Directors must know what they want and how they are going to accomplish it. To coordinate the various aspects of the broadcast, they have to understand the capabilities of the equipment and the crew they have been assigned. The director sets the tone and pace of the production and serves as crew motivator. The director must be able to visually tell the story, to document the event in a way that allows the viewers to feel as if they are part of the action. Occasionally, they

---

Preparing for the Game

Ultimately the key to NBC's successful basketball playoff coverage lies not so much with its equipment and technology as it does with the mental preparation of the director and crew. Our coverage really begins by spending time with the players, coaches, and announcers, learning what the stories are and studying the game. I'm watching NBA basketball literally every night of the week during the season, learning about the players, their moves, their team's style of play. People say, "Oh you just work during the broadcast" but I'll prep all week for that broadcast and I'm prepping the whole season for the playoffs.

Andy Rosenberg, Director, NBC

Creating Magic

For all the engineering, operations, and production services planning that [go] into an Olympics, we only provide the tools for production guys to come in and create the magic. It takes the production guys and the people in front of the camera and us behind the camera to pull of a successful telecast.

David Mazza,
NBC Olympic Vice President of Engineering

Hiring Personnel

When we hire, we are looking for more than just the most qualified people we can find. We need people who understand how their role fits into the bigger picture, who respect the fact that they maybe a guest in different culture, and who are adaptable and can work under pressure in a fast-paced, unforgiving and constantly changing environment. People who can meet these qualifications will be successful in television sports production.

Hank Levine, Executive Vice President of
Administration, International Sports Broadcasting

are also responsible for working with and directing the talent, although this is rare during a sport production. Reports to the producer.

Associate Director/Assistant Director (AD): Assists the director during the television production by keeping track of timing and making sure that camera shots, graphics, and videotapes are ready for the director's cue. One of the major responsibilities of the AD is to maintain constant communication with the studio, coordinating commercial breaks by numerically counting back timing cues in order to smoothly segue between two entities. This person may be assigned some of the same responsibilities that an associate producer performs. Generally reports to the director and the producer.

Unit Manager: Handles budgetary operations, including outside vendors and overtime. The unit manager also handles crew scheduling. This position is sometimes merged with the production manager and/or the technical manager. Reports to the producer.

Production Manager/Operations Producer: Oversees the operation of the production team, including budgets, personnel assignments, transportation, accommodation, coordinating transmission information, and acts as liaison with the venue. Sometimes this job is merged with the unit manager and/or the technical manager. Generally reports to the producer.

Production Coordinator: Responsible for general operations, such as catering, petty cash, runners, credentials, and phones. This position is sometimes merged with production manager. The production coordinator reports to the production manager, technical manager, unit manager or producer.

Stage Manager/Floor Manager: Coordinates everything occurring in the studio or broadcast booth. The stage manager communicates with hand signals when the talent is on camera and sometimes communicates via cards when off camera. Generally reports to the producer but may report to the director in a remote production. *(See figure 2.2.)*

Figure 2.2: The stage manager (middle) coordinates everything with the talent in the field, broadcast booth or studio.

Production Assistant (PA)/Director's Assistant: Handles details for the producer and/or director. These details may include, but are not limited to, overseeing travel arrangements, graphics, show format changes, and distribution of updated information to various staff members. The PA also arranges shipments and pick-up/delivery of food, establishes rights to music, supervises runners, and takes care of anything else the producer and/or director need. Generally reports to the producer and sometimes the director.

Spotter: Advises the production crew regarding important activity or incidents in and around the field of play that may not be immediately evident to the production crew and camera operators. Generally reports to the director.

Statistician: Compiles competition statistics, including past performances and up-to-the-minute competition details. Also gathers general information about current competition conditions, such as weather. Generally reports to the producer and production assistant. *(See figure 2.3.)*

Tape AD: Helps select the appropriate portion of the tape for playback and ensures that VTR operators are cued and ready when the director needs them. Generally reports to the producer.

Technical Director (TD)/Vision Mixer/Vision Switcher: Takes instructions from the director and, using a special effects generator (SEG) or switcher, switches between video images using cuts, dissolves, wipes, special effects, animation, and graphics, sometimes using multiple cameras at the same time. Reports to the director. *(See figure 2.4.)*

Camera Operator: Receives assignments from the director and works to constantly provide the director with the best quality images available for the production. Camera operators are also responsible for transport, set-up, and sometimes general maintenance of their camera. Reports to the director.

Figure 2.3: Statisticians (left) compile up-to-the-minute statistics that are helpful to the on-air commentators and the production personnel.

Figure 2.4: The technical director/vision mixer responds to the director.

Figure 2.5: The camera assistant reacts to movements by the camera operator by providing more cable and/or neatly coiling unused cable.

Figure 2.6: Camera assistants must look out for the camera operator by making sure they don't fall.

Figure 2.7: The Audio Supervisor (A-1) is responsible for patching audio in the mobile unit.

Electronic Still Store (ESS) Operator: Operates equipment used for the capture, storage, manipulation (if needed), and playback of still images from video. Works under the director during the production. Reports to the producer and director.

Camera Assistant (handheld, Steadicam, crane, etc): Protects and assists the camera operator by keeping people from walking into the camera's field of view, eliminating potential obstacles or obstructions, and keeping camera cables untangled and free from traffic. A handheld camera assistant is mainly responsible for reacting to the camera operator's movement during an event by feeding the operator camera cable during the production. In order to accomplish this feat, the camera assistant has to pay attention and learn the over and under cable coiling method. This method greatly reduces cable tangling and ultimately allows the operator to move freely to react to the task at hand. In addition, the camera assistant may collect food for the camera operator, carry extra batteries, and sometimes work as a spotter, looking for shot possibilities or other happenings that the shooter should know about. The camera assistant may also assist with set-up, reposition, and strike of camera equipment. Reports to the camera operator. *(See figures 2.5 and 2.6.)*

RF Assist: A specific type of camera assistant who is responsible for keeping the RF transmitter (used for wireless cameras) aimed at the RF receiver, as well as preventing the cables between them and the camera operator from becoming tangled or stretched. The RF assist is also responsible for looking out for the camera operator, making sure that no one walks between them or blocks the camera's field of view. Reports to the camera operator.

Rigger: Sets up structures to support lighting or camera equipment before the event and then strikes the equipment after the event is completed. Reports to the technical manager.

Audio (A-1)/Mixer/Audio Supervisor: Determines where microphones are to be placed in the field of play, generally patches the various microphones in the inputs/outputs (I/O) patch panel located on the outside of the mobile unit, gives instructions to the A-2, and sets up and/or patches the PL system in the mobile unit. The A-1 also mixes the audio signal from the various microphones, tape decks, digicarts, house feed, public address system, and CD player during the actual production. Reports to the producer and the director. *(See figure 2.7.)*

Audio Assistant (A-2): Receives instruction from the A-1 as to where microphones should be placed on the field of play and sets out the microphones. Other responsibilities may include patching the I/O, assisting the talent with their microphones, and operating microphones on the field of play, such as a parabolic dish. The A-2 also troubleshoots audio problems during the production. Reports to the A-1.*(See figure 2.8.)*

Utility/Grip/Rigger: Before the actual production, utilities assist the engineering crew by carrying equipment, placing cabling during set-up, and assisting during the tear-down (strike). During the production, utilities may be reassigned to work as camera assistants or be placed in other support positions. Reports to the technical manager and to whomever else they are assigned during the actual production time. *(See figure 2.9.)*

Video Operator (VO)/Video Engineer/Vision Control/Vision Operator/CCU Operator/Shader: Responsible for adjusting video levels as well as establishing the color intensity of cameras on the camera control unit (CCU) to obtain the highest quality image. The video operator also works with the engineer-in-charge (EIC) to patch all video sources and phasing/white balance of cameras. Reports to the director and producer. *(See figure 2.10.)*

Videotape Librarian/Archivist: Collates and maintains the videotapes and record of events ready for retrieval on request. This is accomplished by keeping track of the numeric time code clock displaying the exact time and location on the tape where the particular action can be found. They may also be responsible for dubbing. Reports to the producer.

Figure 2.8: An A-2 lays out the audio equipment that will be used during an event.

Figure 2.9: The utility assists the engineering staff is setting-up and tearing-down equipment and cables.

Figure 2.10: Video operators are responsible for adjusting the camera and VTR images to obtain the highest quality possible.

Figure 2.11: Graphics operator and a font coordinator.

VTR Operator: Runs tape machines, monitors audio and video levels, and often operates an auxiliary bus switcher in order to isolate specific cameras on a video recorder. This person may also serve as a slow motion (slo-mo) operator. Reports to the producer and director.

Slo-mo Operator/Super Slo-mo Operator: Operates and maintains slow motion videotape and/ or digital disc recorder/players. Provides the slo-mo/super slo-mo replays as required by the director. Reports to the producer and director.

Editor: Selects, compiles, and cuts video and audio to produce highlights, summaries and feature packages. Reports to the producer.

Graphics Operator/Font Operator/Character Generator Operator: Operates the character generator to put text and graphics on the television screen. Reports primarily to the producer and director. *(See figure 2.11.)*

Font Coordinator: Assists the graphics/font operator, keeping them up-to-date during a production. Responsibilities may include spell checking, updating scores, identifying on-screen personnel, etc. The font coordinator is often one of the production assistants. Reports primarily to the producer. *(See figure 2.11.)*

Technical Manager: Responsible for all broadcast-related technical operations at the venue. Reports primarily to the director.

Engineer-in-Charge (EIC)/Chief Vision Engineer/ Senior Vision Operator: Works for the mobile unit provider and is responsible for keeping everything working in the truck. Also responsible for making sure that all equipment, cables, and supplies that came with the truck are returned to the unit at the end of the shoot. Primarily reports to the technical manager.

Maintenance Engineer: Maintains production equipment in the truck and on the field of play. Reports to the EIC.

Transmission (TX) Manager/Transmission Operator: Ensures the quality and continuity of the television signal transmission. Reports to the technical manager.

Telecom Manager/Telco Manager: Sets up and troubleshoots communication lines (PLs) between the field crew, talent, and the crew in the trucks. Provides and installs telephone lines for outside calls. Reports to the technical manager.

Runner: Responsible for running errands and completing a variety of tasks assigned by the production assistant, producer, production manager, and almost anyone else on the production. This may include being a driver for personnel, getting food or supplies to the crew in the middle of a shoot, making travel arrangements, and undertaking research. Reports to the production assistant.

Figure 2.12: Field loggers must list each shot made by an ENG camera operator.

Talent: Refers to anyone who appears in front of the camera or is heard on air. Reports to the producer. As mentioned earlier, it is very difficult to give an exact definition for each position since responsibilities can vary greatly from event to event and company to company. It is also impossible to create an organizational chart that will fit every situation. The chart in figure 2.13 shows a common television network structure in a remote sports production.

Field Logger: Field loggers are responsible for providing detailed written descriptions and time codes for all footage shot by an ENG camera person. Logs generally identify all athletes, scores, and results shot. These logs are used by the production personnel to identify time codes and to quickly retrieve footage that can be edited and used in packages. Reports to the Producer. *(See figure 2.12.)*

Freelance Personnel

Today it is rare to find a remote production crew that does not have at least a few freelance personnel. Some crews are made up almost entirely of freelance personnel. Freelancers are independent contractors who work for multiple organizations, hiring out their production skills on an as-needed basis.

Many of the positions defined here can be filled by qualified freelancers as opposed to full-time employees.

Freelancers are hired because companies rarely have enough full-time staff to totally crew a remote production. Also, many of the companies that shoot remote productions travel around the region or nation and the least expensive way to staff the crew is to use local personnel. This way the company does not need to pay lodging, travel, and a per diem.

It takes time for freelancers to make the right connections and obtain continual work. However, work is available for skilled freelancers and they can make a good living.

The television industry often relies on verbal commitments when it comes to securing personnel. If the event has fewer than 150 people,

contracts are generally not issued. Employment details are often discussed and finalized over the telephone. For larger events, such as a World Cup or the Olympic Games, written contracts are issued. Freelance contracts generally include description of service the freelancer will provide, period of engagement, compensation, travel, and accommodation (if needed). Contracts may also include insurance information, a confidentiality statement, an intellectual property statement and termination information.

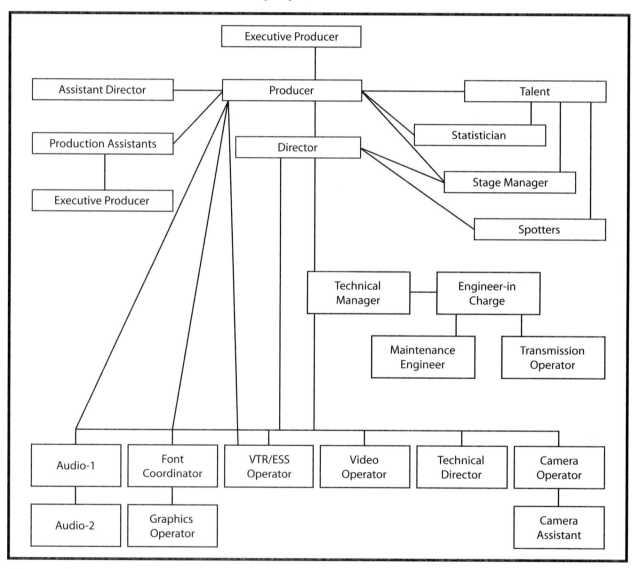

Figure 2.13: Common organizational chart for a network remote sports production crew.

S.L.O. TV SPORTS FREELANCE CONTRACT

CONTRACTOR'S NAME	
COMPANY NAME	
SOCIAL SECURITY NUMBER	
ADDRESS	

CITY		STATE		ZIP CODE	
PHONE #		**EMAIL**		**CELL #**	

EVENT NAME		**CONTRACT #**	
ASSIGNMENT			
S.L.O. CONTACT		**PHONE #**		**CELL #**	
CONTRACT OFFICE		**PHONE #**		**FAX #**	
DATES		**FEE :**			

1.   The Contractor will invoice SLO TV SPORTS for the full amount of the above fee, and that fee shall represent payment in full for the Contractor's services as described herein and shall be subject to deductions as required by law. It shall be the Contractor's sole responsibility to make any deductions or payments required by law. Fee will be paid in one payments of $_____USD due on completion of assignment.

2.   It shall also be the Contractor's sole responsibility, at its/her/his sole expense, to secure and maintain adequate insurance including but not limited to medical, disability, workplace health and safety and life insurance. ***Proof of this insurance must be presented to the Business Manager prior to departure for this assignment.***   The Contractor shall not make any claims, demands or suits against SLO TV SPORTS for employee benefits, pension benefits, severance pay or any other type of termination or other payment which is not specifically mentioned in this agreement, in connection with the services provided hereunder.

3.   Contractor is responsible to the program's Technical Producer, Business Manager or authorized delegate and to provide his/her services as stipulated above.   The Contractor agrees to report to the designated remote production location at the designated start time. It is the Contractractor's responsiblity to be available for the transportation provided by SLO TV SPORTS.

4.   The Contractor will be responsible for the care and custody of any SLO TV SPORTS equipment or vehicles which he/she may use in the performance of his/her services herein.

5.   All right, title and interest in connection with the services of the Contractor shall vest in SLO TV SPORTS at all times.

6.   The Contractor agrees to abide by the regulations, instructions, directions and program policies of SLO TV SPORTS.

7.   The Contractor agrees to indemnify SLO TV SPORTS against any claims or actions for infringement of copyright or otherwise in connection with the broadcast of material contributed by the Contractor under the terms of this Agreement or otherwise, provided that this indemnity shall not extend to claims for infringement of copyright based upon broadcast of material supplied by the Contractor and in respect of which it/he/she has advised SLO TV SPORTS in writing that it/he/she does not hold rights.

8.   This Agreement may be cancelled, without penalty, by either party prior to the start of the assignment provided there is mutual agreement.

9.   No substitution shall be made for the Contractor in the provision of the services herein.

10.   This Agreement embodies the entire agreement between the parties with regard to the matters dealt with herein and no understanding or agreements, oral and/or otherwise, exist between the parties except as expressed herein.   The Contractor acknowledges that he/she has read the Agreement in its entirety, understands the content and accepts the foregoing, as acknowledged by the Contractor's signature below.

11.   Invoice must be sent to _____ at the following addresses:

_____

_____

_____

_____   _____
Signature of Contractor / Date   **Signature of SLO TV Representative / Date**

Figure 2.14: Freelance personnel often sign some type of contract when working for a production company.

Working as a Team
Dateline: Thursday, 21 February 2002; Place: Salt Lake Ice Centre

The final group of women is about to take the ice for the warm-up of the free skating event at the Olympic Games. The hand-picked team we spent two years putting together is in position. My top requirements as the director are talent, experience, positive attitude, a sense of humour and the passion to give 100%.

We are 13 days in. The programs have been taped and blocked. I have visualized each shot and screened each top skater's routine with my camera operators, communicating my vision to them. The producer and the experts in videotape have planned potential replays. The team responsible for the truck, video, audio and graphics has been fine-tuning every step of the way. The TD is standing by for the cues. The skaters are ready for their night… and so are we. I am ready to go out onto the edge of the envelope because I trust every member of my team and I know each of them will go there with me.

Sarah Hughes flies through her program and the audience senses that what they are seeing might be the biggest upset in skating history. We are with her every stroke of the way… through the two breathtaking triple/triple jump combinations, the graceful inside spiral, her sweeping lay-back spin, and even the brief moment when she looks up midway through her program, right into camera 2…we see a tight shot of her face… and an expression full of promise. As the music builds and the audience rises to their feet, camera 2 gets the tight shot at the end as she throws back her head with a flourish. Then there is unrestrained jubilation as camera 3 pushes past Sarah's face to her exuberant coach jumping up and down, with Sarah in the foreground; rack focus. The rack focuses again and pulls back to see Sarah in all her glory. This becomes the replay of the Olympics. But before we roll it in, there are the flowers and the ovations and the heady shots of joy as Sarah leaves the ice. While others cut away to replays, we stay with it live. And then I notice her coach turning her away from "kiss and cry." Cut from handheld 8 to camera 3. Sarah's coach is doing something unusual and I know her and I know what she is doing. Camera 3 captures the moment when her coach whispers in her ear as Sarah takes in the cheering arena full to the rafters. We can't hear her, but we know. She is saying to Sarah: "Remember this. Stop and take this in. Remember this moment for the rest of your life."

Forty minutes later the last skater has skated and her scores are up. They are not good enough. Sarah Hughes has won the gold and we see her and her coach off in a locker room as they fall to the floor in shock—crying and laughing and hugging each other. Their victory was captured by the only two camera operators allowed inside by the officials, Sarah and her coach to witness this private moment. They were permitted because they had gained their trust over the years by honoring the skaters during their most difficult times. They were there because they were the best—as camera operators and as people. They brought Sarah's triumphant moment to the world.

It's over. I walk alone from the truck to the arena to be with my team. As I descend the steep hill, I can see figures in the doorway, backlit from the glow inside. A slow, wide smile spreads across my face. It is my camera team and they are walking and laughing together. It is a stride I recognize.

I call it: "the astronauts walk from The Right Stuff"…and they have it, not just the walk but the camaraderie…and at that moment I stop and take it in. I am so proud of every member on our team.

Meg Streeter, *Director,* 12 Olympic Broadcasts

CHAPTER 3
The Television Media

New technology are not in opposition [to television] but they are complementary.

Jacques Rogge, IOC President

Traditionally television directors and producers knew how their final program would be viewed, generally on a 19" television set. Today there are many options including standard definition (SD), high definition television (HDTV), Internet, cell phone, and even a personal digital assistant (PDA).

How many types of screens have you used in the last 48 hours? The TV in your home, the large public television screens now common in stores and airports, the PC on your desk or at home, the laptop, the PDA that keeps your schedule, and maybe even your cell phone. Today's broadcasters have to deliver content to all of them... and that presents quite a challenge.

That means that the whole production process needs to be rethought. Productions shot for HDTV are different than those shot for SD, you have to keep the small monitor in mind if the program is going to be primarily watched on the cell phone and pan shots don't look great on today's Internet...although that will change in the near future. Producers also have to realize that the various media do not have to compete against one another. Patrick Chene, Director of Sport for France Television believes the "the Internet has added value as a product on demand whereas the telephone has the added value of mobility. We go for dinner, we are in a taxi or getting off the plane and you want to watch the goal just scored by your team on your mobile. TV owners have realized that

it is not television versus mobile phones. They are not competitors but complementary." That's obvious as we see more and more networks making their programming available on cell phones and the Internet.

Networks used to use a multiprong programming strategy, which meant that each medium did their own thing. The changing landscape of sports production is requiring a layered approach, requiring networks and stations to have downloadable supporting print material, web based, cell based, as well as the normal broadcast coverage. The layered approach may also mean that some programming is originally seen on one media and then available on another media whenever the viewer decides to view it.

We have a very mobile society. People are used to technology and are not afraid to use it. Their expectations are only going to continue to rise. Those companies who provide the layered programming will not only survive but will flourish. Michael Grade, Chairman of the BBC, in a speech to the Interactive TV Show in Barcelona, stated that he "used to think that the problem of convergence was how to make everything work for that single predicted devices. In fact, we all now know, the problem turned out to be rather different. It turned out to be how to tailor our content so that it works for each device as though it had been uniquely created for it."

This type of layered programming does require changes that we are not really used to. It means we have to change from our focus on a 19" real time box to focusing on what the viewer needs in order to understand the event... using whatever devise they have at the time. Here are some of the shifts that have to occur in order to produce sports programming not only in the future...but now.

1. According to Andrew Thompson, Head of Development in News Media and Sports at the BBC, the key words are "choice" and "control" moving increasingly to the viewer. The audience wants to direct their own sports coverage. This means rethinking coverage plans.

2. Television producers need to learn new skills ...how to seamlessly integrate the cell coverage, web coverage (including possibly creating downloadable print material) and television stations so that the viewer is fed all of the information they need, wherever they are located around the nation...and world.

3. Networks and stations can no longer afford to have different departments or farm out the Internet stuff when covering sports. The web producer needs to sit in on the production meetings from the beginning of the planning phase and also at the site when the television producer has a production meeting with the remote crew. Multimedia, or the Internet, is incredibly time consuming...labor intensive, the hardware is constantly changing, the software is changing at an even faster pace, the staff need to be sent for updated training on a continual basis and if the content on the site isn't changing pretty fast then today's society thinks that the site is stale.

Jacque Rogge, President of the International Olympic Committee, summed it up this way: "I believe that the public in the future will choose the [visual] platform according to the moment of the day. If you are in your car, you will want to look at the results on your mobile phone. If you want to follow a table tennis match, you will not use your mobile phone because you will not be able to see anything.

Figure 3.1: Japan's NHK network has introduced this Ultra High Definition/Super Hi-Vision camera that is capable of capturing 4320 scanning lines.

If you really want to watch a match or competition in its entirety and in comfortable, enjoyable conditions, you will be on your couch in front of your big TV set with a very good stereo environment... That is the way you are going to enjoy sports. If you are in the office and you want to login quickly on the webcasting, you will do that. So everything will have its sequence according to the moment of the day..." The following is a summary of some of the different media:

HDTV

The wider 16:9 aspect ratio makes a big difference in covering football. With the old 4:3 aspect ratio screens it was often tricky to cover the defense. In HDTV they are already in your picture, so you can see more of the play develop.

—Norm Samet,
HD Director,

High Definition Television (HDTV) is a production format that has 720 to 1250 scan lines compared with an analog format (SD) that has 525 to 625. There is even an Ultra High Definition Television/Super Hi-Vision format that sports 4320 scan lines that is currently in the experimental stage *(see figure 3.1)*. Numerous different HDTV systems are available. Japan uses a 1125-line system. European systems use 1250 lines and the United States currently uses both 720p and 1081i systems. The 720p system uses progressive scanning where the beam scans every line from top to bottom. The progressive systems have a smoother image and are better for motion (fast moving scenes) and less image flicker on a large screen. The other systems mentioned use interlaced scanning systems where the beam scans every other line from top to bottom. The interlaced systems have sharper images with the 1080i format having 12% more information capacity than the 720p format. While each system has advantages and disadvantages, these systems all have comparable quality.

Shooting HDTV

- HDTV uses a 16:9 image format.
- The incredible clarity of the image means that focus is critical.
- Don't crush the blacks because if this is done in the camera it is irreversible. Save this for post-production.
- The best for narrative storytelling is 1080, whereas 720 is good for sport.
- Obtain the most accurate exposure possible. If unsure, err on the side of under-exposure.
- HDTV generally provides too much depth of field. Keep in mind that focus is an important tool in production, allowing you to isolate players, etc.
- HDTV sometimes shows too much detail in make-up, sets, and wardrobe. Tiny imperfections on a set can suddenly become obtrusive.
- HDTV has a tendency to see more fine detail in the shadows or blacks.
- An HDTV camera offers more technical control than standard video cameras. These controls are generally accessible by menus or remote control units.
- HD or film lenses should be used on an HDTV camera. Normal television lenses do not have adequate resolution for HDTV.
- The HDTV 16:9 format may not lend itself to the camera positions generally accepted in the 4:3 format (tennis is an example). Directors will need to experiment with a new way of shooting some events.

Adapted from *Cinematography and The Guide to Digital Television*

HD Baseball Directing Strategy

Mike Fox, HDNet director on directing in HD: The images are so sharp on HD that in one long baseball shot that you can see the detail on the batter, catcher and the umpires faces ...something not possible on standard def. Fox's goal is to eliminate camera movement as much as possible. Since the HD image is obviously wider and has more detail, he believes that it is much more compelling as a still image ... that the viewer can actually watch the action occur within the frame. His technique is to use more static shots, cutting from camera to camera more frequently.

Photo courtesy of BBCi

BBCi Interactive Television

The BBC's interactive television goals are to be able to deliver all programming as a download for seven days after a broadcast and to allow the audience to access as much of the content in as many diverse ways as possible. During recent projects, BBC Interactive has had approximately 100,000 unique users per day on the weekends.

During the Olympics, viewers had access to over 1200 hours of extra TV footage, available for 15 hours a day. They could follow live video from up to four events at once, listen to audio commentary from BBC radio, review the latest events, and select special highlights packages. More than nine million viewers went interactive during the Olympics. Of those nine million viewers, half were still interacting after 25 minutes and a third after 45 minutes. The previous record had been set at Wimbledon with roughly 4 million viewers.

The BBC's Andrew Thompson said: "Before we had the interactive option, hundreds of hours of footage disappeared down a black hole. But now…viewers have up to four extra sports to choose from and, judging by the initial figures, the viewers are taking full advantage of that." Interactive television has provided the BBC with the chance to show complete start-to-finish action from sports that would not have been shown on linear television coverage.

Lessons the BBC learned from covering the Olympics using interactive television:

1. *Our audience does not come to us for great distribution. They come to us for great content. It is fatally easy to become mesmerized by new technology for it own sake. But technology is only a means to an end—and the end is great content.*
2. *The production values of the interactive material have to be exactly the same as the linear material. Though different in kind, it has to look as good, it has to sound as good, it has to be just as creative in concept and execution. You cannot get away with using second-class interactive material to support first-class linear material.*
3. *Stop thinking about interactive TV as an add-on and start embedding it into the creative process right from the start. At the BBC, the interactive people were at the table right from the start of the planning process and stayed there*

through the end. In the main television control room, the director dealing with the output for the BBC broadcast channels sat at the same desk as the director dealing with the interactive channels. If you want converged output, start with converged input.

4. *Once you start down the interactive path, there is no going back. The BBC has now created the expectation among its audience that certain kinds of events, particularly multi-event live sport occasions like the Olympics, Wimbledon and other landmark programs, will come with a powerful interactive component. When they televise these events the audience question is no longer "Why interactive?" but "Why not interactive?"*
5. *They found that they had to spend a significant amount of time helping viewers understand how to use the system. Their biggest problems were not with the content…it was hand-holding the audience to get into the interface of the system.*
6. *Viewers are driven by the schedule. In Athens the staff were not prepared for the continual requirements of updating the schedule. Since the schedule changed due to weather, frustrated viewers often complained when sports did not appear as advertised. More attention needs to be put on the schedule system.*
7. *"Live" is what draws most people to interactive TV. Recorded events do not have the same draw.*

Patrick Dalzell, Editor of BBC Sport Interactive, says that they are working to increase the amount of dependency between the two broadcast channels and the interactive service. While only partial events may be shown on the broadcast channels, the broadcast channels will then advertise that viewers should go to the interactive TV to watch the entire event.

Interactive/Internet Television

The key words are "choice" and "control" moving increasingly to the viewer.

—Andrew Thompson,
head of BBC New Media

Interactive television, also known as enhanced television, is television with interactive content. It actually combines traditional television viewing with the interactivity that is enjoyed by those communicating through a network like the Internet. Programming can include links to web sites, forums for discussions, trivia questions, sports related games, interactive advertising, instant messaging, email, athelete and coach bios, interactive program guides, polls/surveys, a variety of camera angles, replay options, opportunities to purchase sports related items, and in-depth statistics. Viewing experiences can be personalized to the individual, allowing the sports fan to select the information they want to view or hear. As a platform for in-depth editorial content, interactive television provides easy access to commentators and writers from different perspectives. All of these options actually allow the sport fan an opportunity to participate in the coverage or possibly virtually participate in the sport. Interactive television can be available on television, wireless phones, and the Internet. It provides incredible opportunities for sports television.

One of the most popular forms of interactive television is personalized multiple-camera angles, or interactive point-of-view. Interactive television content providers can make it possible for the viewer to select the camera angles when viewing a specific sport. This way the viewer is able to view different perspectives during the game. The cameras could range from a wide-angle shot, a close-up of the coach, to a POV camera located in a helmet. In 2002 DirecTV Latin America deployed 23 cameras to shoot a single soccer game in the World Cup, allowing viewers to select their own views of the game.

We shouldn't be trying to compete with television. But if we do deliver audiovisual content, what will be the reason that people pay? It will be because they are either at work, expatriates, can't access a TV or the content isn't available on TV.

—Simon Denyer, from TWI
Interactive (London)

Interactive Sports Fans

Rachel Church, from the Sports Business Group (London, UK), has reported that their research has shown that interactive sports fans:

- *Spend more online than non-sports fans*
- *Have higher disposable income than non-sports fans*
- *Own more mobile phones, iTV and Internet appliances than non-sports fans*
- *Have more leisure time*

Figure 3.2: The use of cell phones to receive television programming continues to grow. (Courtesy MobiTV)

Television for Mobile Phones

TV in a handset is a whole new paradigm. The whole face of TV is likely to change. On your living room TV, prime time is at night. Prime time on a mobile phone might very well be commutes.

—Bill Krenik, Texas Instruments

In 2003, MobiTV, the first television service for mobile phones, teamed up with industry leaders to deliver programming that meets the demands of a television audience on-the-move. Since that time other companies have begun providing television services to mobile phones. Sports content has included news, regional sports coverage report, flips from sports entertainment programs, and exclusive footage of nonaired events.

While each medium discussed in this chapter has its advantages and disadvantages, the mobile phones currently do have some of the severest limitations. Dan Herlihy, from British Telecom, believes that 99% of what is seen on television is not suitable for mobile consumption. The telephones can handle from 2–15 frames per second, a far cry from the 30 frames per second in broadcast television. While the telephone screens are improving, they are not even close to the quality that you would find on a laptop. Sitting and watching a screen for a long period of time can be extremely wearing. It is also difficult to read small text on the screen. Some wireless networks are slow enough that the television program can resemble more of a slide show of photos instead of full-motion video. These limitations must be considered when creating programming specifically for the mobile phone. Close-up shots are best, graphics must be large and programming may need to be in shorter segments.

The primary advantage is its mobility, which cannot be matched by any other medium. Some phones even have enough memory and processing power to create a TiVo-like video recorder that fits in a pocket. This feature allows the viewer to stop watching the program (while recording it), take a phone call and then resume watching, without missing any of the action.

Ross Levinsohn, Senior Vice President of the Fox Sports Channel, says that mobile phones "give us the ability to deliver our sports programming 24 hours a day. It's an 'always on' sports programming channel."

Personal Video Recorder

Producers need to create sports programming with the personal video recorder (PVR) in mind. The PVR is where a combination of hard disk technology, interactivity, and a sensible navigation system provides more control and more power to the viewer. This technology allows a viewer to program a scheduled recording, watch sports in the format they want to watch, when they want to watch it and on the platform they want to watch. What sets the PVR apart from a standard VCR is that it can record and play back at the exact same time. This record/playback function can be used to record live programming, stop, play back in slow motion and then go back to the program at the point where it was stopped.

The International Olympic Committee (IOC) President Jacques Rogge recently stated that the PVR can allow the viewer to have a normal life, tuning into the Games at the moment that suits them best. "I think this is a great development … I think in terms of behavior, that is the behavior of the future."

Media Summary

With the variety of media now available to the television producer, we've begun to redefine the art of event coverage. Media producers do have to keep in mind that ultimately it is not the technology that wins viewers. The media that succeed, according to Michael Grade of the BBC, "will be the ones developed by listening intently to the audience, by really understanding our audiences—and by offering them wonderful personalized content that engages and delights."

CHAPTER 4
Mobile Unit/OB Van

The mobile unit is the nerve center of a sports production. It is where everything comes together in order to effectively communicate the competition.

Dan MacLellan, Technical Manager, Four Olympic Games

A mobile unit, often referred to as a remote truck or outside broadcast (OB) van is a mobile television control room. Mobile units come equipped with a video switcher, intercom, graphics, audio, record/playback decks, and all the engineering equipment required to maintain a quality signal.

Remote trucks come in a variety of sizes and are equipped accordingly. Many are not even trucks. Although they may be referred to as trucks, mobile units may be trailers, buses, 16m tractor–trailers, RVs, bread trucks or vans. The typical size of a large mobile unit is around 16 m long by 2.6 m wide. However, in order to provide more space for the production crew, some trucks are expandable to 6m wide, utilizing a large shelf room that expands out of the main chassis. *(See figure 4.1.)*

Mobile units can be built by specialty manufacturers or assembled by the engineering department of a local television station.

The bigger the production, the larger the mobile unit required. Figure 4.2 shows the typical layout of a large remote production truck.

Smaller trucks contain similar equipment to that found in the larger mobile units however the quality, quantity, and the equipment's capabilities may differ greatly.

Large trucks may be able to support 20 cameras while a smaller unit may be able to handle only two or three. In addition, some trucks have multiple slow motion replay machines, while others may not even have that capability. The

Figure 4.1: Mid-size remote production truck (top); full-size truck (bottom)

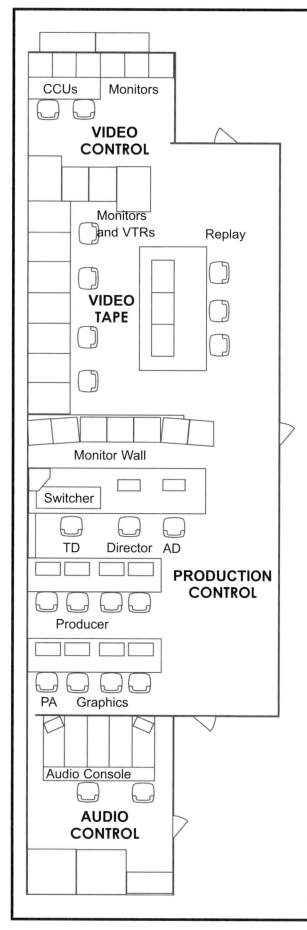

Video Control Area

Video Tape Area

Production Control

Audio Control

Figure 4.2: The four parts of a mobile unit/OB van.

size of the truck and equipment is based on the end usage.

Larger productions may require the use of multiple mobile units/OB vans. The primary mobile unit is designated as the "A" unit, while secondary mobile units/OB vans are referred to as "B" units. These "B" units are generally not equipped as well as "A" units, but they provide additional space for the tape, graphics, and storage/maintenance. *(See figure 4.3.)*

Some events may not be large enough for a second mobile unit. Under this circumstance, a makeshift "B" unit is created by "out boarding" graphics or audio to a separate area. *(See figure 4.3.)*

At very large events, an additional unit may be included which would be an engineering support unit (ESU). *(See figure 4.4.)*

Inside a Mobile Unit/OB Van

The four primary areas of a mobile unit/OB van are production, audio, videotape, and video control/transmission. Although layout and size of each of these areas differ from unit to unit, it is essential that each truck include these areas. *(See figure 4.2.)*

Production Area

The production area is where the actual production decisions are made and the show is created.

This area includes the space for the director, producer, and their assistants; the technical director and the switcher; and sometimes the font coordinator, graphics operator, and graphics equipment.

One of the most significant parts of the production area is the monitor wall. The monitor wall includes the following:

- Preview monitor (an off-air monitor that allows the director and technical director to preview a video image before going to air)
- Live or on-air monitor (shows images going on air or to tape)
- Camera monitors (one for each camera)
- VTR monitors
- Graphics monitors
- Still store monitors
- Routed monitors

Most walls are programmable so that any video device can be routed to any monitor giving directors the freedom to customize the wall

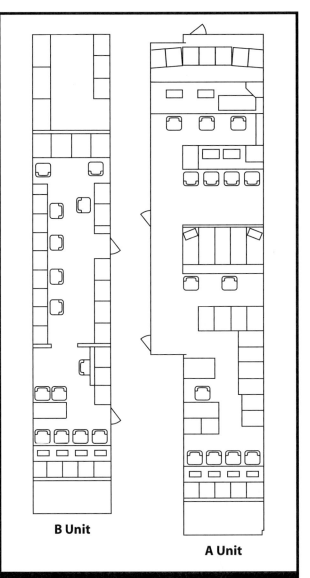

B Unit

A Unit

Figure 4.3: 'B' units used for large events where additional space is required

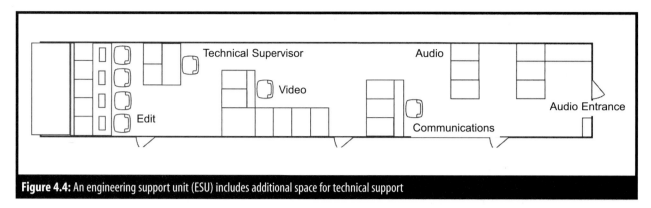

Figure 4.4: An engineering support unit (ESU) includes additional space for technical support

to their own liking. *(See figure 4.10.)*

A new development in monitor walls is the large high definition flat screen. One virtual monitor wall screen replaces multiple monitors. The director can define the layout of the virtual monitor wall with multiple inputs including a clock, audio levels, analog and digital inputs, and 4:3/16:9 aspect ratios. *(See figure 4.11.)* The advantages of these large programmable monitors is that they are compact, light, and consume little power.

Audio Area

The audio area includes:
- Audio mixing board
- Patch panels
- Video and audio monitors
- Sources (such as CD player)
- Storage for microphones and patch cables
  The intercom is also patched in this area. The A-1 is usually the only person working in this area.

Videotape Area

The videotape area includes:
- VTRs and their remote control units
- Routing switchers to route various video signals to VTRs
- Electronic still store (ESS) equipment used to capture, store, manipulate (if needed), and play back still images from video. The ESS can capture a still from any video source, such as camera, videotape or computer, and store it on a hard drive. A large ESS system can store thousands of these still images, allowing instant retrieval.
- Digital disc recorders (DDR), sometimes called Elvis (slang for EVS, one of the original DDR manufacturers), allows the operator to record and play back from the hard drive at the

Figure 4.5: This production crew has out boarded their audio area in order to have more room

same time and provides instant playback ability via random access. In fact, some DDRs will record and play back two different sources at the same time. *(See figure 4.8.)*

Video Control Area

The video control area includes space for the video operators, camera control units, and test equipment. The goal for the video operators working here is to make sure that the cameras provide the highest quality image possible.

Transmission equipment is sometimes included in this area as well.

Outside a Mobile Unit/OB Van

The outside of the mobile unit gives access to large storage areas that are used to transport cameras, tripods, and miscellaneous production gear. The storage space is also used to house the stairways and ladders that allow access to the various truck areas.

The other primary area that is on the outside of the mobile unit is the inputs/outputs (I/O) panel. This panel is used to patch audio and video in and out of the truck. It generally has a variety of connector types and may even include phone patch blocks. *(See figure 4.7.)*

Communication Devices

Communication at a remote production is essential. Without it, directors cannot give directions to production personnel, and producers cannot communicate to the talent, graphics and tape operators. Without quality communication, a production will come to a grinding halt.

The intercom is one of the most commonly used communication devices. Routed by the A-1, the intercom may have one to eight or more channels. Each channel is patched/routed only to those crew members who need to hear that specific channel. Intercoms can be wired to each other, patched to telephone lines or can even be wireless.

An interruptible fold back (IFB) system is the type of intercom system used by production personnel to give directions to on-air talent. While talent may be hearing the program in their headsets, the producer can interrupt the program in order to give talent instructions in their headset.

Two-way radios are essential wireless commu-

Figure 4.6: This Alfacam surround sound truck, used for audio for the broadcast of the Torino Olympics, has a capacity of 192 audio imputs.

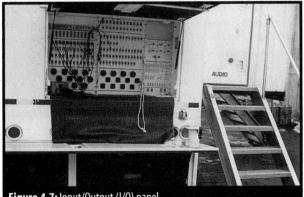

Figure 4.7: Input/Output (I/O) panel.

Figure 4.8: Digital disc recorders (DDR), such as this EVS unit, record and play back from a hard drive at the same time.

Figure 4.9: Inside a medium truck—note that the switcher, tape, and graphics all share one fairly small area.

nication devices that are used by production support, engineering, and field production units. These radios allow a person to move away from the more "wire" style of communication of the intercom yet remain accessible.

Types of Mobile Units/OB Vans

As stated earlier, mobile units come in a variety of sizes. The size required will depend on the needs of the production. They are generally equipped for a specific purpose.

A large mobile unit typically includes:
- Video switcher (64 inputs with multiple mix/effect buses)
- Digital video effects (DVE)
- Still store
- High-level graphics generator
- 1–8 studio cameras
- 1–6 hand-held cameras (including pan heads, tripods, lenses)
- 6–8 VTRs
- Slo-mo controllers
- Disc recorder (DDR)
- Audio console (roughly 120 inputs)
- Dolby surround sound
- A full inventory of microphones (shotgun, lavaliere, hand-helds)
- Sportscaster headsets and boxes
- Multiple digicart players
- CD player
- Compression/limiters
- 12 channel intercom
- 12 channel IFB system
- Multiple phone hybrids
- Multiple line phone system
- 8–12 two-way radios
- 12–28 frame synchronizers
- 20–40 distribution converters
- 8–12 outboard monitors
- Multiple four instrument light kits
- Camera cable 6000 triax, 4000 coax
- Audio cable 3000 DT12

In contrast, medium sized mobile units generally are minimally equipped with a switcher, tape decks, and graphics equipment in a fairly small area. *(See figure 4.10.)*

In some cases, productions require only a small mobile unit—sometimes as small as a mini-van—that is generally equipped for a specific purpose. *(See figure 4.11.)*

Another type of mobile production unit is a

Figure 4.10: The production control area of an HDTV truck.

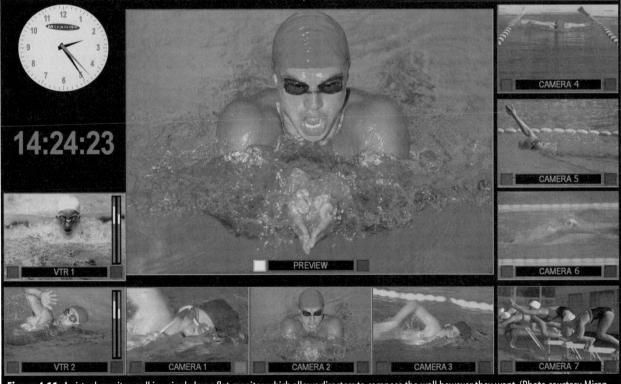

Figure 4.11: A virtual monitor wall is a single large flat monitor which allows directors to compose the wall however they want. (Photo courtesy Miranda Technologies Inc.)

Figure 4.12: Production trucks come in all shapes and sizes. Production companies need to find the one that fits their needs.

Figure 4.13: The outside and inside of a small production truck

Figure 4.14: A flypack is a control room that can be crated easily.

"flypack." They include much of the same equipment that mobile units have, however the equipment racks are built into shipping cases that can be assembled like building blocks and then wired together to make a portable production unit. These units can be shipped by standard air freight making them a cost-effective alternative to shipping a production truck. When considering using a flypack for a production, it is important to keep in mind that they do take more time to assemble on-site and are sometimes more expensive to rent. These units are sometimes referred to as fly-away kits, grab-and-go packs, air packs and cube-type units. *(See figure 4.14.)*

Flypacks typically contain the following:
- Small video switcher
- Graphics generator*
- Digital video effects (DVE)*
- Still store*
- 1–6 cameras (including studio kits, pan heads, tripods and lenses)
- Wave form/vectorscope
- Monitors
- Distribution amplifiers
- Inventory of microphones (shotgun, lavaliere, hand-helds)
- CD player
- Minidisk
- 1–4 channel intercom (including belt packs and headsets)
- Frame synchronizers*
- Scan converters*

These items may not come with the standard configuration.

A number of truck diagrams, from a variety of companies, can be found in Appendix I.

The Compound
The mobile unit may stand by itself at a smaller event, or may reside as just one of the units in a broadcast compound. *(See figure 4.15 and figure 4.16.)*

"Compound" is the term used to describe the production/technical area at a large event. The compound may include any of the following:
- One or more mobile units/OB vans.
- Technical management and operations, which could include a full mobile shop that has the tools to repair all the equipment while on

the road.

- Support services, which would include the personnel needed to arrange catering, transportation, lodging, and other related services, and probably include space for catering to serve meals under cover in case of inclement weather.
- Transmission facilities and personnel, such as an uplink truck or microwave unit.
- Temporary offices and meeting rooms for production and technical staff.
- Temporary trailers that could house post-production equipment, out boarded graphics equipment, and/or VTRs.
- Security
- Generators for primary use or as backup power supply.
- Toilets

Figure 4.15: Television compound at the Indianapolis Motor Speedway.

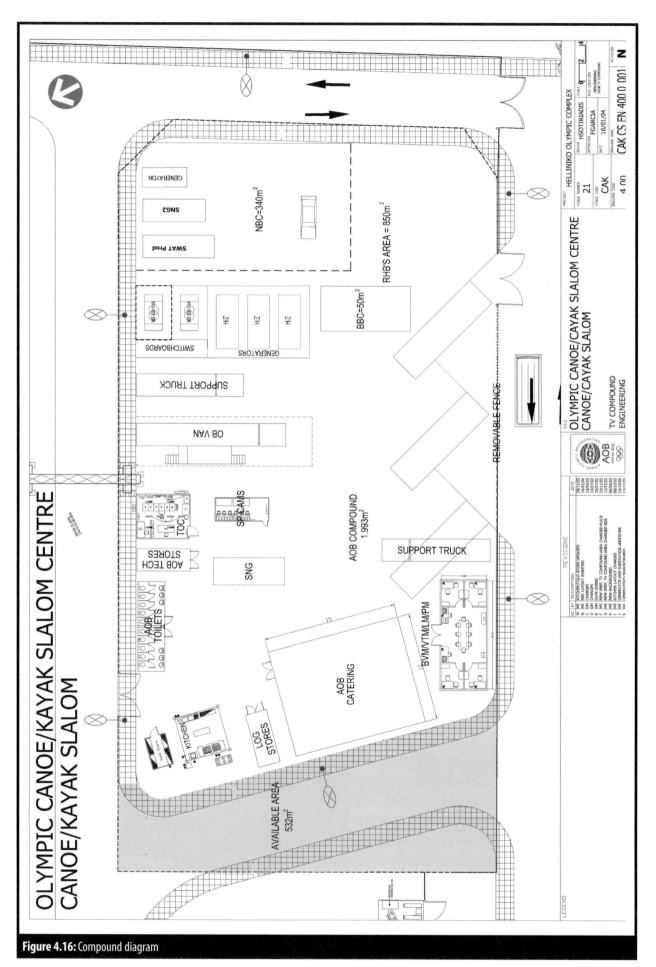

Figure 4.16: Compound diagram

Safety: The Mobile Unit/OB Van and the Remote Production

Safety during production refers to avoiding any unnecessary risks or danger. Implementing safety procedures and establishing a safe work environment for your crew is one of the fundamental aspects of the production plan.

—Helen Borobokas-Grinter,
Deputy Producer,
Athens Olympic Broadcasting

Health and safety must always be considered when working on a remote production. A healthy crew is essential for a successful remote production. Remotes may require more endurance than other productions because equipment has to be unloaded from the mobile unit and then placed on the field of play. For example, at an Alpine event the camera crew may need to ski into positions and then stand for hours in freezing weather. Remote production crews may have to set up heavy cameras in freezing or sweltering temperatures or may have to carry equipment up high scaffolding. Most injuries at an event do not happen during the event, they occur from crew members either lifting too much weight or falling before or after the event.

When working at a remote production, keep in mind the following aspects of health and safety.

Hearing. Some events, such as auto racing, may have very high levels of noise. Crew members should take precautions to protect their hearing by wearing ear plugs or noise-cancelling headsets.

Electrical Power. Mobile units require a large amount of electrical power. The truck engineer is the only person who usually deals with that power, especially when hooking up the truck. Normally, no one else should be near the power area. Otherwise, power in the truck is like plugging something in at home.

Contact with overhead electric lines can be lethal. Work near overhead power lines must be only undertaken where there is a horizontal safe distance of 30 feet. The safe distance must take into account the reach of camera booms, crane/jibs, ladders, and scaffolding.

If a radio mast, crane jib, scaffold pole, ladder, camera boom or similar object makes contact with power lines, an electric current can flow that can cause a risk of fatal or severe shock or

Figure 4.17: Don't take chances when lifting heavy equipment. Get help.

Camera Platform Guidelines:

1. *Personnel should have both hands free when climbing an access ladder to a platform. One person may be on the ladder at a time.*
2. *Avoid carrying too much at a time since overloads increase the risk of tripping or dropping articles.*
3. *When using a hoist, do not exceed the working load of the equipment.*
4. *Personnel must stay inside the guardrails of the platform.*
5. *No equipment should be extended outside the line of the guardrail unless it is properly anchored to a secure point on the platform to prevent it from falling.*

First Live Summer Olympic Broadcasts

In 1948 the BBC made summer Olympic broadcast history when they provided live television coverage of the Olympic Games for the very first time. Although television was still in its infancy, track and field events, show jumping, and Opening and Closing Ceremonies at Wembly Stadium were covered by an OB van with four cameras. A van with three cameras shot swimming and diving at Wembly Pool. Simplistic and modest by the standards today, but history-making in a first, giant step.

Olympic Television Production

burns to any person in the immediate vicinity. This can also occur with objects made from material such as wood or plastic, which are normally regarded as electrical insulators. If damp or dirty, these substances are capable of transmitting sufficient current to cause dangerous or fatal electric shock.

Cables. Mobile unit cables need to be protected so that people, cars or equipment do not rub or walk on them, wearing the insulation thin or breaking the wires. The cables also need to be secured in such a way that they do not pose a hazard for the crew or visitors. All cable connections need to be protected against the weather by wrapping them in plastic or placing them under cover. In some areas, local codes dictate how cabling is done.

Weather. Bad weather can create a problem at any remote production. In remote situations, lightning can strike the truck, cameras or crew members. Freezing weather creates ice, causing hazards for the crew and possibly adding weight to hanging cables. If rain gets into connections the moisture could cause electrical shocks.

Heights. Remote productions invariably require crew members to be at high vantage points on the roof of a truck, on scaffolding or climbing somewhere to run cables or hang lights.

Precautions need to be taken to ensure that crew members do not fall from these areas. Most injuries on remote sites result from falls. A safety harness should be used when a crew member is in a high area.

It is not uncommon for a camera person to concentrate so much on their shot while following a subject that they don't realize they are about to step off the scaffolding.

High cranes and microwave transmission masts are other production areas that present height obstacles. When setting up this equipment, it is critical to avoid any power lines. Each year people die from hitting power lines with television remote equipment.

Hazardous Areas. Many areas of a remote production can be hazardous and require caution. For example, working as an RF camera operator in the pit of an auto race is a fairly dangerous place. Personnel placed in hazardous areas have to be especially aware of what is going on around them at all times and be prepared to move out of the way of the action when necessary.

PART 2: Planning

CHAPTER 5: Planning the Production

CHAPTER 6: Pre-production and Set-up

CHAPTER 5
Planning the Production

television has undergone many changes. One of the things that hasn't changed is the need for thorough preparation. A good director or producer goes to the control room prepared..

Roone Arledge, ABC Television,
Live TV: An Inside Look at Directing and Producing

The planning process is always much more time consuming than the actual production process. In fact, some have stated that 99% of a producer's time is spent planning or in pre-production, leaving 1% for the actual production process.

While the production process is the most glamourous part of the business, the planning phase is where the majority of the decisions are made. The purpose of the planning process is to review the various available options and prepare a plan that will provide the best television coverage of the event. The plan has to include the technical and production components. Planning for a small local event may take only a few days, whereas planning for the coverage of the Olympic Games may take four or five years.

Creating goals for the production is an important step in the planning process. Once goals are determined, they provide a benchmark that can be used to measure the success of your television program. Television network ESPN created the following series of television sports coverage goals that are exemplary.

Accuracy. Be informative while never compromising accuracy.

Fairness. Be fair in the coverage. Get both sides of the issues. Be objective.

Preparing to Cover Sports

How to prepare to cover sports:
- *Know the rules of the sport*
- *Know the participants*
- *Know the venue/field of play*

Decision areas:
- *Cameras/lenses*
- *Graphics*
- *Mount-platforms*
- *Lighting*
- *Audio*
- *Medal ceremonies*
- *Start and finish protocols (run-ups/run-down)*

How the production plan is created:
- *Production planning meetings with group who will be producing that event*
- *Production meetings with production staff*
- *Seminars with International Federations*
- *Sports events- test events at that venue (test lighting, graphics, etc.)*
- *Rehearsals right before the event*

Adapted from **Pedro Rozas**,
Head of Production, 1992 and 2004 Olympics

Analysis. Tell why and how things happened. Lend perspective to the events as they unfold.

Documentation. Capture the event, including the color, pageantry, and excitement. Help the viewer experience the event. Innovate in audio and video to show events from a new perspective.

Creativity. Develop story lines. Take the viewer beyond the obvious. Entertain and inform using a variety of methods (graphics, etc.).

Consistency. Maintain your level of ambition throughout the season. Do not become complacent. Don't fall victim to patterns that may diminish creativity.

Flexibility. Follow established formats, but treat every game as a new event.

Condensed from ESPN/Catsis, Sports Broadcasting

Coordination Meetings

Coordination meetings are essential to the planning phase of a production. These meetings provide a forum for all parties involved in the production to share ideas, communicate issues, and ensure all details are in line for the production. Coordination meetings will involve applicable sports organizations, venue management, television production personnel, and any other party involved in the production. By organizing a pre-competition meeting, each group begins to understand each other's role and the issues confronted by each. The meetings allow the various groups to compromise and work together for the best remote coverage. Relationships that are helpful to the production crew when something goes wrong during the event can be forged in these meetings.

The International Amateur Athletic Federation created a series of guidelines for television coverage of athletic events. One guideline clearly states the importance of a coordination meeting:

A coordination session well in advance of the event is absolutely imperative. All parties that may take an active role in the meeting should be present—television with all departments involved, organizers, timing, computers, telecommunications. All demands and wishes should be voiced, discussed, and resolved at this early stage. A long report of the planning session keeps all the involved parties informed of decisions. However, even the most careful preparation of the coverage of a one-day event is no insurance for a trouble-free show. It is necessary to be ready to act or react if cameras fail, if the computer breaks down, because the show must go on.

Remote Survey

When discussing venue surveys I'm reminded of an old commercial that states: "You can pay me now, or you can pay me later," meaning that while it seems expensive at the time, it will cost you more in the long run if you don't do it. That's the essence of surveys...sometimes they are expensive and seem a bit like a boondoggle, but they're really the only way that your interests and costs can adequately be determined. You can learn more in an hour about the location and the organization than you could in a month of email and telephone calls.
—Joe Sidoli, Director of Production Resources,
Canadian Broadcasting Corporation

The production team generally has a good idea of how the event will be covered. However, until the venue is visited by the survey team, final decisions cannot be made.

The survey team is there to assess the venue and determine how, where, how many, who, what, and how much. The answers to these questions will provide the foundation for the production's planning.

A remote survey, or venue survey, is generally completed far in advance of the event especially for large-scale competitions. For an event such as the Olympic Games, remote surveys may occur four years in advance.

A small, local event survey may occur as little as a week in advance. However, unless engineers are fully familiar with the facility, it is essential to complete a detailed survey. *(See figures 5.1 and 5.2.)*

Horror stories abound about people who did not check the power supply or look at a venue at the correct time of day.

The purpose of the remote survey is:
- To determine the location for the production.
- To determine where all production equipment and personnel will be positioned.
- To determine whether all the production's needs and requirements can be handled at the remote site.

Figure 5.1: A broadcast venue survey team reviewing an Olympic venue three years before the Games.

Figure 5.2: Site surveys may include putting on skis and skiing the course. Here a producer and director survey a mountain venue for a winter Olympics.

Leni Riefenstahl, on filming the 1936 Olympic Games

After months of negotiating with different officials, Riefenstahl finally got permission to build two steel towers in the infield. These enabled the cameramen to take good all-around panning shots and, with the telephoto lenses, some of the big close-ups Riefenstahl wanted. But wherever the cameras were put they seemed to block someone's view and provide new objections. Eventually she was given permission to dig pits around the high jump and at the end of the 100 m sprint track. From these the cameramen could gain good low-angle images of the competitors without distracting anyone. The pit at the end of the 100 m track proved too close for comfort, and in one of the heats shown in the final film Jessie Owens can be seen nearly running into it. The officials were furious and made the production team remove all the pits from around the track.

The shooting techniques used by Leni Riefenstahl have become standards for Olympic filmmaking and television coverage ever since.

Olympia
Broadcasting the Olympics

Numerous people who may be involved in the remote survey including the producer, director, EIC or technical person from the remote truck company, site contacts, and, ideally, the lighting designer and audio engineer. It is important to visit the venue at the same time of day that the event will take place. This allows personnel to assess the lighting, hear the sounds at that time of day and identify other possible distractions. Selected portions of a planning document from one event of an Olympic Games can be found in Appendix II.

The Contacts

It is essential to establish who the event/venue contacts are early in the planning phase and how to reach them in case of an emergency. The crew may need access to additional power or restricted areas at any time. In this case, it is essential to be able to contact the appropriate personnel immediately to prevent a complete breakdown in the production.

It is important to establish an alternative contact person as well. A contact list should be created identifying as many ways to reach the individuals as possible by office phone, fax, pager, cellular phone, home phone, and email.

Also important is identifying the appropriate contacts for all aspects of the event—venue, hotel, credentials, catering, specialized equipment, mobile unit, electrician, generator company, security, golf carts, transportation, officials, satellite provider, phones, uplink truck, and possibly even the sanctioning body for the event. Contact lists can become long but are necessary and should be distributed to everyone working on the production.

Venue Access

Without the correct access to the facility the production can come to a grinding halt. The crew needs access to the venue so they can do their work before, during, and after the event. During the planning phase, the following access issues need to be addressed:

• When does the crew need access? Can they get in very early and stay very late? Is there any procedure—for example, a special pass—that must be completed in order to move them in or out at odd hours? Do they have

Remote Survey Form

Client: _____ Date of Survey _____
Shoot Date _____ Time of Shooting _____
Program Name _____ Air Date(s) _____
Location _____
Director _____ Producer _____ TD _____

Location Contacts:
Primary Contact _____ Phone _____
Secondary Contact _____ Phone _____
Permits Needed _____ Phone _____
Truck Location _____
Other Parking _____
Credentials Contact _____

Cameras: (add sketch of camera locations at event)

	Camera	Position/locations	Lens	Cable run
1				
2				
3				
4				
5				
6				

Audio: (add sketch of microphone locations at event)

	Mic Type	Location		Mic Type	Location
1			6		
2			7		
3			8		
4			9		
5			10		

Lighting: (add lighting plot if needed)
Available Light _____
Talent Light _____
Special Instructions _____
_____

Power:
Location Electrician Contact _____
Program Requirements _____
AC Outlets

	Location	Voltage	Connect. Type		Location	Voltage	Connect. Type
1				4			
2				5			
3				6			

Communications:

Type/Style   Location(s)
Camera Headsets _____
_____
Intercoms (PL) _____
_____
Business Phone _____
_____
Wireless _____
_____

Location Sketch: (should include important dimensions, location of props and building, truck, power source and sun during time of telecast)

Figure 5.3: Sample of a small event remote survey form.

access to adequate parking? Can they easily get to their positions during the event? Can camera crews move in and out of locations during the actual production of the event?

- Do engineers have access to cable runs?
- Make sure that the mobile unit can be driven onto the location, especially if it is of the 15m+ variety. Are there any small bridges, low overpasses or very narrow roads that could cause access problems for large vehicles? Can the access route handle a more than 36,000 kg production unit?
- Where can the mobile unit be parked so that it is close to power, within cable length of your cameras and not blocking traffic?

Location Costs

Every location has its unique costs. It is important to identify what those costs are in advance of the production.

- Are there costs for crew parking?
- Does space need to be rented in order to provide the amount of area needed for the production?
- Does anything need to be built or modified at the location?
- Are there any local ordinances that will affect the production? If ordinances limit the production hours or access to the facility, the budget may need to be increased to include additional days.
- Is additional insurance required by the city or facility?
- Are there permits that are required by the city, county or facility? Facility management should know what is required. However, it may be worth checking with the local police department and/or fire department to make sure that the necessary permits are in order to park on public property or on a public street. Sometimes permits can take days to process.
- Are security bonds required by the city, county or facility?
- What is the cost of housing at this location?

Other Areas for Survey Consideration

Broadcasting an Olympics is like putting on a few Super Bowls every day for 17 days straight. It is an enormous logistical challenge and we have one chance to get it right...

—*John Fritsche,*
NBC Olympic Vice President of Operations

Food/catering. Who is supplying the food, how many meals are required, and where are they going to set up the meals?

Lodging. How many rooms are needed and how close are they to the venue?

Parking. Is sufficient parking available for rental cars and golf carts? Parking should be marked on the location sketch.

Security. Where should guards be? Do they need special parking? Where will they be located in inclement weather?

Program transmission. Who will provide transmission services and where will their equipment be located at the venue? Do they have any special needs?

Construction. Does anything need to be constructed? If so, is there space allocated for the construction crew to build the required elements? Does the construction have any special needs?

Video and audio feeds. Who needs video and audio feeds outside the mobile unit? Are additional cables needed to meet the requirements?

Telephones. How many lines are required? Where should the lines be installed? How many cellular phones are needed? Are any dedicated lines required?

Medical. Are there medical facilities at the venue? Is there a hospital within close proximity? Is there a first-aid kit nearby for minor injuries? Does an ambulance need to be nearby? If so, where would it be located?

Areas that Significantly Impact the Survey

There are a number of areas that need to be considered for both the remote survey and planning the production. The rest of this chapter will include areas that significantly impact the survey—camera, lighting, audio, electrical power, program transmission, and backup plans. All of these need to be thought through before completing the location sketch.

Cameras
Camera Positions

It is hazardous and erroneous to believe that the more cameras there are, the better the show will be. The number of cameras alone does not guarantee good coverage. Close-ups are interesting. They show faces, details, and reactions, but the sports fan also likes to see how the competition develops.

—International Amateur Athletic Federation Television Guidelines

A major function of the remote survey is to determine where cameras are going to be placed at the venue. Camera placement needs to be determined early since many other decisions are based on it, such as where the cabling will be run or if the venue is already cabled, the number of days it will take to set up, the coverage plan, and any additional facilities that will be needed.

Here are some of the questions that need to be addressed about cameras and their associated equipment.

- If a dolly is needed for a mobile camera, what kind is required? What is the ground/floor like where the dolly will be located? Is the ground level?
- How many cameras are required to give adequate coverage of the event?
- What type of camera should be used in each position (fixed, tracking, ENG, etc.)?
- Where can camera cables be run? Will cables be protected from people, cars, weather etc.?
- What kind of camera mounting devices, platforms or scaffolding are needed? (*See figures 5.4 and 5.5.*)
- Are any special lenses required?
- If cranes or jibs are needed, where can they be placed with maximum action radius?

Camera Placement

One camera is all that is needed to cover a sports event, all of the other cameras (Steadicam, slow-mo, etc.) are for ambience.

—Pedro Rozas, Head of Production, 1992 and 2004 Olympics

A number of factors should be taken into consideration when placing cameras. For example,

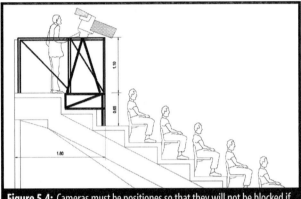

Figure 5.4: Cameras must be positiones so that they will not be blocked if the audience should stand up or move.

Figure 5.5: Scaffolding is often used to provide high angle camera shots

Pop-up Cameras

Capitol Broadcasting System (CBS) has also installed in-field pop-up cameras along the track. These miniature cube cameras are mounted in spring assemblies over a hole in the ground. Should a crashing car roll over a camera—not an unlikely occurrence—the camera will be pushed into the ground. The system is designed so the camera should pop back up undamaged, but that is not always the case. "They work very well for us," Ken Aaggaard, Senior Vice President of Operations and Engineering at CBS Sports, said, "but usually a few of them get wrecked before the race is over."

Plenty of Horsepower for Daytona 500 Coverage

Figure 5.6: Fixed or hard camera

Figure 5.7: Hand-held camera

cameras cannot be placed on opposite sides of the field of play except for isolation (ISO) cameras.

Other questions that should be asked when determining camera placement include:

- Where can cameras be placed that provide the best coverage for both action and isolation coverage? Make sure that you can provide the necessary wide shot of the event.
- What locations provide the best lighting?
- Where is the sun located at an outdoor event? The angle of the sun will be a factor when determining the angle from which to capture the event. Cameras should be positioned with the sun behind them.
- Are there signs or billboards in the background of this shot that could be distracting? Will anything be changed on the day of the event that could become a distraction?
- Will cameras block the spectators' view?
- What locations are available that are not in view of the other cameras?
- Does anything obscure the camera shot required by the director? If so, can anything be done about it?

Veteran sports director Lee Henry has this advice about determinging camera placement: "In planning where to place cameras at an event, there come a point where the basics are covered and you have to consider where the niche cameras will go. The best producers go for camera angles that better cover their story lines. The best directors want this plus the ability to place cameras in locations that provide additional options/angles for a higher percentage of use. A balanced approach lets you consider both issues. Here is a formula that can be used to determine where to place the camera: Balanced Approach = (Story Line Need) x (Percentage Used). Its what I call the B = S% (or BS% for short)."

A variety of camera diagrams may be found in Appendix III.

Types of Cameras

A variety of cameras are used in remote sports productions. Figures 5.6 and 5.7 illustrate the cameras used in the Olympic Games. While some cameras are used only at the highest level of sports production, the following list

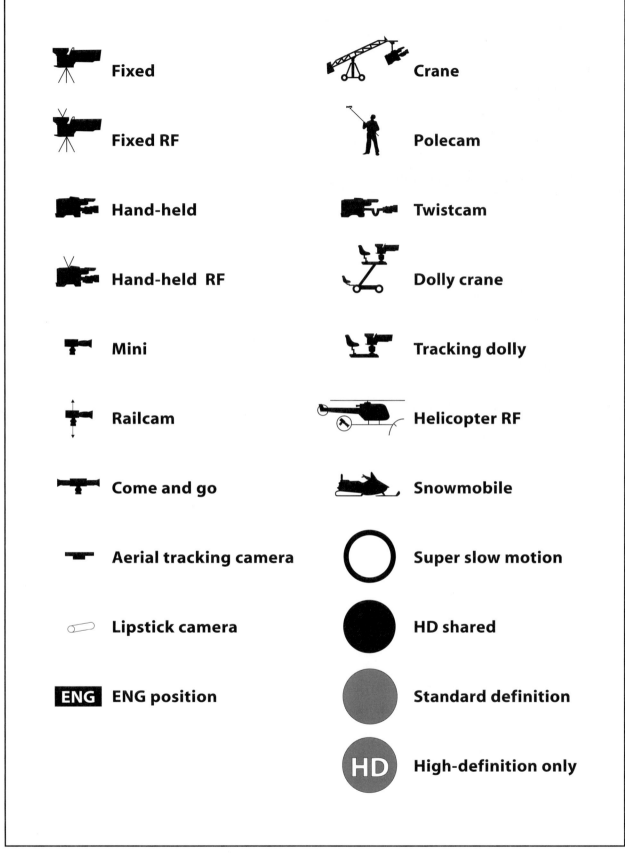

Figure 5.8: Camera legend used for the 2002 Winter Games in Salt Lake City.

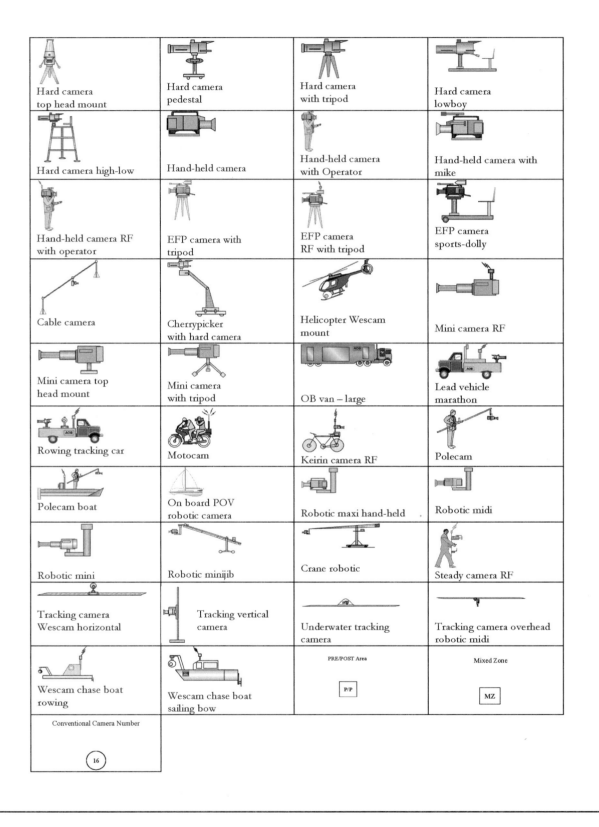

Figure 5.9: Camera legend used for the Athens 2004 Olympic Games.

gives an overview of the types of cameras that are currently available.

Fixed or Hard Camera. A camera that is mounted on a camera mount in a fixed position. These are generally large, heavy cameras that can be equipped with long telephoto lenses and require extremely stable built-up platforms to prevent shaky shots. The larger cameras provide the operator with a larger monitor as well as more control on the camera head. The camera mount may be stationary or it may have wheels. Walking or climbing on these camera platforms/scaffolds should be avoided. *(See figure 5.8.)*

Hand-held Camera. A camera held by the camera operator. *(See figure 5.9.)* These cameras are much smaller than hard cameras, making them more portable and easy to reposition. They can be used as part of a multi-camera production or docked with a recorder so that they become an ENG camera. Generally this camera would include an RF transmitter that would be handled by an RF assistant.

Tracking or Rail Camera. A camera that follows the motion of the object it is shooting. These can be automated or manually controlled. They are mounted on rails or other devices allowing them to synchronize movement with the subject. It is easier to repeat shots accurately using a tracking camera because the track does not move. These cameras are extremely stable, silent, and can be moved safely at slow or fast speeds. Tracks and rails can be curved or straight. *(See figures 5.10–5.13.)*

Mobycam. Manufacturer name for an underwater remote controlled camera that can move underwater along the length of a swimming pool.

Figure 5.10: Tracking or rail camera

Figure 5.11: The Mobycam is a type of tracking camera.

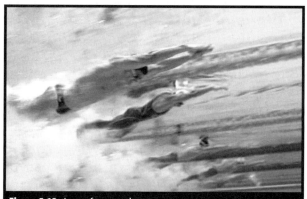

Figure 5.12: Image from a mobycam

Figure 5.13: The sideline camera is a different type of tracking camera.

Figure 5.14: Camera crane

Figure 5.15: POV camera

Figure 5.16: A mini POV camera was added to this referees helmet.

Figure 5.17: Image obtained by a POV camera inside a hockey net.

Camera Crane/Jib. A camera crane or jib is used to move a camera (and sometimes operator) to high, medium, and low shots. A crane movement is when the camera is moved up, down or side to side. Cranes have become very popular for their ability to give a production a special vantage point at an affordable price. They are also transportable when broken down into cases. Cranes are generally operated by one or two assistants and a camera operator. *(See figure 5.14.)*

Mini Point-of-View (POV) Camera. This camera is used when space is limited, restricted or when it is not essential to use a camera operator. As a point-of-view camera, the mini-camera is often placed in unusual positions to give the effect of being part of the action or competition. These cameras can be set in a fixed position or remote pan/tilt controlled. POV cameras provide a unique vantage point for the viewer, such as attached to football goal posts or underwater for swimming competitions. These cameras are usually reasonably inexpensive (often placed in hazardous positions where they may be damaged), rugged, very small, and have average technical specifications. They are sometimes called "lipstick" cameras due to their shape and size. The camera is operated from a remote location. *(See figures 5.15–5.17.)*

Slow Motion/Super Slow Motion Camera. These television cameras have special capabilities which capture high quality slow motion images with reduced blurring. "Standard" slow motion is 25 frames per second. "Super" slow motion records 75 frames per second, which further reduces the speed of the action with less blurring.

Steadicam. A device designed to stabilize a camera. The camera is attached to a special vest, which is worn by the camera operator. An accomplished Steadicam operator has the freedom to walk or run and still provide fluid shots. Steadicams at large events generally are attached to an RF transmitter allowing totally wireless operation. "Steadicam" is the brand name of the most popular body-stabilized camera support. There are other brands available as well. *(See figure 5.18.)*

Skycam or Cablecam. Manufacturer names for

cameras that hang from a system of cables over a venue. The camera is then remote controlled to cover different locations within the venue. The controls for the camera also include remote pan and tilt. *(See figure 5.19.)*

Pole Camera. A small camera attached to a long pole. The pole can be attached to a camera support or to a belt/strap on the camera operator. The advantage of this camera is that it has a very portable jib arm that can obtain high or low angle shots. It can also be used to obtain above and underwater shots. *(See figure 5.20.)*

Stabilized Camera. A camera that is equipped with a stabilization system such as a gyro, optical stabilizer, digital stabilizer or counter-balance of some type. These cameras are often used with helicopters, boats or other moving camera mounts.

RF Camera. Any wireless camera that uses radio frequencies to transmit the video signal. Prior to the actual production, RF camera operators must complete a walk-through wherever they will be going during the broadcast. The reason for this is to find "dead spots" or areas that are not conducive to a quality video signal.

Motocam. A motorcycle equipped with a stabilized television camera and RF transmitter. *(See figure 5.21.)*

Vehicle Camera. A vehicle equipped with a stabi-

Figure 5.18: Steadicam.

Figure 5.19: Skycam

Figure 5.21: Motocam

Figure 5.20: Pole camera

Figure 5.22: Boatcam

Figure 5.23: Helicopter equipped with a stabilizer remote-controlled camera. (courtesy Gyron systems)

Figure 5.24: Remote-controlled helicopter utilized by CBS Sports at the Daytona 500 (courtesy Flying Cam)

lized camera and RF transmitter.

Boatcam. A boat that is equipped with a stabilized television camera and RF transmitter. *(See figure 5.22.)*

Helicam. A helicopter that is outfitted with a stabilized, remote-controlled television camera. Generally the helicopter is also equipped with a microwave transmitter. These cameras can be mounted on full-size helicopters or can be carried by small remote-controlled helicopters. *(See figures 5.23 and 5.24.)*

Electronic Field Production Camera (EFP). An EFP camera is a lightweight camcorder that is not connected to the mobile unit. These cameras are used for the production of news stories or short reports. They are used for immediate post-production and editing, but the pictures could also be transmitted live from the field. *(See figure 5.30.)*

Why POV/Robotic Cameras?

Many of the cameras previously mentioned are robotically controlled. These cameras have become increasingly popular in the production of sporting events. They are used when:

- It is impossible to fit a camera and operator into a location.
- It may not be physically safe to have a camera operator present—for example, a POV used under a jump at an equestrian event.
- A unique perspective contributes to a viewer's overall understanding of an event—for example, a POV camera in a hockey net.

Figure 5.25: EFP camera

TVNZ Sports Coverage

Television New Zealand's (TVNZ's) broadcast coverage of the 2003 Louis Vuitton Cup Finals and the America's Cup match will include "two camera helicopters, two chase boats, one camera on the organizational committee boat and five onboard cameras per race yacht." The onboard cameras are "stabilized and dampened to reduce the effects of the boat movement." The panning, tilting and zoom are controlled by remotes from the International Broadcast Centre.

Mark Hallinger, TV Technology

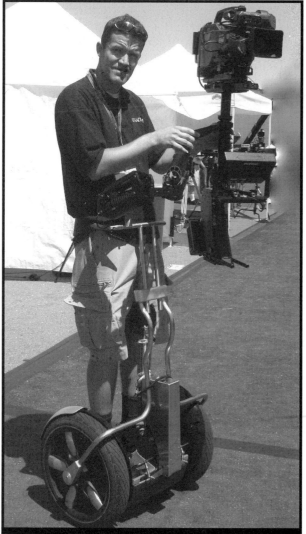

Figure 5.26: New technology is opening new options for getting the shots that are needed. In this instance, a Segway has been combined with a Steadicam for increased mobility and smooth shots.

Designing a Specialty Camera

During the 2002 Winter Olympics, International Sports Broadcasting's specialty camera creator, Mike Hampton, was interviewed about the process of designing some of the unique cameras used for the Olympics.

Question: What were some of the interesting cameras that you created for the Winter Games?

Answer: I had to design a come-and-go gate camera (two cameras in one pole) that was created to fit inside an actual official World Cup ski gate pole (34 mm in diameter) for the downhill slalom competition. The other camera that was a challenge was designing a camera, power supply, and video transmitter that would fit inside a (23 cm) high orange cone used in speed skating.

Question: What did you first think about in the design process?

Answer: What is its function? Where is it going to be? Does it have to be in the field of play? Does it have to be a specific size? Does the camera need to be protected? What kind of shot is required (wide or close-up)? All these things need to be considered as you begin the project.

Question: What kind of limitations were you given?

Answer: Everything required to capture the image and get it back to the truck had to be contained in either the gate pole or the cone. Anyone should be able to look at the gate camera and not know that it is there. The camera cannot be distracting to the athletes. It must be approved by the appropriate sport governing body. The camera had to be able to handle very cold weather. The cameras had to be durable enough to be able to be hit occasionally by an athlete.

Question: How did you know where to start and where did you get the parts?

Answer: Don't try to reinvent everything. The key is to keep it simple. Try to use something that already exists and then adapt it to work for you. This will save money and time. I generally look through automotive supply catalogues and surplus stores.

For a lift mechanism for a camera used in the Opening and Closing Ceremonies, I used a headlight lifter from a car.

Question: How did you choose a camera?

Answer: The camera needed to be small enough to fit inside the pole and cone. It had to be color and it needed to have adjustable settings. I chose the highest resolution camera for the physical size that I needed. I ended up using a single-chip camera since a three-chip camera would have been a little too large for the space that I had to deal with. The single-chip camera was also much less expensive.

Question: What were the design stages that you work through?

Answer: First, you have to gather all of the parts. For the gate camera, we started with an official gate pole so that we knew that it had already been approved by the ski federation. We did the same thing with the cone camera and the skating authorities. Second, you build a working prototype and then test it. Generally, multiple prototypes have to be created until we get one that does what we want. Then the design is refined. This refining would include "cleaning up" the look and design, or it may even include something like adding an additional small exhaust fan. Third, a blueprint is created.

Question: What were some of the difficulties you had to deal with?

Answer: We originally built the inside of the cone camera from aluminum but found it was just too heavy. I had to go back and design it out of Styrofoam. The Styrofoam also helped cushion and protect the camera and video transmitter from damage when it was kicked by a skater.

The gate cameras had to deal with the possibility of falling snow. I ended up placing a miniature fan above the camera and a second fan below the camera (inside the pole). These fans not only kept the camera cool but forced air through the pole and out around the lens of the camera. The goal was that the forced air would keep snowflakes from landing on the lens. If it kept one snowflake off the lens and captured one great shot, it was worth it. (See figures 5.27a, b, c and d for examples.)

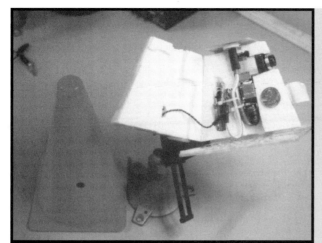

Figure 5.27a: The final come camera was encased in foam to provide protection as well as reduce overall weight.

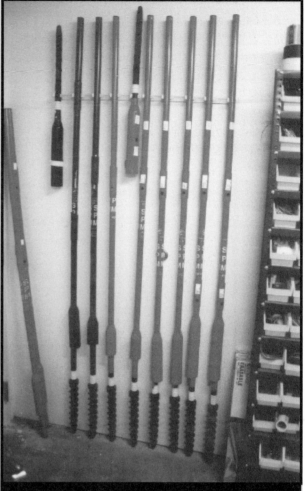

Figure 5.27d: Gate cameras were used in a number of the ski events at the Winter Olympics. The 34 mm poles housed one or two cameras. The black spot shown on the pole is actually the lens of the video camera.

Figure 5.27b: The cone camera in use during the Olympics

Figure 5.27c: The actual cone camera shot used during the Games.

Divecam

With the invention of the divecam, viewers can now follow the twists and turns of the dive. The camera falls at the same rate as the diver and then follows the diver underwater. Divecam, a three-chip broadcast-quality camera encased in a 16 m glass tube, rides on six wheels on a track mounted inside the tube. The tube is attached to the aquatic center roof and runs 2.5 m under the water, mounted to the floor with a platform and weights. The tube, filled with air, and the camera weigh approximately 364 kg when out of the water.

Divecam's view of the diver both in the air and underwater is through a 10 cm window of smoked glass that runs the entire length of the tube. Attached to a rope, the 0.7 kg camera is released by a technician who watches the dive on a monitor. The one-way pulley lets the camera drop at the acceleration of gravity—the same forces that rule the diver. A second technician, the pilot, moves the camera and stays with the dive. The picture remains clear underwater because the tube keeps the camera from hitting the surface.

A cord providing the signal and power to the camera follows the camera down the tube and returns to its position when the camera returns to the start position. During the course of the dive, a scant few seconds, a joystick remote control tilts the camera to follow the dive.

Divecam gives both the announcers and viewers a different angle to show each intricate element of the dive. In addition, the use of slow motion further enhances the ability to highlight or critique the technique. As the camera falls at the same rate as the diver, viewers get a sense of the split second accuracy and precision of the diver's complicated moves.

NBC's coverage of the Games of the XXVI Olympiad

Figure 5.28: The black vertical line between the diving boards is the divecam

Product Innovations

The Olympics have a rich heritage of testing new technology for covering the sports action. In 1984 the American Broadcasting Company (ABC Sports) created three types of specialty camera vehicles. (See figures 5.29–5.31.)

James Hay, Olympics Television Production

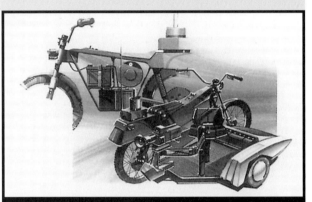

Figure 5.29: Two of these electrically powered motorcycles were designed and rebuilt for use in the marathon coverage. Fuel-powered vehicles cannot be used because of fumes. The RF camera and the operator are positioned in the sidecar.

Figure 5.30: This electrically powered camera car was specially designed for use in the marathon. The car is equipped with two cameras on specially designed gyro mounts and a hand-held, with positions for a commentator.

Figure 5.31: This is one of two specially designed camera boats to be used for coverage of canoeing and rowing. The boat is actually two rowing shells (eights) uniquely married in a catamaran effect with the camera platform raised 3m above the boat. The design effectively reduces the amount of wake that might affect the competition and provides a steady platform for the two cameras. The power is provided by two 50 HP outboard engines. The two cameras are mounted on gyro platforms for stabilization.

Lighting

A famous architect once said: "Without light there is no architecture." We can say the same for television: "Without light there are no pictures." The challenge is to make the lighting produce natural three-dimensional visual sensations of the action at any position on the field of play. I know my job is done when the pictures look fantastic and nobody mentions the lighting.

—David Lewis, Lighting Director,
2000, 2004, and 2006 Olympic Games

As mentioned earlier in the camera placement discussion, lighting is one of the primary considerations when determining camera placement. Cameras need a basic level of light to operate. In addition, the creative aspects of lighting can help set the mood of the production. Below is a review of some of the issues that need to be considered for indoor and outdoor venues.

Indoor Venue

- Does the venue have adequate lighting or are additional lights required?
- Will the heat generated by the lighting instruments be too much to handle for the air conditioning system in the venue?

Outdoor Venue

- Will the event be shot during daylight or at night?
- What kind of lighting is already available?
- Where will the sun be located during the production?
- Does lighting need to be added to illuminate dark shadows on the field of play? It is important to view the venue at the same time of day you will be shooting the event in order to correctly evaluate the lighting conditions.

Other Lighting Concerns

- Can the electrical system handle additional lights? If stadium lights are turned on at night, can the electrical system handle the increased load of a mobile unit/OB van?
- Does talent require special lighting? If so, where does special lighting for the talent need to be located (booth, field, mixed zone, etc.)?

Field of Play Lighting at the Sydney Opympics

- **Light Level.** Field of play (FOP) should be 1400 lux (130 fc). Some sports, particularlythe martial arts, require a minimum of 2000 lux (185 fc).
- **Uniformities.** Lighting must be uniform to ensure balanced and even illumination of the FOP.
- **Modelling.** Lighting must ensure good modelling and natural looking scenes.
- **Panning.** The lighting has been designed to ensure smooth illumination over the breadth of the action during panning.
- **Replays.** Mindful of the ever-increasing use of replays in production, areas on the FOP have been identified that will probably be the focus of highlights and replays. Definitive quantitative tolerances have been set for the quality of the lighting in these zones.
- **Spectators.** The contrast between the foreground and background has been specified for picture composition and to capture the emotion of the crowd.
- **Glare.** Stringent guidelines have been designed to control glare and spill light to ensure minimal lens flare while keeping athletes happy.
- **Super slow motion.** Higher light levels have been requested in SSM areas. A plan has been devised to reduce the usual flicker effects of AC-supplied lighting equipment when captured by slow motion cameras.

Production Guidelines

High Definition Lighting

Because of the clarity of the picture, the 16:9 ratio and everything that goes with HD, lighting is a lot more critical. HD cameras need more light and they need better directed light.

Ken Aaggaard, Senior Vice President of Operations Engineering, CBS Sports, March Madness

Figure 5.32: Sometimes lighting is used to boost the little light that is available.

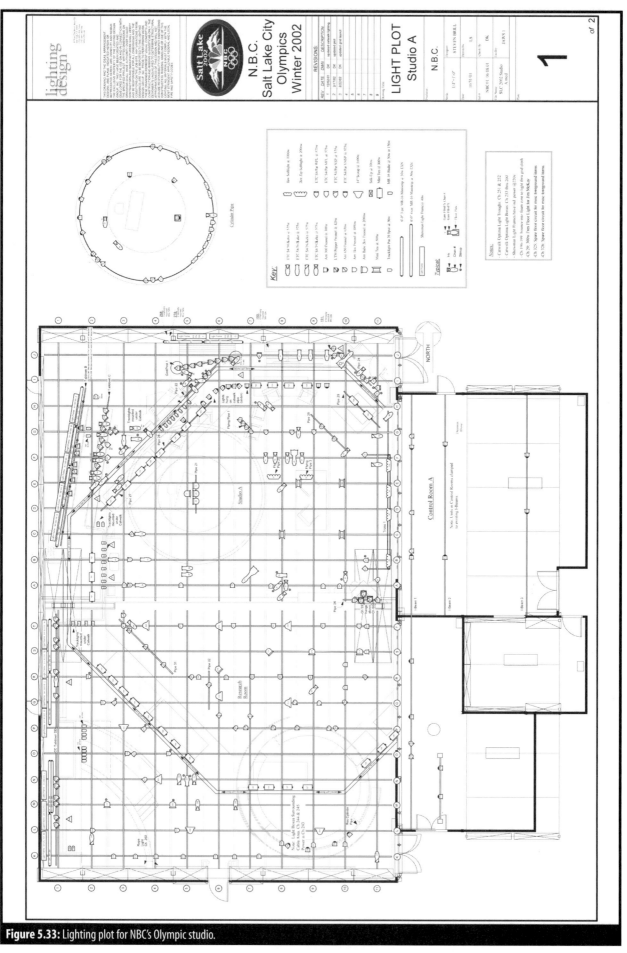

Figure 5.33: Lighting plot for NBC's Olympic studio.

Lighting the Commentators

Lighting a commentators broadcast area takes an enormous amount of work. Lighting Design Group's (LDG) has worked on five Olympics, lighting NBC's sports commentators. LDG's Senior Lighting Designer, Steven Brill, described the lighting process in five stages: pre-production, pre-production implementation, hang & focus, rehearsals and finally, the production. Throughout the entire process LDG's staff worked with NBC's producers, directors, senior management, production designer, talent, make-up/hair, and video operator. Each one participated in the process from their unique angles.

The pre-production phase included logistics and design. Logistics operations included determining how many locations, where the locations were geographically, how many talent were used at each location, what was the background, where the available power, was and what the time frame was? A significant issue was whether the location would be interior or exterior.

The majority of the pre-production phase was actually in lighting design. LDG worked closely with NBC's production designer and NBC production to establish the look that was needed. The goal was to create a concept that fits the event, using texture and color. It is also important to know who the talent was going to be at each location since different people require different lighting.

Once the lighting concept was complete, the plan moved from concept to reality, the practical installation of the lights on a document called the lighting plot. (See figure 5.33.) With the concept and lighting plot in hand, LDG went back to logistics so that they could work together on making the lighting look the way they wanted it to look.

The second stage was pre-production implementation. In this phase LDG worked to obtain all of the equipment that would be needed, which included lighting instruments, grip gear, perishables, patterns, and spare lamps. LDG used theatrical

NBC Sports' Olympic coverage studio. (courtesy of LDG/NBC)

type of instruments (ellipsoidal, softlights, and freznels) since they bring out the texture in the background. Outdoor venues primarily used HMI since they are brighter and balanced. NBC's sets utilized light boxes (background scenery photos) with fluorescent lights. LEDs and fiber optics were used as edge lights for glass and furniture. Fiber was used to enhance sets as tiny point lights that added sparkle.

The third stage of lighting was hang and focus. This was the phase where all lights were hung on the grid and positioned as shown on the lighting plot. Gels and patterns were also put in place.

Rehearsals occurred in the fourth stage of the lighting process. Now that the lights had been hung and were positioned, the director actually looked at the lights on camera. As each camera shot was examined, the lighting was modified to improve the image. After the director was satisfied with the lighting, the talent was brought in to make sure that they looked good. Again, modifications will be made all along the way.

The final stage of the lighting process was the production phase where; mixed with cameras, microphones, and an incredible crew, the show was broadcast.

Lighting an Olympic Venue

David Lewis, who has worked as a lighting director for tele-vision in Australia as well as two Olympics, was responsible for taking the sports lighting basics (see the Lighting the Night sidebar on page 63) and turn them into a detailed specification (list of requirements/wants) for each sport that is carefully aligned with the production plan. (See examples of sport lighting specifications in Appendix VII.)

This first phase of detailed specifications required that he spend a significant amount of time with the coordinating producers to determine key cameras and where super slo-mos were going to be. For example, in swimming 70% of the television production came from the railcam that ran along the side of the pool. Since the railcam was the key production camera for swimming, Lewis especially focused on that camera when determining light levels and the reduction of reflections and glare. Once the key camera was lit as well as possible, then lighting was adjusted for the remaining cameras.

Once the detailed specifications had been created, Lewis had to explain and sell those specifications to the organizing committee, the individual sports federations, and the various managers that will deal with lighting. This was not an easy task since these people were not always knowledgeable about television production processes and requirements. This was a very time-consuming task that took years to finalize. When the specifications had been approved, the Olympic committee then got an external lighting designer to create a venue lighting plan that met the list of specifications.

The Olympic committee's lighting plan was then submitted to Lewis for evaluation. This 150+ page report had to be carefully analyzed, thinking through what it will look like through a camera. The key was to make sure that it met the detailed specifications. The positioning of each light was critical due to each specific camera's angle of view. AOB then responded to that plan, negotiating the placement of lights to get the best pictures. The Olympic committee was responsible for arranging for the lights to be installed so that they matched the final plans. Once the lights had been installed, the broad-casts had to verify that the lighting did meet the specifications. Final verification and approval of the lighting occurred when

each camera shot was reviewed on a video monitor, using game time camera positions. Lights were then fine tuned to maximize the quality of the image.

Lighting was also tested at each outside venue when the sun was located in the same position it would be during the Games. For example, the April sun was at about the same position as the sun was going to be during the Olympics in August. Lewis looks for shadows and reflections. Sometimes errant reflections caused the timing of the event to be changed. An example was that the glass wall near the swimming pool had a glare at 3:30 in the afternoon, but not any other time. The specific time for the event needed to be changed to avoid the glare.

Camera placement dictates light placement.

Lighting work does not just stop at the venue. Lewis also created a lighting lab where he tested samples of the items that would be located on the field of play to see that they contrast and show up correctly. His lab consisted of a camera and the type of lights that would be used in that venue. Some-times he recommended that colors be changed. For example, in one test he found that a magenta flower actually looked blue on a video monitor. He finally tested eight different color dye combinations to find the best color for television. His tests also included reflectivity.

Lewis says that his "challenge is to make the lighting produce natural three-dimensional visual sensations of the action at any position on the field of play. I know my job is done when the pictures look fantastic and nobody mentions the lighting!"

Lighting the Night: An Interview with David Lewis

Lighting Director David Lewis has developed lighting plans for three Olympics as well as other sports events around the world. We talked to him about the challenges of lighting at night:

Question: How are outdoor night venues different from indoor venues?

DL: *Indoor venues make it easier to get an overall consistent light. Light bounces off of the ceiling and the walls. With all of that bounce, the lighting is more uniform. Indoor, the contrast is relatively easier to create with the building interior surfaces. Outdoor venues, on the other hand, are difficult to light. There is nothing on the sides to bounce the light off. That means that we deal with more shadows. Another problem with lighting the outdoor venues at night is that we don't want the images to show the field of play lit with everything around it black. The contrast can be severe. This means that we have to light the background and people to create more of an ambience. This requires more beauty or decorative lighting than we would*

normally do for sports. We also have to be much more careful of where we place our lights. We don't want athletes or the cameras to be "blinded by headlights" during the competition. That means that the positioning of our lights is very critical.

Lighting must be kept out of the athlete's eyes and the camera lens

Question: How does HDTV impact your lighting plans?

DL: *Lighting is different for HDTV. It used to be that more lighting was needed. However, with the newer HDTV cameras, they now require about the same amount of light as SD cameras. The big difference is the need for smoother lighting across the venue. However, HDTV's film-like quality is unforgiving; it shows every change in lighting. That means that there can be no compromise on our part, which is something we could do with SD.*

Lighting an Olympic venue is difficult enough as it is. Lighting an outdoor venue at night when it will be shot in HD has prompted David to emphasize his motto "Not more light but better light."

See Appendix VII for a sports lighting plan.

Lights must also be kept high in order to give smoother lighting across the field of play.

Roone Arledge, Production Innovation

In 1960, Roone Arledge (1932–2003) wrote a production plan for how he thought American football should be covered by television. His innovative plan included previously unheard of suggestions, such as directional microphones, hand-held cameras, isolated cameras, game analysis, split screens, and the use of prerecorded interviews and stories. His ideas intrigued the network's programming and sports directors who allowed him to begin experimenting with his ideas. Since those early days Arledge has been credited with transforming sports coverage. He introduced "instant replays, slow motion, advanced graphics, as well as the introduction of journalistic values and the personalization of athletes to sports broadcasting." Dick Ebersol, an Arledge protégé who later became president of NBC Sports said "Before Roone Arledge there were no replays. There were no slow-mo machines. There was absolutely no prime-time sports on any network. He encouraged others to see the unscripted drama in sports."

When asked how he determined when to use "electronic wizardry" in his sports coverage, Roone's response was "the answer is simple: You must use the camera—and the microphone—to broadcast an image that approximates what the brain perceives, not merely what the eye sees. Only then can you create the illusion of reality." His example was an auto race where, even though cars may be traveling over 200 mph, the perception of speed is absent when a camera with a long shot is used. However, when a POV camera is placed much closer to the track than spectators would normally be allowed. The close camera and microphone give the television viewer the sensation of speed and the roar that a live viewer would perceive by sitting in the stand. "That way, we are not creating something phony. It is an illusion but an illusion of reality."

CBS Sports President, Sean McManus, says that Roone's "greatest accomplishment was his ability to tell a story. He understood that to get someone interested in gymnastics, track-and-field, auto racing, and even the Olympics, the viewer had to care not just about the score, but perhaps more important, about the athletes themselves. It was Roone's keen sense of storytelling and his ability to make even the most unknown athletes fascinating and compelling that truly separated Roone from all the other sports producers who came before him."

ABC News.com and sportsline.com

- Can lights be hung on existing structures?
- Can windows be covered or filtered in order to block out daylight or reduce glare?

Most professional sports venues have special lighting specifications. For example, the International Olympic Committee Broadcasting Guide specifies the following: "In general, the lighting level should not be less than 1400 lux measured in the direction of the main television cameras. Special care must be taken to match color temperature in the case of venues where there is a mix of artificial light and daylight. Additionally, at indoor venues where windows and translucent roofs may cause daylight interference, this problem must be addressed to prevent negative effects."

Audio

My production philosophy is "if you see it, you should hear it."

*—Peteris Saltans,
Senior Audio*

Audio is one of the least appreciated yet most important aspects of television. The audio can make or break a production. In order to be prepared to capture the highest quality audio, there are a number of questions that need to be asked:

- What does the audience need to hear? In order for the audience to hear the necessary audio, who and what needs to have a microphone?
- Can the microphones appear in the shot?
- Must the TV audio be coordinated with the public address audio system being used at the event?
- How many microphone cables are needed? How long do they need to be?
- Do you need wired or wireless microphones?
- Is the natural sound a problem?
- What are sources of probable audio interference? Recognize that they will vary widely with the time and day. Are there any problems with existing acoustics?

The final decision about the type and placement of microphones is generally the responsibility of the A-1. The decision is not always an easy one. There are a variety of types of microphones and placement techniques. In

Troubleshooting Audio in the Field

Effective troubleshooting is a methodical approach that eliminates one potential cause at a time.

Television sports production by its very nature introduces variables that will inevitably interrupt the function of audio equipment. Wet weather is one of the most common problems given that many televised sports are played outdoors and will continue in the rain. Problems will arise and you will find yourself in the middle of trying to determine exactly why a piece of equipment is not functioning properly. Electrical components are amazingly reliable and television equipment is built to very durable specifications. Most problems are in the interface and specifically in a piece of wire and/or connector. Here are some of the most common field audio problems.

Wind noise: *A common problem with outdoor sport is wind. Wind blowing across the diaphragm of a microphone causes a fluttering low frequency sound that is heard as periodic rumbling distortion in the sound program. Foam and specially designed encasements are used to reduce this noise. Always use windshields but be careful because they are fragile and expensive to replace. (See Figure 5.50.)*

Isolation/Insulation of each microphone: *A microphone generates minute amounts of AC electrical voltage. Alternating current (AC) has the same characteristic as common house voltage. If you grab an electrical wire that has fallen on the ground you will be electrocuted because you complete the natural electrical path to ground. Birds are not electrocuted when they sit on one wire because the circuit or path to ground is not complete. If a microphone casing or connector completes a path to ground, a hum will be induced. Similarly, if a microphones touches a metal fence or mounting post a ground may occur between the microphone and earth, and a ground hum can be induced.*

Waterproofing: *Do not leave audio connectors on the ground or exposed to weather because a ground hum can be induced into the sound when the metal jacket or moisture conducts to earth. Always wrap connectors with a plastic sleeve that is taped along the jacket of the cable. The jacket connection to the sleeve should be seamless and without gaps to ensure no water can trickle down.*

Troubleshooting Microphone Cables

- *Check the obvious. Is everything plugged in correctly to the appropriate piece of equipment and patched to its destination?*
- *Examine the wire. Television audio uses two distinctly different types of cable—shielded and unshielded. Good quality shielding around audio wire minimizes outside electrical or magnetic interference that may be in proximity to the microphone cable. The longer the cable the more likelihood of interference.*
- *Check the ends of the cable. A steady buzz or intermittent crackle usually indicates a problem around the connector. Connectors are either soldered on or screwed down on terminal blocks or binding posts. Solder joints are prone to become brittle with age and abuse.*
- *If a cable makes a crackling sound when flexed back and forth, the cable may be old or cheap. Do not use it.*

Suggestions for preventing audio problems:

- *Always test cables before you leave the broadcast area. A three-light test box will tell you if there is a continuous circuit. This type of box, however, will not tell you if it is a noisy cable.*
- *Audio cable paths must avoid close proximity to high voltage, transformers, dimmers, and lighting. A constant hum is indicative of close proximity to an electrical cable or circuit.*
- *Never run audio or electrical cables in parallel with high voltage electrical cables or bundles of studio camera cable. This will induce a 60 hertz hum into your audio.*

Dennis Baxter, Audio Supervisor,
four Olympic Games

Olympic Surround Sound

Torino Olympic Broadcasting's (TOBO) 5.1 discrete surround sound mix is defined as front left, front right, center, rear left, rear right, and LFE (Low frequencies). However, the center speaker will not be used by TOBO because this is normally reserved for Rights Holders (networks who own the broadcast rights) announcers. Basic elements of the Sports production are:

1. *Sports Sound Effects—mono and stereo "Field of Play" microphones.*
2. *Atmosphere—HD surround atmosphere and crowd will consist of a front crowd mix and a separate rear crowd mix.*
3. *Camera Microphones—Handheld cameras will have stereo shotgun microphones.*
4. *Videotape playback—Opening Animation Music was produced as a 2 Channel Stereo mix.*
5. *Music was produced as a 2 Channel - Stereo mix. TOBO will "Up-convert" the music for the opening ceremonies to 5.1.*

Sports Sound Assignments to the Surround Channels

Sound Elements	Front Left	Front Right	Center	Rear Left	Rear Right	LFE
Sports Specific Sound	•	•				•**
Atmosphere	•	•		•**	•**	
Camera Microphones	•	•				
Videotape Playback	•	•				
Music	•	•	•**	•**	•**	•**

*Certain Microphones; ** If music is "Up-converted"

Sports specific sound effects will be assigned to the front stereo speakers depending on the visual orientation. Any image placements or movement will be from left to right or right to left. TOBO is examining certain sports where the camera perspective lends itself to some front to rear or rear to front movement depending on the desired effect. Short Shotgun Microphones will be used in a XY Configuration or Spaced Pair to feed Atmosphere to the front speakers. Large diaphragm studio microphones will be strategically places around the venue to provide an atmosphere mix for the surround speakers.

Hand-held camera microphones will be assigned to the front stereo speakers. Most hand-held shots will probably be close-ups and fill the screen so the desired effect is to focus the audience's attention toward the screen. TOBO is using D-Cam's and there is a delay.

The LFE channel may be used depending on the sonic characteristics of the sound effects. This is because the LFE channel can create the desired impact without overloading the speakers or amplifiers. The LFE channel will be effective at sports such as Ski Jumping, Freestyle, and Ceremonies.

addition to microphone placement, the A-1 has to make sure that the signal can be transmitted back to the truck. The A-2 is responsible for the physical placement of microphones on the field of play.

Stereo audio is increasingly becoming more popular as it allows the television viewer to experience the sound that spectators hear at the venue. Stereo audio utilizes matched pairs of microphones called XY pairs.

Stereo Audio for Television

Stereo sound is very natural to the listener since they already hear things in stereo through two ears. Stereo gives the viewer the ability to localize the direction of the sound and judge the distance of the sound source. The ability to localize the direction of the sound gives the viewer a sense of depth, a spatial awareness of the visual image and the sound.

Most people are used to the constant left-right sound and picture orientation. However, some sports events to do not lend themselves to this type of coverage. For example, camera coverage of gymnastics, baseball, and athletics tend to be head-on looking at the athlete, plus over the shoulder and wide shots. In these situations stereo sound generally consists of an open, non-specific ambience with sounds emerging from the left and right sides of the screen with the athlete sounds front and center. Tennis, basketball, and football easily lend themselves to a good left and right sound image.

Stereo microphones on hand-held cameras have been one of the biggest improvements in stereo sound for television. Stereo microphones on hand-held cameras deliver close, crisp, definable field of play sport sound, while giving a depth of field and spatial orientation to the pictures.

Basic 5.1 Surround Sound

When mixed correctly, surround sound can provide a sense of envelopment, a feeling of being there. The basic requirements for 5.1-channel mixing/production is a mixing console with six discrete output buses: Left Front, Right Front (sometimes called Stereo Left and Right), Center, a subwoofer for Low Frequency Effects (LFE), Left Rear, and Right Rear speakers (sometimes called Surround Left and Right). Surround sound is obtained by the A-1 panning between the five main channels and routing to the LFE channel. This set-up offers the greatest flexibility of sound placem67ent in the surround field. The Olympic Surround Sound case study will give you an inside view of how surround sound for sports is set up.

Traditionally, the A-1s mix surround sound to the following speakers:
- Announcers voices are on the Left Front, Center, and Right Front speakers.
- Sound effects are usually on the Left Front and Right Front.
- Atmosphere/ambience microphones are routed to the Left Rear and Right Rear speakers.
- Music is usually routed to the Front Left and Right and the Rear Left and Right speakers.
- The LFE track is usually used for rumble from the effects tracks.

Audio Levels

Audio levels are generally talked about in terms of decibels (dB). "0" decibels has been established as the standard. However, "0" on a VU meter is a relative scale. It is always referenced to some standard level such as +4 dBm or +8 dBm. The most commonly used is +4 dBm.

There are basically two groups of audio signals—line level and microphone (mic) level. Line level is "0" on the VU meter, which is +4 or +8 dBm. Most audio outputs from machines (VTRs) are line level.

The second type of audio signal is called mic level and is within the range from -50 down to around -60 dB on professional microphones. Most microphones fall into this group. Anything more than -70 is generally considered to be noise.

These two different audio levels are not compatible. Mic level cannot be heard on line level and a line level would greatly distort a mic level input.

Microphone Pick-up Patterns

There are two primary types of audio pick-up patterns:

Omnidirectional Pattern. The omnidirectional microphone is sensitive to audio coming from all directions—front, sides and back. Omnidirectional microphones resist wind noise and mechanical or handling noise better than unidirectional microphones. *(See figure 5.34.)*

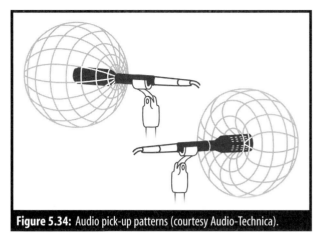

Figure 5.34: Audio pick-up patterns (courtesy Audio-Technica).

The Audio Field Kit

1. *Leatherman-type tool: A combination tool that generally includes a knife, pliers/wire cutter, various screwdrivers, and a file. There are all kinds of variations of these.*
2. *Punch tool*
3. *Turnarounds and barrels*
4. *Tweaker: Greenie*
5. *Screwdriver*
6. *Roll of white tape and a permanent pen used for marking cables*
7. *Portable listening device—for example, Q-Box—to check intercom power on XLRs*
8. *Gloves for cable pulling*
9. *Extra fuses, assorted batteries, extra audio cable, soldering kit, and gaffer tape available from the truck and should be carried by audio personnel*

Unidirectional or Cardioid Pattern. The unidirectional or cardioid microphone primarily picks up audio coming from one focused direction. There are basically two types of unidirectional patterns—the super-cardioid is a short shotgun microphone, while the hypercardioid is considered a long shotgun microphone and has a narrower pick-up pattern than the super-cardioid. Unidirectional microphones are used as camera-mounted microphones since they are highly directional and generally do not pick up camera noises. *(See figure 5.34.)*

Microphone Sound Generating Elements

There are basically two types of microphone sound converting mechanisms used for sport remotes—dynamic and condenser.

Dynamic. Dynamic microphones are by far the most durable. They can withstand high sound levels without distortion or damage and they are generally the top choice of ENG/EFP production personnel. Dynamic microphones need little or no regular maintenance. However, they are not quite as high quality as the condenser microphone mentioned below.

Condenser. Condenser microphones are very sensitive when it comes to weather conditions or physical abuse. They must be powered by a power supply, an inboard battery pack or a phantom powered audio board. The electric condenser microphone uses a polarizing voltage that is impressed into the diaphragm or back plate during manufacture. The charge remains for the life of the microphone. This type of microphone usually has a higher quality audio sound than the dynamic microphone, even when placed at a greater distance from the audio source.

Condenser microphones have two other design advantages that make them ideal for sports broadcasting—they weigh much less than dynamic elements, and they can be much smaller. These characteristics make them the logical choice for shotgun, lavaliere, and miniature microphones of all types.

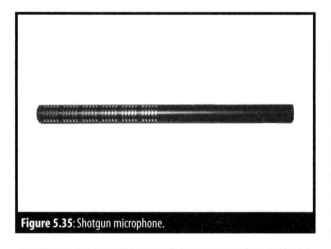

Figure 5.35: Shotgun microphone.

Figure 5.36: Hand-held microphone.

Types of Microphones

Shotgun Microphone. The shotgun or line microphone, usually a condenser, is probably the most commonly used microphone on sport remotes due to its ability to pick up quality sound from a distance. It is especially used to pick up sounds from the field of play and to mic the audience. The shotgun is very sensitive. It must always be carried in a shock mount to avoid picking up extraneous sounds made by the person holding it. This microphone is also very sensitive to wind noises so windscreens must be used when working outdoors. *(See figure 5.35.)*

Hand-held Microphone. The hand-held microphone, or stick mic, is primarily used by talent reporting from the field of play or conducting an interview. It can also be used in a parabolic dish. Most hand-helds are designed to be held from 15–30 cm from the mouth. Talent should speak across the mic, not into it and hold it at roughly a 45 degree angle to the mouth. Differential hand-held microphones require a close proximity, allowing the talent to talk directly into the microphone. This close proximity to the microphone allows the talent to talk over loud background sound. *(See figure 5.36.)*

Headset Microphone. The headset microphone is used by sportscasters who need to have their hands free. Headset microphones ensure the microphone will be the same distance from the announcer's mouth at all times, allowing more freedom of movement and consistent audio quality. This microphone allows their hands to be free for working with notes. *(See figure 5.37.)*

Lavaliere Microphone. The lavaliere or "lav" microphone is generally used by on-camera talent. It is also often used in a parabolic dish. The lavaliere is clipped onto clothing approximately 15 cm below the chin and is most often used as a wireless microphone. This mic is popular because it is always at a consistent distance from the talent's mouth yet is not as bulky as the headset microphone. It is important to conceal the microphone cord so that it is not seen by television viewers. Lavaliere microphones can be as small as about 3 mm. *(See figures 5.38 and 5.39.)*

Lavaliere microphones are also used to pick-up sounds in places where the mic should not been seen. For example, it is commonly used on basketball backboards to pickup the sounds

Figure 5.37: Headset microphone.

Figure 5.38: Clip lavaliere microphone.

Figure 5.39: A lavaliere microphone is connected to a basketball backboard to pick-up the sound of the ball hitting the board, hoop and net.

Figure 5.40: A contact mic being buried in the sand at the Olympic

Figure 5.41: Holophone surround sound microphone.

Figure 5.42: Digital processing microphone.

Figure 5.43: Clip microphone.

Figure 5.44: Boundary microphone.

of the ball hitting the hoop or the sound of the ball going through the hoop.

Contact Microphones. Contact microphones listen to vibrations, not acoustic sounds. These microphones can be buried in the sand at sports such as beach volleyball and at events in athletics. It gives a completely different impact sound that should be subtly mixed into the program. This mic's sound must be layered, it cannot stand alone. The sand microphones are generally mounted on plexiglass and buried in the pits. *(See figure 5.40.)* Contact microphones can also been screwed into a wooden surface such as a basketball court, attached to gymnastics equipment or frozen into the ice for speed skating.

Holophone Microphone. The Holophone is the only single microphone capable of recording up to 7.1-channels of discrete surround sound without additional processing. This one microphone terminates into eight XLR microphone cable-ends (Left, Right, Center, Low Frequency, Left Surround, Right Surround, Top, and Center Rear). *(See figure 5.41.)*

Digital Processing Microphone. Digital processing microphones use an analog mic capsule with digital processing of that capsule. The mic can reject certain frequencies, allowing it to pick up a specific sound like the kick of a ball, the punch of a boxing glove or the landing of the shotput. *(See figure 5.42.)*

Clip microphones. Clip mics are used for close-microphone situations where it is imperative to place a hidden, or low profile, microphone

Sydney Olympic Games Field Hockey Audio
Once the requirements for a mic position are determined, a number of choices need to be made. For example, if a goal mic at a field hockey match is needed then a directional mic should be used to block out (reject) any crowd noise from behind the mic. Level also needs to be considered. The slap of the puck in the back of the net can create a very high, very quick audio peak. If a mic that is overly sensitive is placed too close to the sound source then it will distort within the mic, precluding a clean signal anywhere along the chain. Therefore, a medium shotgun would be the appropriate mic in relation to its sound response patterns.

Host Broadcast Training Program:
Trainee Audio Assistant

close to the source of the sound. Examples of how this small microphone has been used include clipping it to a landing mat for gymnastics or a net in volleyball. *(See figure 5.43.)*

Boundary/Pressure Zone Microphone (PZM). While the pick-up technology is very different, these two microphones are used similarly. This type is especially useful for being a low profile microphone that has the capability of picking-up quality ambient sounds. The PZM microphone can be mounted on a hard surface to increase the pick-up distance. *(See figure 5.44.)*

Commentator's Noise Cancelling Ribbon Microphone or Lip Microphone. This was designed by BBC engineers in the mid-1950s. This "lip ribbon mic" is used for reproducing high quality commentary from noisy surroundings by cancelling out a high degree of background noise. Although this is probably the highest quality commentary mic, it must be handheld, unlike the headset mics that allow the commentator to use both hands for papers. Another disadvantage is that the mic obscures the commentator's mouth, which is not great for television. *(See figure 5.45.)*

Specialty microphones. Just as specialty cameras are designed to cover specific sports situations, specialty microphones are created to fit unique audio events. Existing microphones can be adapted or rebuilt to capture audio that cannot be heard in any other way. Figure 5.46 shows a specialty microphone that was specifically designed by Audio-Technica to capture the sounds of yachting at the 2004 Olympics. The wireless and waterproof microphone was mounted on a buoy in the water.

Phantom Power

All types of microphones can be "phantom" powered. Phantom microphones require voltage that is supplied to them through an audio mixer, recorder or camera. There are two different types—P and T. The P (Phantom/ Symplex) standard, requires a balanced 48 volts. The T, often referred to as A–B powering, is unbalanced 12 volts. These two types of microphones are not interchangeable and will not work if the incorrect voltage is attached. In fact, microphone components may be damaged if interchanged. The T standard was created

Figure 5.45: Commentator's Noise Cancelling Ribbon Microphone.

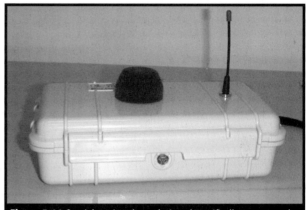

Figure 5.46: Specialty microphone designed specifically to capture the sounds of yachting.

Figure 5.47: Wireless Microphones.

Audio Plan for Swimming
- *Crowd microphones*
- *4 competition center lanes starting block microphones*
- *4 competition center lanes flip turn microphones*
- *Splash microphones as needed*
- *Underwater microphones as needed*
- *EFX microphone on dolly camera*
- *Starters microphone*
- *2 RF microphones for coaches*
- *Interview microphone w/IFB at finish area*

New York '98 Goodwill Games Production Manual

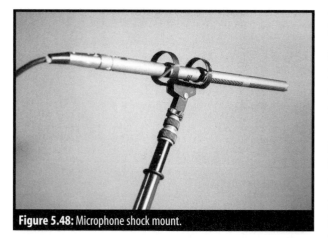

Figure 5.48: Microphone shock mount.

Figure 5.49: Parabolic dish.

Figure 5.50: Microphone windscreens. (courtesy Rycote Windshields)

primarily for television so that a camera head, which had trouble supplying 48 volts, could supply the power to a microphone. Some manufacturers actually put a T or P as part of the microphone model number for easy identification.

Microphone Accessories

Wireless. The wireless could be considered as a type of microphone, however, almost all of the microphones we have mentioned can be wireless. Lavaliere microphones are probably the most commonly used wireless microphones because they allow the talent to have unrestricted movement while speaking. The wireless lavaliere is great for capturing an athlete's words or breathing during a competition or for picking up the calls from a coach or referee. Wireless microphones actually work on radio frequencies (RF) and many are "frequency programmable," allowing the audio personnel to select the best transmission frequency for a specific location. Some wireless microphones can transmit as far as 305 m. However, it is essential that audio personnel test the various locations where a wireless will be used in order to check for dead spots that either deteriorate or block the audio transmission. It is also occasionally possible to pick up other transmitting devices, such as police radios, or have interference from other wireless microphones. Since these microphones operate on batteries, it is important that new batteries be installed before each production and that crew members have spares available during the production. *(See figure 5.47.)*

Shock Mounts. Shock mounts reduce mechanical noise transferred to a microphone through its mounting hardware or physical contact. *(See figure 5.48.)*

Parabolic Dish. A parabolic dish uses an omnidirectional microphone aimed directly at the focal point of the dish, providing an extremely narrow pick-up pattern. *(See figure 5.49.)*

These work well to screen background ambiance in a venue, allowing the audio personnel to pick up the sounds generated by the athletes during a competition. Hand-held or lavaliere microphones can be used with parabolic dishes. A wireless microphone is especially useful since

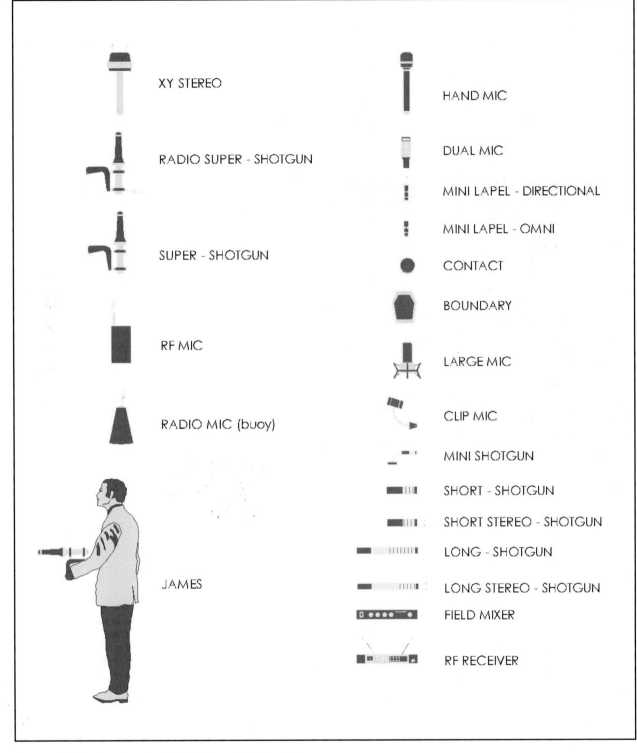

Figure 5.56: Microphone legend used for the Athens 2004 Olympic Games.

Figure 5.51: XY Stereo mic configuration.

Figure 5.52: Audio Technica's XY mic takes the place of two shotgun mics.

the dish may need to be moved up and down the field of play. Although the quality of the audio is not always the highest, it works well for background or ambient sounds. It would not be good to use a parabolic dish for commentators. The keys to obtaining good sound with a parabolic dish are:

- Find a position that provides a clear path to the field of play. The microphone must be aimed directly at the field since the dish cannot pick up sound through a crowd of people.
- Stay alert and focused on the action occurring on the field of play.
- Listen closely to the microphone so that it can be finely tuned (aimed at the sound). Sounds will be very clear when the "beam" is in the right place.

Windscreen. Windscreens protect The microphone sound-generating elements from the wind or air generated by the talent's mouth. When working outside, windscreens are essential for every type of microphone. While windscreens cannot protect the microphone from all wind noises, they can significantly reduce unwanted rumbling sounds. Windscreens take a variety of forms from foam rubber to the shaggy variety known as the windjammer. *(See figure 5.50.)*

Microphone Placement

The key to microphone placement is finding the location that will allow you to capture the specific audio you want. Considerations include analyzing the port from a sound perspective, the type of microphone, sound sources, whether

Athletics Sound Coverage Philosophy

Television sport sound has benefited from the addition of many varieties of high-quality, small microphones. Beginning at the 1996 Games, flat plate microphones were laid on the field of play and miniature microphones attached to all apparatus. The close proximity of microphones to an athlete gives a very close and personal perspective of the sport and eliminates shotgun microphones from the visible field of play. The challenge in the sound coverage of athletics is simultaneous competition on the field of play. Crowd reaction has a tendency to confuse a television audience because the stadium crowd may react to an event or athlete that is not on the television screen. AOB's goal is to achieve a significant level of separation by placing microphones very close to the apparatus and athlete

and "zoning" the crowd. The crowd sound will be miked with a ring of short shotgun microphones around the stadium so that any quadrant of the stadium ambience can be mixed into the specific sport or into the integrated program.

Microphone Placement

Track and field sounds are often very faint and difficult to be heard over ambient noise that tends to dominant or mask any relevant athletic sounds. Close miking is a technique that places the microphone as close as possible to the desired sound. Close miking permits the mixer to bring to the foreground the minute sounds of a particular activity, a technique that can effectively punctuate a sound mix.

Audio Production Plan, Athens 2004 Olympics, 2003

the microphone can be seen by the camera, and whether sounds are present that you do not want to record. When determining microphone placement, place the microphones as close as possible to the audio source to ensure the highest quality sound. The farther the distance between the microphone and the audio source, the poorer the sound quality, and the possibility of picking up unwanted sounds is increased. Christopher Lyons, Senior Audio Engineer, Shure Audio, recommends that the lowest number of microphones possible be used. "People sometimes have a tendency to over-mike a shot, using three or four microphones when one or two would be sufficient. Excess mics mean more background noise pick-up, greater chance of feedback or tin-can sound, and more levels for the operator to keep track of. If additional mics don't make things sound better, then they will probably make things sound worse."

Camera Mounted Microphones. Camera microphones, generally shotguns, are attached to the camera so that the viewer will hear exactly what they are seeing from that camera. *(See figure 5.53.)*

Talent Microphones. Talent, meaning anyone who appears on camera, uses specific microphones for different situations.

- In a broadcast booth, commentators usually use headset microphones to keep their hands free for notes and to have the ability to keep the microphone at a consistent distance from their mouth.

- Lavaliere microphones are generally used for interview situations or when the talent is on a set. The lavaliere's prime advantage is that it is small and unobtrusive.

- Hand-held directional microphone is especially popular for interviewing on the field of play. The hand-held gives the interviewer the ability to control the interview by directing The microphone at the subject. Hand-helds are valuable because they can be placed very close to the mouth when there are loud background noises. They will help pick up what the commentator is saying and diminish background sound. *(See figure 5.54.)*

Fixed Microphones. A variety of fixed microphones are used to capture specific sounds.

- Shotgun microphones may be used when

Stereo Microphone Placement for Basketball

Sound coverage for basketball is exactly like all court sports where the action moves left to right across the TV screen (handball, basketball, and hockey). The sound mix must follow the action on the field of play with the combination of microphones on camera, stationary microphones, and microphone pointers. Stereo microphones will be used on all hand-held cameras to deliver close sport–athlete sounds while giving a depth of field and spatial orientation to the pictures. In addition to the camera and crowd microphones, stationary microphones will be used at courtside to capture the action through the middle court as play moves side to side. This microphone placement should give crisp, definable, present field of play and sport sound. Microphone operators will be used during the competition schedule. Often there is a shot of the coaches from a camera across court and consequentially this audio is often never heard. Additional microphones will be placed in the vicinity of the coaches to give sounds of the game from the off-court area. The sneaker squeak has become so prevalent that it is necessary to equalize the floor sound to try and reduce the harsh squeaky sound.

Stereo Imaging

Camera coverage of basketball typically starts wide, showing side-to-side action. This view lends itself to a good left-right sound and picture orientation. Stereo crowd microphones, stereo microphones on the hand-held cameras, and two miniature microphones under the basket will give a wider sound dimension to the home viewer. The sound mixer can adjust the spread to give addition depth to the picture. Stereo microphones will be hung at various distances from the crowd to give a full stereo image to the sport and atmosphere. There are three stereo microphones that are spaced along the stands for a large stadium sound and a pair of short shotguns for an XY stereo configuration for a tighter defined sound. (See figures 5.51 and 5.52.)

Audio Production Plan, Athens 2004 Olympics

Figure 5.53: Camera mounted microphones.

Figure 5.54: Talent microphones.

Audio Terminology

2-Wire: A two-wire communication circuit that is bidirectional (talk/listen).

4-Wire: A four-wire audio communication circuit which uses one pair of wires for talk and one pair for listen.

Attenuation: The amount of audio or video signal loss from points A to B or through a device.

Barrel: Also known as a turnaround or gender bender, a barrel is an adapter that allows identical cables to be connected together (male to male or female to female).

Binding Post: Converts a dry pair to an XLR (three pin shielded audio connector).

Bridging: A high-impedance method of connecting destination components in parallel where there is no measurable signal level loss from the source.

Dry Pair: A pair of wires without any electrical voltage.

Impedance: The vector (scaler with direction) sum of the resistance and reactance in a circuit.

PL: Abbreviation for any type of communication circuit that serves as an intercom system.

Punch Block: A panel used to connect or separate audio/ telephone cable.

Resistance: Opposition (reduction) to the flow of signal in a circuit.

Wet Pair: A standard telephone cable that has a twisted pair with roughly 70 volts.

trying to capture specific sounds on the field of play.

- Hand-held microphones are generally used to capture ambience sounds. Avoid placing the microphone where it will pick up specific people or the public address system.
- Due to the small size of a lavaliere microphone, it is sometimes used when the microphone needs to be hidden. For example, if the A-1 wanted to catch the sound of hands on the rings during a gymnastics competition, the lavaliere could actually be mounted on the chain holding the rings.

Wireless Microphones. Wireless microphones can be used with umpires or referees, in parabolic dishes, and anywhere else that audio cables would get in the way or be difficult to run. *(See figure 5.47.)*

See Appendix IV for examples of audio microphone placement diagrams.

Communications (Intercom) Systems

While microphone signals flow to the OB van for the on-air program, communication between producers, camera operators, and other television engineers is accomplished through another set of wires that make up the intercom. This television intercom communications system utilizes equipment that functions very similarly to a telephone. The A-1 is responsible for the intercom system for the remote production crew and routes the various channels to the appropriate personnel.

To communicate from production and engineering to field operators, a headset and intercom box is plugged into a cable that runs to the OB van. This cable is plugged into an intercom channel so that operators can talk to the truck.

Intercom systems may comprise many different types of intercoms and sub-systems. The three basic systems can be categorized as party-line, matrix and wireless systems, as well as any combination of the three types.

Adapted from Handbook of Intercom Systems Engineering.

Wired party-line systems involve a number of participants in the same conversation. Everyone can speak to and hear each other in a "public" conversation. This system may be referred to as party-line (PL), two-wire (TW) referring to the two wires required, or a conference denoting the type of activity taking place in the conversation.

A wired **matrix** system is an intercom system in which a large number of individuals have the ability to establish private individual conversations from point A to point B at the same time. The matrix system is not limited to simple point-to-point communications. Like telephone systems, they also have other functions and capabilities including conference, call waiting, and busy signals. This type of system is also referred to as a cross-point intercom, point-to-point system, private line or some of the various brand names, such as McCurdy, Adam™, Zeus™, and others.

Wireless systems encompass all sorts of systems from the most basic pair of walkie-talkies to mobile phones to dedicated professional intercoms. The most basic feature of wireless intercoms is that they are not tethered by wires. Wireless intercom systems are employed where their limitations—interference, battery life, lack of range, and lack of security—are outweighed by the freedom of being cordless. A wireless intercom can be designed, installed, configured, and operated in PL or matrix configurations, and may be connected to a hard-wired PL or matrix intercom system at some point. They can range from a simple single pair of units talking to one another, to a system in which 24 or more different portable units are dynamically switched between conversations. *(See figure 5.55.)*

There are basically two types of intercom user stations. These include belt packs and master stations.

Belt pack. This portable single or two channel intercom headset box is designed to be worn on a user's belt, but is often fastened to the underside of consoles, taped to a structure near the user or mounted on a piece of equipment. The intercom headset plugs into the belt pack, as does the connection to the rest of the intercom.

Master station. The master station allows a director to access multiple channels. This allows different crews to be monitored, cued or updated. The master station includes both an intercom user station and an intercom system power supply combined in one package. *(See figure 5.57.)*

Cables should be organized so that the inter-

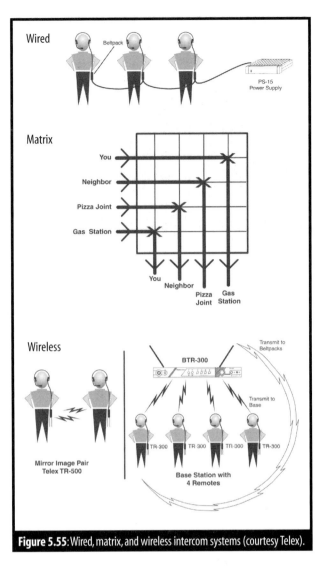

Figure 5.55: Wired, matrix, and wireless intercom systems (courtesy Telex).

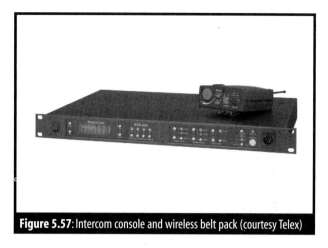

Figure 5.57: Intercom console and wireless belt pack (courtesy Telex)

com signal flows in the direction of the male connector. This is the way the equipment that you must attach to the wire is usually designed. Microphone signals flow toward the truck or camera. Intercom signals flow away from the truck.

Most mobile units/OB vans have from 12 to 24 channels of intercom and an additional 12 interruptible fold-back (IFB) channels that are used to communicate to on-air talent. In most cases, only the producer, director, and possibly the spotters will need to communicate with the on-air talent.

It is not uncommon to have backup transmission equipment actually transmitting the same program on a different microwave link or satellite. That way, if something happens with your primary transmitter, the production still gets to the intended distribution source. Although backup plans may seem like an unnecessary expense, if a problem occurs you will have saved yourself the cost of losing the production.

The producer will determine which crew members need to talk to each other and whether they should use an intercom channel or a two-way radio. Most of the time, the producer will be talking with the director, assistant director, font coordinator, technical director, and tape and RF camera operators. The intercom will be programmed so that the producer can talk to all of them or individually. Also, producers will have an "all call" switch that allows them to talk to everyone on IFB.

The director will primarily want to talk with the camera, graphics, and videotape operators. The technical director will want mainly to listen to the director and talk with camera operators, videotape operators, and the A-1.

Electrical Power

Surveying the electrical power on location is essential. It is important to find out if there is sufficient electrical power for all the equipment being used and if anyone else is planning to share the power with you. Engineers should not take anything for granted and must make sure that all electrical outlets actually work. During the electrical survey, it is important to determine the following:

• Where are the breakers? How will the crew access them?

- How many extension cords are needed?
- Is a portable generator needed? If shore power (power on site) is available, is a generator needed for redundancy?

Program Transmission

Unlike the 1964 Olympic Winter Games, today there are quite a few ways to get the video image to the distribution point. Currently, there are primarily five ways to transmit an audio and video signal:

- **Coaxial Cable.** Can be used for relatively short distances but is more susceptible to outside interference.
- **Fiber Optics** (optical fiber). Video signals can be transmitted up to 16 km on a fiber optic cable with virtual immunity to interference. Fiber cable has a high capacity for transmitting information. In addition, it does not leak and can withstand temperature variations. The cable is very small and lightweight, low in cost, and very reliable.
- **Microwave Link.** Microwave transmissions use Radio Frequencies (RF) usually in the Super High Frequency (SHF) band and must be line-of-sight; snow and rain can degrade a video signal that is transmitted by microwaves. The microwave transmitter has a highly directional signal with a maximum transmission of approximately 120 km. However, a series of repeaters can be created to transmit the signal around obstacles or increase the distance. Microwave transmitters can be hand-held and can be so small that they fit on the top of a camera (for short distances). For long distances the transmitter is generally mounted on a vehicle or a building. *(See figures 5.58 and 5.60.)* Sports coverage sometimes necessitates the use of a moving vehicle (helicopter, boat, motorcycle) to transmit live video images. Since it is very difficult, or impossible, to keep a normal transmitter/receiver aligned, these vehicles are equipped with special omnidirectional transmitters which transmit to a modified dish that can receive signals over a broad area. Today's transmitter/receivers have been programmed to automatically align themselves for maximum quality.

Figure 5.58: Microwave truck.

Figure 5.59: On-camera transmitters are available for SD and HDTV cameras. (Courtesy RF Central.)

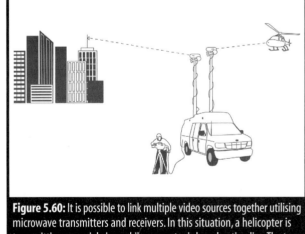

Figure 5.60: It is possible to link multiple video sources together utilising microwave transmitters and receivers. In this situation, a helicopter is transmitting an aerial view while a reporter is broadcasting live. The two video signals are mixed, using a small switcher in the van, transmitted to a microwave receiver/transmitter mounted on a high structure and then relayed back to the production facility, station or network.

Figure 5.61: Flyaway satellite uplink. (courtesy Swe Dish Wahlberg Selin)

Figure 5.62: Satellite receiving dishes

Figure 5.63: Satellite uplink truck

- **Satellite links** are optimal when working in a remote site since they overcome the distance and line-of-sight problems. The transmitter "uplinks" the signal to the satellite. The satellite receives the signal, amplifies it and then "downlinks" it back to the receiver. Satellite transmitters for multi-camera sports productions are often mounted onto trucks. *(See figure 5.63.)* A flyaway satellite unit is used when a location is not accessible for satellite trucks. These transmission units can be as small as a suitcase. Flyaway satellite units are not commonly used for large sports productions. *(See figure 5.61.)* The satellite signal is received by a satellite "downlink" dish, which comes in a variety of sizes. *(See figure 5.62.)*

- **Webcasting** is a rapidly emerging transmission method which streams audio and video on the web. Although the transmissions are not broadcast quality at this time, the quality continues to improve each year. Figure 5.64 shows webcast equipment installed in a remote production truck.

Backup Plans

It is imperative to have a thorough backup or redundancy plan in place in case something goes wrong with the production. Most production companies make sure that they have backup equipment, generators, graphics, and even a backup audio feed. When developing the backup plan, it is important to determine how the plan will impact space requirements—for example, where the additional generator will be parked.

Joe Maar, television director, recently stated in *Television Broadcast:* "sometimes, it's even important to have a backup for your backup plan. For example, some networks have one primary and two backup systems to get the game clock on the air during a sporting event. Their primary system is a direct cable connection to the stadium's scoreboard clock, the secondary system is a visual recognition system that changes the character generator clock with the scoreboard clock. A dedicated camera shoots the scoreboard for the recognition software."

It is not uncommon to have backup transmission equipment actually transmitting the same program on a different microwave link or satellite. That way, if something happens with your primary transmitter, the production still gets to the intended distribution source. Although backup plans may seem like an unnecessary expense, if a problem occurs you will have saved yourself the cost of losing the production.

Location Sketch

The location sketch is used to help staff identify camera, microphone, cabling, crew parking, and truck/office placement. As the name implies, the location sketch is not a refined drawing. Rather, it is a rough map of the remote telecast locale. The location sketch for an indoor remote production should include:
- Room dimensions
- Furniture
- Props
- Talent broadcast locations
- Window locations
- Power sources

An outdoor remote location sketch should include:
- Location of buildings
- Talent broadcast locations
- Compound location
- Power source
- Location of the sun at the time of the telecast

Budgeting for the Remote

A budget is very similar to a survey but is really a numeric evaluation of the production plan.
—Hank Levine
Executive Vice President, ISB

Budgeting for remote productions varies greatly from event to event. We chose to use a medium sized event as our case study. This way smaller production personnel can review the costs of a medium production and adapt them for a smaller event.

For this rough production budget, we have assumed that a freelance crew has to be hired and a large mobile unit/OB van needs to be rented. The event, a small auto race, will require three days on site and the final product will be two hours of programming shown on a national network. The amounts shown are based on 2003 costs in the United States and

Figure 5.64: Mobile unit equipped with servers for webcasting

Budgeting
Creating and managing a good working budget requires part foresight, part discipline, and a lot of experience. When developing a project budget, for instance, you need to have a plan for every situation while also realizing that every situation will not actually happen. A budget should be used as a planning tool and, if used properly, it will challenge the team to focus their energies on ensuring that the resources are used in appropriate ways to enhance the production.

Hank Levine, Executive Vice President of Administration, International Sports Broadcasting

are given as an example for studying the budget process.

Equipment Rental

Mobile Unit/OB Van: $19,500

This cost ($5000–8000/day) generally includes eight cameras (some hand-held and some hard cameras), truck personnel (EIC, maintenance engineer, and driver), and the cost of transporting the unit to the location.

Cameras: $650/one additional camera

The cost for cameras that are in addition to the cameras that come with the truck are generally around $500–800/camera (for equipment only). However, keep in mind that every camera the producer adds requires additional cable, possibly an additional microphone and a camera person (daily pay, per diem, flights, and lodging). This additional cost of a camera rapidly moves from $500+ per camera to approximately $2400+ per camera if you have to use outside, nonlocal personnel.

Cable Truck: $3000

Sometimes called a "race package," the cable truck is used primarily at events that require massive amounts of additional camera cable, such as an auto race. It is generally a flat rate added to the cost of the mobile unit/OB van.

RF Unit: $10 500

Wireless audio and video equipment is being used more often in remote productions. Most RF trucks are available for roughly half the cost of the mobile unit/OB van. The RF unit provides everything other than the cameras and takes roughly 10–14 crew members to operate.

Uplink Truck: $4800

Uplink trucks are available in C-band (lower transponder frequencies) and KU-band (highest frequencies used by satellite transponders). A KU-band truck is $2400 for the first day and $1200 for each additional day. A C-band truck generally rents for twice the cost of a KU-band truck. The truck's staff comes with the truck and are included in the cost.

Satellite Rental: $1500

Satellite rental time usually runs around $500/hour for KU-band time and $650/hour for C-band time. Time is booked in advance of the production by the hour. This event will require two hours plus an additional 30 minutes before air time for tests. Additional time is usually scheduled in case the event goes into overtime.

Graphics

Many productions require rental of additional graphics equipment. Again, adding graphics equipment increases the number of staff required, thereby increasing per diem, lodging, and transportation costs. For our sample production budget we will not be incorporating any additional graphics.

Generator: $4000

Generator costs vary ($2500–8000) based on whether the production requires a small generator to backup shore power, or if the entire production must be powered by generator.

Lighting

Some productions will require additional lighting for the commentator booth or on the field of play. For our sample production budget we will not be using additional lighting.

Office Trailers: $5000 for two

Trailers may need to be rented to house production and operations personnel. They generally cost around $2500 each.

Housing

Housing: $16,200

Generally $120/night is budgeted for each crew member to have their own room. The budget for 25 crew members for three days would total around $9000. However, in addition to providing housing for the production crew in our personnel list, the production company is also usually responsible for providing housing for:

- Talent (generally around 3 people)
- Mobile unit crew (3 + people)
- RF unit crew (10–14 people)
- Uplink truck crew (2 people)

This adds 20 additional people at a cost of $7200 to the housing budget. The total budget for housing this production crew would be approximately $16,200 for three days.

Personnel

Approximate Personnel Cost: $30,375

Personnel costs vary based on whether you are using in-house or freelance personnel. Whether you hire local or nonlocal personnel will also impact the budget. As mentioned in the camera section, nonlocal personnel can be very expensive when you include the daily rate, per diem, lodging, flights, and on-location transportation. A basic crew needed for our case study of a three day, on-location, production providing two hours of network programming is as follows. Keep in mind that these are approximate costs used only for pre-planning purposes. The actual cost will vary depending on the location of the event.

Overtime, if not watched carefully, can turn into a very large amount of money. It can be incredibly difficult to estimate. It usually depends on how familiar the crew is with the venue, weather, and unexpected equipment difficulties.

Per diem: $3375

Per diems average $45 per person per day for nonlocal personnel.

Transportation

Flights: $9600 average, $400/person
Rental Cars: $3300
Roughly 15 cars will be required for three days.

All senior personnel and talent generally require a car.

Other Costs

Tent, tables, and chairs: $1000/ three days

Includes a large tent (including set-up and tear down), 50 chairs, and 10 tables.

Catering: $1500

Generally, catering is provided only on the actual day of the competition. However, it is often worth catering the day before the event so that you don't lose your crew for two hours if they need to go off-site to find restaurants.

Golf Carts: $3200

This cost would include 16 golf carts for three days.

Phone Lines: $440 for 3 lines

$30/line plus an installation charge of $150/line

Tape Stock: $1500–2000

Wardrobe: $1000

Hats and shirts for crew and possibly additional clothing for the talent.

Production Insurance: $3000 for one event

Many companies who do remote productions on a regular basis pay an annual policy that

		Salary of Personnel on a Sports Production Crew		
# Needed	Position	Approx. Pay/Person	3 day total	Total Cost
1	Producer	$1000/day	$3000	$3000
1	Director	$3000/event	$3000	$3000
1	Associate director	$500/day	$1500	$1500
1	Unit manager	$550/day	$1650	$1650
1	Production coordinator	$250/day	$750	$750
1	Technical director	$475/day	$1425	$1425
8	Camera operators	$350/day	$1050	$8400
1	ENG camera person	$400/day	$1200	$1200
2	Videotape operators	$350/day	$1050	$2100
1	Video operator	$350/day	$1050	$1050
1	Graphics	$400/day	$1200	$1200
1	Font coordinator	$275/day	$825	$825
1	Senior audio (A-1)	$475/day	$1425	$1425
1	A-2	$300/day	$900	$900
2	Utilities	$250/day	$750	$1500
1	Runner	$150/day	$450	$450
Total: 25 Crew Members				Total pay: $30,375

302 disciplines / 38 sports + 57 digital OB vans x 18 cameras + explosion of the cost of broadcasting facilities − best ever TV coverage + 40 billion viewers x global economic downturn + 40 venues / 3500 employees − shared crews / venues / equipment + logistics expenses x 3700 live transmission hours x less is more + quality = budgeting of the Athens Olympic Games.

Anna Chrysou, Deputy Producer,
Athens Olympic Broadcasting

covers all productions for the year. An annual policy would substantially reduce the cost of insurance.

Weather Insurance: $600
Covers all production costs in case inclement weather causes the event to be cancelled or postponed.

Miscellaneous Budget: $2000
Covers snacks, office supplies, and other unforeseen expenses.

Security: $1200
Covers two security officers to be present from 6 p.m. until 7 a.m. They generally receive around $15/hour and are on duty whenever the crew is not at the venue.

Portable Restrooms: $1000
General rule is to provide one facility for every 15 people working at the location.

Overhead: $11,500
A 5%–13% overhead fee covers the cost of people booking the crew, administration, office space, and related costs.

Production Fee: $15 000
The production fee, generally around 10% of the budget, is the amount of money a production company would make as a profit for producing the event.

Contingency: $6500
The contingency is generally 5% of direct costs (not including an overhead figure).

Total Rough Budget: $162,000
For three days on-site with a freelance crew and rented mobile unit/OB van.

CHAPTER 6
Pre-production and Set-up

The production must show the world both sides of the sport, human and emotional. Our cameras need to be placed in the best locations to follow the athletes as well as capture the excitement of the moment. To accomplish this task, production meetings bring together the director, broadcast manager, venue technical manager, logistics manager, engineer-in-charge and the production manager—that is, all the people who will have responsibility for the coverage of the Games will get together to discuss, study and create the best television coverage.

Pedro Rozas, Head of Production,
2004 Athens Olympic Broadcasting and 1992 Barcelona Olympics

Production Meetings
Pre-production or production meetings are an integral part of the production process. Usually run by the producer, these meetings should include representatives from each area including:
- Director
- Talent
- Art director
- Production assistant
- Engineering supervisor

These meetings are designed to provide an overall vision of the production, receive feedback from the participants, determine how they may be impacted by production decisions, and discuss deadlines and budgets.

Production meeting frequency depends on the event. For the Olympic Games, production meetings may actually begin four years before the actual production. A local station covering a regularly scheduled event may meet the week or day before the event. Networks sometimes have two meetings each day the week before a large event in order to allow the producer to keep up with the various components of the production.

The Show Format
Scripted pre-game shows allow a producer and director to create a detailed format that gives a shot-by-shot and second-by-second description of the entire show. These formats seem to have a life of their own, evolving through a number of versions. The formats generally specify:
- Image source (videotape, graphic or on-camera)
- Audio source (sound on tape, live ambience or live talent)
- Description of image (talent who will be on camera, image content, and location)
- Segment time
- Total elapsed time

The program format lets each crew member know their responsibilities throughout the pre-game show, allowing them to anticipate the action, and reduces the number of instructions the producer and director need to give over the

The Game Plan

Broadcasters cannot simply walk into a venue, set up their cameras and microphones, and start broadcasting. Instead a broadcast game plan is created. This plan not only includes the broadcast of the actual event, it includes building a program around the sporting event. Live sport coverage cannot be scripted. A basic plan, however, still needs to be thought out and communicated to the production team by the producer and director. Elements of the broadcast game plan may include some of the following:

- *Show opening*
- *Introduction to the event*
- *Introduction of the participants*
- *Setting*
- *Atmosphere and the crowd*
- *Closing*

Figure 6.1: Cameras are placed on sleds to be skied into position at an Alpine event.

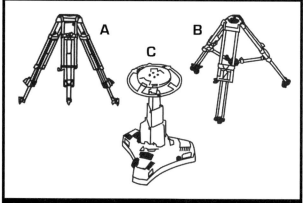

Figure 6.2: Camera supports are integral to getting solid steady images. While they do have their limitations, camera supports are used as much as possible to reduce operator fatigue as well as camera shake. Support A is an EFP tripod (sticks) used to hold lighter hand-held cameras. Support B is an in-studio pedestal used for heavy studio cameras. Support C is a hard camera heavy duty tripod, used to hold heavy cameras in the field. (Courtesy of Vinten Camera Support Systems.)

intercom. The format also helps RF camera operators and talent, who may need to move from one location to another. *(See figure 6.1.)*

Equipment Set-up

The equipment set-up (ESU) time varies from under a day for a small event to more than a week for a larger, more complicated event. Other factors that determine the ESU is the complexity of the terrain (alpine event), whether the venue is precabled, and the size of the set-up crew. The ESU includes running all audio and video cables and the transport and set-up of cameras, monitors and all audio equipment.

During set-up, the crew should always keep the strike (tear down) in mind. Equipment and cables should be removed from the truck and placed such that it will be easy to put them away after the shoot.

Setting Up a Camera

- Set up the tripod or other type of camera support.
- Check that the pan/tilt head is firmly attached to the mount.
- Level the tripod and pan/tilt head.
- Check that the pan/tilt head is locked.
- Attach the camera to the head. There are three basic ways to attach the camera: screws, wedge plate or quick release plate.
- Adjust the center of gravity of the camera on the tripod.
- Check the friction adjustments for the pan and tilt. These should be set at your comfort level.
- Make sure that the lens is tightly mounted on the head.
- Set the zoom controls at the right speed.
- Test the focus control to make sure that it is working.
- Attach the camera to the CCU cable and power up the camera.
- Check the monitor and adjust the contrast and brightness.
- Check the back focus to ensure that the image stays in focus from long shots to close-ups.
- Attach the intercom headset and test to make sure that it is working.
- If everything appears to be working on your end, wait for further instructions from the mobile unit.

TRU Victory Tour Indoor Soccer

One Hour Program Airs: 21/11/99

Segment 1

Tease	0:00:45
Locator/title (arena wide shot)	0:00:10
Talent on camera/discuss 2 US players and lead sound bite	0:01:00
US player pre-taped sound bite	0:00:25
Talent on-camera/discuss 2 world players	0:00:30
US team starting line-up and subs (gfx)	0:00:20
World team starting line-up and subs (gfx)	0:00:20
Begin game/1st quarter action (insert gfx: indoor soccer rules at 1st stop of play)	0:03:30
Opening billboard	0:00:25
Segment 1 Total	0:07:25

Segment 2

Welcome back/1st quarter action (throw to role model feature at stop of play)	0:02:00
Role model feature	0:02:00
1st quarter action>end 1st quarter	0:02:30
US team bumper: coach comments on 5 players w/b-roll and music	0:00:40
Segment 2 Total	0:07:10

Segment 3

In Bump: US player hi-8 clips on the road	0:00:30
Welcome back/2nd quarter action (throw to player feature at stop of play)	0:03:30
Player feature (Mia Hamm or soccer mothers)	0:02:00
2nd quarter action>end of 2nd quarter	0:02:30
US team bumper: coach comments on 5 players w/b-roll and music	0:00:40
Segment 3 Total	0:09:10

Segment 4

Main title rejoin	0:00:10
Welcome back/halftime sponsored element/throw to halftime interview	0:00:30
Alexi Lalas interview with US player/s	0:00:45
Halftime statistics	0:00:20
3rd quarter action	0:02:00
Player soccer tip	0:00:45
Segment 4 Total	0:04:30

Segment 5

3rd quarter action (throw to player feature at stop of play)	0:02:00
Player feature (Mia Hamm or soccer mothers)	0:02:00
3rd quarter action>end of 3rd quarter	0:01:45
US team bumper: coach comments on 5 players w/b-roll and music	0:00:40
Segment 5 Total	0:06:25

Segment 6

In bump: US player hi-8 clips on the road	0:00:30
4th quarter action (throw to player mini-feature at stop of play)	0:02:30
Player mini-feature (Brandi Chastain)	0:00:50
4th quarter action	0:02:00
US team bumper: coach comments on 5 players w/b-roll and music	0:00:40
Segment 6 Total	0:06:30

Segment 7

Closing billboards	0:00:25
4th quarter action>end of game	0:03:50
Final score/throw to Alexi interview	0:00:10
Alexi w/US player/s post-game interview	0:00:45
Goodbyes/courtesies/copyright (roll out)	0:00:30
Segment 7 Total	0:05:40

Total Program Time	0:46:50

Figure 6.3: Production format for CBS coverage of women's soccer (courtesy of Gary Milkis, Producer).

Figure 6.5: Set-up crew anchors a camera to a platform to minimize shake.

Figure 6.6: Winter coats on placed on cameras when shooting in sub-freezing weather.

Video versus Modulated Video

The highest quality video image is obtained from the standard video out from the camera or recorder. This standard video is often referred to as baseline video. Modulated or RF video is when video is mixed with the audio and both are then transmitted via RF. Video uses a BNC connector while modulated or RF video uses an RF connector.

- Make sure the appropriate filter is set.
  Color Correction Filters:
  – 5600K outdoor in daylight or indoors utilizing a lighting source that simulates daylight (generally includes fluorescent lighting)
  – 3200K tungsten lighting (indoor)
  Neutral Density Filters:
  – ND-1 reduces light by one f-stop
  – ND-2 reduces light by two f-stops
- Make sure that the camera is color balanced. This may include setting up the appropriate test chart and selecting the correct filter.
- When the camera is not in use, the front lens cap should be left on the camera.
- Familiarize yourself with the weather gear so you can put it on or take it off easily. If the weather looks as though it might get bad, put the weather gear on before the production begins. It is difficult to put weather gear on the camera during the production. *(See figure 6.6.)*

Cabling

Cables used in television broadcasting vary from simple coaxial configurations to very complex multicore cables. Triax cable is used by most mobile units/OB vans.

Fiber optic cable is frequently used to carry signals over long distances with minimum degradation. There are also a variety of cable connectors used in remote television production.

The following is a list of things to keep in mind when cabling:

1. Run cables neatly and, if possible, parallel. Try to group them together so the cable run is obvious and well defined. Lay cables as close to the production truck as possible so that the production crew will not trip or continuously walk on them.
2. When running camera cable, make sure that the correct end is toward the camera.
3. Cable connectors must be protected from the elements to ensure signal quality. If a cable connector must be exposed to the elements, try to support the connector so it is hanging downward or, preferably, wrap it with plastic and tape it. However, only tape the plastic on the top end, allowing air to come in underneath to prevent condensation in and

Figure 6.7: Organizing camera cables, known as dressing cables, is an important part of a technician's job. Tangled cables can be easily snagged by other cables or someone passing by. This can cause a safety issue, crimped cable or disconnected cable or connector. When cables are neatly organized into groups, tracing problems is much easier. Also note that to reduce electrical interference, power and audio/video cables need to be separated.

Figure 6.8: King triax connector. As a standard television production trucks use cameras utilizing triaxial cables. Generally referred to as tri-ax, these cables are thinner and lighter than multicore cables. Triax uses RF for signal transmission and can reach a maximum distance of around 5000 ft (1525m).

Figure 6.9: Lemo Triax connector (courtesy Lemo Connectors).

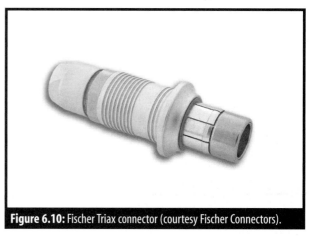

Figure 6.10: Fischer Triax connector (courtesy Fischer Connectors).

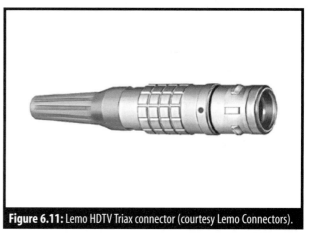

Figure 6.11: Lemo HDTV Triax connector (courtesy Lemo Connectors).

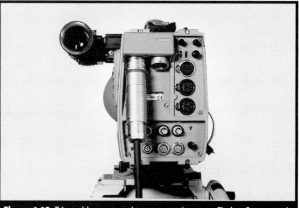

Figure 6.12: Triax cable connected to a camera (courtesy Fischer Connectors).

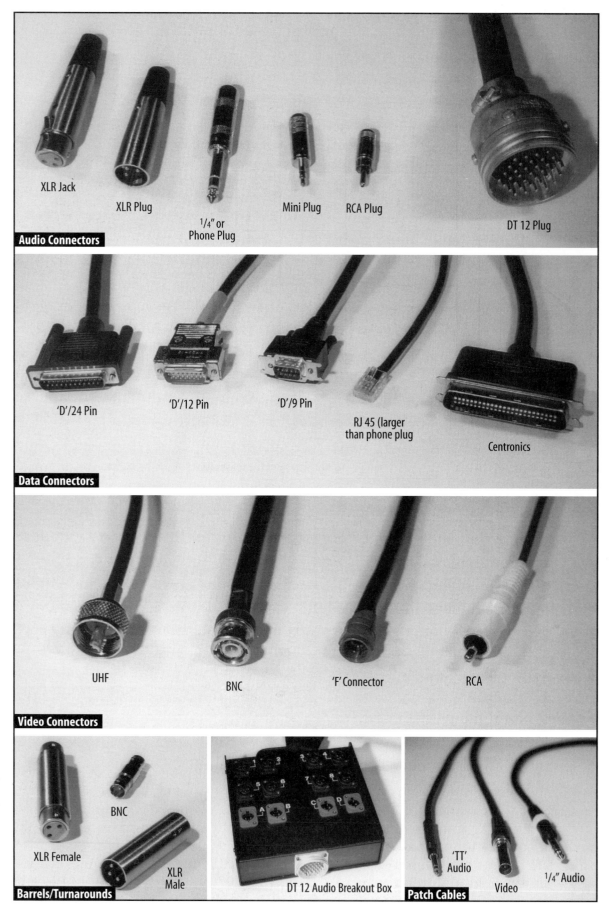

Figure 6.13: Audio data and video connectors.

on the connector. Do not allow the ends of cables to lie where water may puddle in the event of rain or melting snow.

4. Label all cables, for example, "Cam 1."

5. Report damaged cable to the supervisor. It is far easier to solve problems in the cabling phase than try to troubleshoot the problem during a competition.

6. Excess cable should be placed on the ground in a figure eight pattern or the over-and-under method so that the cable will not kink or tangle. A knotted cable can cause significant stress and subsequently irreparable damage to the cable.

7. Do not run a cable around any object that requires a tight bending radius. An extremely tight bend could damage the cable.

8. Avoid running video and audio cables close, and parallel, to power cables since these cables may be subject to a buzz. Video and audio cables that must cross over power cables should do so at a 90-degree angle to minimize the impact of the power on the video and audio signals.

9. Do not suspend tightly stretched cables between two points for much of a distance. Cables must be supported to ensure the cable is not damaged due to tension. Cables should be pulled and supported by the cable, not the connectors.

Camera Meetings

The camera meeting gives the director a chance to convey the nuances of his or her show.
—Brian Douglas, Head, Host TV Productions, 2002 and 2006 Olympics

Camera meetings are run by the director and are attended primarily by the camera operators. Other attendees include the camera assistants and maybe the associate director. These meetings, which last from 10 minutes to an hour, serve a variety of purposes. Primarily, the meeting allows the director to communicate his or her vision and also discuss with the camera operators how their shots fit into the overall production. The director describes the types of shots expected from each camera including framing details, cutting patterns, and specifically what the camera operators are to

---

The Basic Tech Kit:
What every technician should carry on a shoot
1. *Leatherman-type tool, a combination tool that generally includes a knife, pliers/wire cutter, various screwdrivers and a file*
2. *Gloves*
3. *BNC barrels*
4. *Roll of electrical tape*
5. *Roll of white tape and permanent pen used for marking cables*

Pre-game Meetings
It's important at pre-game meetings to give a thought process as to what is important, what are our goals. It's always been important for me to allow the technicians – camera operators especially – to have as much freedom as possible and let them express what it is that's coming from within them. From my perspective, we try to take a level of emotion and dedication to what our common goal is and bring it out every single week.

Craig Janoff

Figure 6.14: T66 audio punch block.

Figure 6.15: Krone audio punch block.

shoot. Often, directors create detailed shot sheets which describe the camera's anticipated shots. Some directors use video prints and/or photocopy the media guide so that camera operators can familiarize themselves with the key individuals they need to cover. Camera operators can then clip the sheets to their camera for easy visual access. In addition, the video prints show the type of shots and framing. *(See figures 6.16 and 6.17.)*

Shot sheets can be created from a production storyboard. Occasionally a director will have a storyboard created for the preshow, post-show or other related event. *(See figure 6.18.)* Appendix V includes two different sport-related storyboards. One of them was used for the medals ceremony at the Athens 2004 Olympics and the other is from the Emmy-winning Opening Ceremony of the 2002 Salt Lake Olympic Games. It is rare to storyboard sport-related programming but it is sometimes done when the show is extremely complex.

The camera meeting is also an effective tool for building teamwork. Mark Wolfson, Executive Producer/Director of KRON-TV in charge of Oakland As baseball, says in *Strangers in the Night* that the purpose of the meeting is to establish a relationship and an attitude with the crew. You need personal contact. The crew has to see that you're serious about what you're doing—without trying to imply that what we're doing is brain surgery.

Facilities Check

The facilities check or FAX is a check to see that all equipment is working correctly. Every facet of the production equipment should be tested, from intercoms to monitors. It is critical that the communication system, intercoms and two-way radios are working properly so the crew can hear who they need to hear and are able to respond. Other items that need to be checked during the FAX include:

1. Producer verifies camera feeds appear on the correct monitors on the monitor wall in truck.
2. Camera operators verify that they can see the return.
3. The video operator verifies that the cameras have the correct color match.
4. The technical director ensures that each VTR

Camera Three and Four
(left and right hand-helds)

Cable enough to make it to locker rooms if possible (including lights).

1. Stay wide/zoomed out all the way when ball gets near the basket or paint on your side. Resist the temptation to zoom in as ball moves around the perimeter.

2. Player makes fast break down court toward your basket—we will cut to you live.

3. Hero shot on shooter (coming toward you), include jersey # and zoom to face if he's looking toward you.

4. Switched on ISO Y from 3 to 4 (will use switch on replays). Also sometimes in replay when ball is on perimeter on other side of court.

5. Free throws on your side: Show shooter tight (leave room for super, then zoom in). Occasionally you'll follow ball on second shot of a two-point foul.

6. Free throws on opposite side: Get coach on your side. (Also look for occasional shots of cheerleaders or fans.) We rarely follow free throws from your reverse angle but be able to do so.

7. Watch/listen for substitutions, get player(s) leaving floor when the ball is NOT on your side of the court.

8. On time-outs/non-shooting fouls: Go for player huddles. If none, then get coach shots or other color (band, cheerleaders, etc.). Also, cue cheerleaders to perform out of break or we'll roll on them during a break. Please sell me on your color shots!

9. During breaks: Shoot huddles (if allowed) and well ISO shots for replay out of break.

10. Drama shots: Close-up of coach, post-game celebration inside players hugging, tight on basketball on ground, close-up of faces with sweat or ultra-wide with zoom-in when ball is on opposite side of court (i.e., during free throws). During time-outs, try to get into huddles if allowed.

11. Pre-game taping: Camera 3 on tripod shoots talent standing up at sideline position (with court/far basket in background).

12. At half-time: Camera 4 shoots announcers at table once only when we come back from studio update. Camera 3 gets color shots for 1st half stats or Nevada bench.

13. At end of game: Camera 4 shoots post-game interview with Nevada coach (color announcer will arrive with :30 remaining in game). Please check that the interview area has working monitor, mic, lights, and IFB. Camera 3 shoots announcer who stays at table. Also look for post-game fun shots on your way over as we will not take you until interview is over.

14. Break at half-time for 5 minutes.

15. Be aware that we have viewers watching during breaks on satellite in the clear.

Figure 6.16: Directors shot list for hand-held cameras from a basketball game. (courtesy Joseph Maar, Director/Producer).

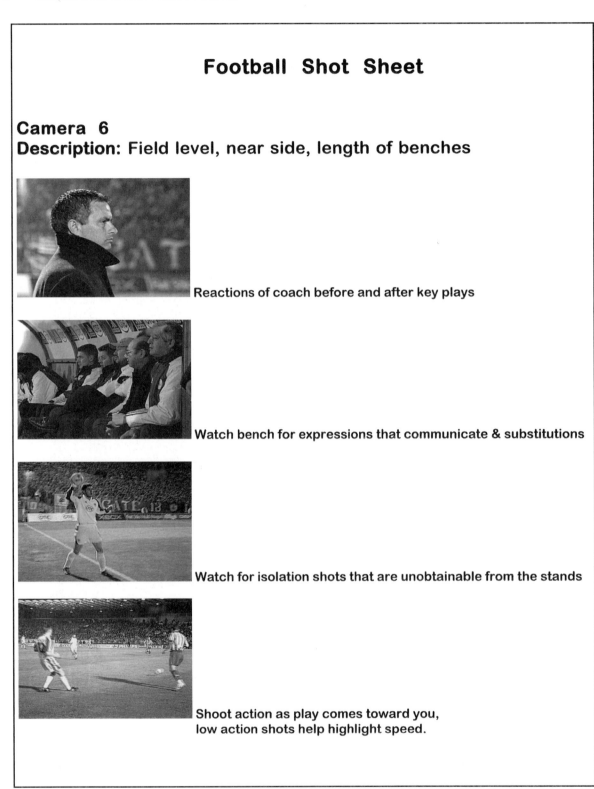

Football Shot Sheet

Camera 6
Description: Field level, near side, length of benches

Reactions of coach before and after key plays

Watch bench for expressions that communicate & substitutions

Watch for isolation shots that are unobtainable from the stands

Shoot action as play comes toward you,
low action shots help highlight speed.

Figure 6.17: Visual shot sheet shows the camera operator the types of shots wanted from camera #6.

Medal Ceremony Coverage

The final element of Olympic competition is the medal ceremony in which outstanding achievements are acknowledged and celebrated. AOB production has coordinated with ATHOC ceremonies to ensure the multilateral coverage conveys the power and emotion of the moment. Fixed and portable cameras, graphic identification for athletes, international federations and IOC presenters, and other production design elements have been carefully evaluated and specified. Regardless of the sport or venue, the coverage of medal ceremonies should conform as closely as possible with the outline below. The order of presentation of medals will be bronze, silver then gold.

Wide shot of venue – victory ceremony ID graphic

Medium shot, low – procession of IOC, athletes and medal bearers

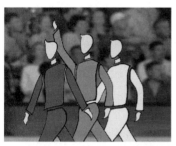
Close-up, hand-held camera – medallists walk and wave to crowd –

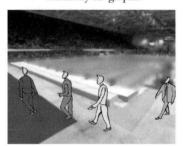
Wide shot – procession

Medium shot – IOC members, medallists and medal bearers

Close-up medallists behind podium – victory ceremony medals graphic

Close-up of IOC members presenting the medals to athletes – IOC ID graphic

Close-up – each bronze, silver and gold medal winner standing on platform when announced

Medium shot – bronze, silver and gold medals awarded

Close-ups of presentations to medallists – victory ceremony medal ID graphic

Three shot – medallists on the podium

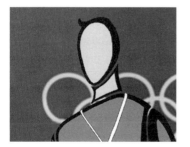
Close-up – gold medallist faces flags during anthem

Figure 6.18: Storyboards are often used to pre-visualize segments of a show.

Medal Ceremony Coverage (continued)

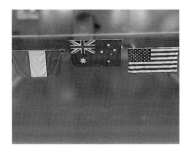

Close-up – country flags of
medallists

Close-up – gold medallist

Close-up – country flag of gold
medallist

Three shot – medallist during
anthem

Close-up – country flags of
medallists

Close-up – gold medallist at the end
of the anthem

Wide shot – crowd

Medium wide shot – medallists
posing for photographers

Medium shot, low – IOC members,
athletes and medal bearers exit
procession

Close-up, hand-held camera –
medallists walking

Wide shot – file out procession

operator receives the correct feed.

5. The A-1 and A-2 verify all audio and communication channels.

6. The engineer-in-charge verifies with the transmission facilities that they are receiving the feed.

Schedule

Production schedules vary depending on how familiar the crew is with the venue, how much equipment is already in place, whether the venue is already cabled, and the level of difficulty of the production. The level of difficulty is determined by the number of cameras and specialty cameras, the venue (cabling the side of a mountain or a small basketball court), and the complexity of the actual production format. Cabling crews usually arrive one or two days before the mobile unit, especially if the cabling is difficult—for example, skiing venue.

Productions take teamwork. Each member of the production crew is assigned a specific task. In many cases, one person may not be able to begin their task until another member of the crew has completed their portion of the set-up. At times, this means that some of the crew have to wait for hours until they can do their part. The production schedule helps the crew better plan, knowing exactly when each part of the production must be complete. See figure 6.20 for a sample production schedule for a figure skating competition at the 2000 Winter Goodwill Games.

Rehearsals

You can't "rehearse" a ball game, so you have to pre-plan. People used to tell me my camera rehearsals were too short. I told them that once the camera crew knew the shots I wanted, we'd rehearsed. I could do in seconds what some people needed minutes for—and the difference was knowing what I wanted and communicating it thoroughly.

—Tony Verna, Director, five Super Bowls, 12 Kentucky Derbys, Live TV: An Inside Look at Directing and Producing

Television rehearsals take many different forms. If the crew is shooting a scripted event, then theoretically, the order of events is known

Figure 6.19: ABC Sports personnel rehearse the Indy 500 pre-game show

First Color Olympic Broadcast

The first color broadcast of an Olympics occurred in 1968 when ABC Sports covered both the winter and summer Games. Although 1964 was black and white, we knew that we would be doing color by 1968—so we were expecting the changes. But not everything in Grenoble—where the winter Games were held—was color because some things such as bobsleigh, luge, and ski jumping, were taped and therefore still black and white. The most difficult thing about it all was that we had to go without triax, just a 200 foot multicable which was a horrible job. It weighed a pound for every foot, so for 200 feet, it was 200 pounds.

Jules Barnathan, Broadcast Operations,
ABC Sports, 1968 Olympic Games

and the crew can practice the details of the production. Live events present a unique challenge in that anything can happen. The crew must rehearse for the unexpected. Generally, the pre-game and post-game shows are fairly scripted, allowing for some rehearsal. Rehearsals provide an opportunity for the director to make sure the camera operators are providing the required shots. It also gives RF talent a chance to determine if they have enough time to move from location to location. Also, during rehearsal, it is important to check the RF camera paths, verifying their transmissions stay intact throughout the entire area in which they will be shooting.

At the Indianapolis 500, ABC Sports used runners and PAs to serve as "drivers" and "cars" to rehearse the detailed pre-game show. Runners wear the name of the driver on a placard around their neck to allow the director to identify who is being interviewed. *(See figure 6.19.)*

Day	1	Management and production trailers park and power	
	2	Phone installation	
	3	Furniture, fixtures, and equipment (FF&E) delivered	
	4	Staging and platform construction	
	5	Mobile unit/OB van park and power	
	6	7:00–5:00	Equipment set-up
	7	7:00–Noon	Transmission tests
		Noon–5:00	Results, data, and timing test
	8	6:00–7:00	Equipment set-up
		7:00–Noon	Rehearsal
		Noon–4:00	Equipment set-up
	9	Competition Day	
		8:00–10:00	FAX
		10:00–11:00	Meal
		11:00–Noon	Pre-production
		Noon–3:00	Production
		3:00–5:00	Reset and FAX
		5:00–6:00	Meal
		6:00–8:00	Pre-production
		8:00–11:00	Production

At the end of the multiple-day event, tear down is scheduled for two hours.

Figure 6.20: A set-up and production schedule from the 2000 Winter Goodwill Games.

PART 3: Creating the Production

CHAPTER 7
Production

Content is still king. Technology is a secondary thing for us. The responsibility of documenting—creatively, emotionally, journalistically—the games itself is really our goal.

Craig Janoff, Director,

Producing the Remote

There is no set worldwide programming strategy formula for producing a remote. NBC's Olympic Games coverage primarily consists of packaged programs. Other countries however primarily program live, staying away from prepackaged material.

At an IOC Olympic television symposium in 1998, Yosuke Fujiwara, Senior Producer for Olympic Operations at NHK in Japan, made the following statement: "We believe that the essence of the sports broadcast lies in live coverage ... we believe that the unscripted drama exists in sports itself, and live broadcast is the best way to show such drama."

Each producer and director must analyze their audience, the sport, and the available broadcast facilities to determine the best programming strategy for their specific audience.

Several coverage strategies will be discussed in this chapter. Coverage strategies are constantly evolving, changing with the type of sport, the anticipated audience and the skills of the crew.

Better Than Being There

Andy Rosenberg, Coordinating Director of the NBA on NBC stated: One thing that television does exceptionally well is take you to places that you cant get to otherwise. By placing cameras in a variety of locations throughout the stadium, and having some of them fitted with very long lenses, we were able to achieve an intimate view of the players and the game that you just can't get from a fixed seat location in the building.

NBC Blends Drama with Technology
in NBC Playoff Coverage

NBC's Olympic Television Philosophy

The National Broadcasting Company's (NBC's) broadcasting philosophy was born out of hundreds of hours of research, examining the preferences, expectations, and hopes of thousands of Olympic television viewers in the United States. Throughout the research, many of the same themes kept surfacing—story, reality, possibility, idealism, and patriotism. These five themes—which correspond to the five Olympic rings—serve as the foundation of the NBC Olympic television philosophy.

Ring 1: Story
Viewers want a narrative momentum, a story that builds. Stories make connections with reality, among facts, and between the subject and the viewer. This is what the viewer takes away from the telecast.

Ring 2: Reality
Perhaps the major hook for Olympic viewers is the unscripted drama of the Olympics, the idea that anything can happen, both of an athletic and a human nature. People look for real stories and relativity, things that apply to them. They are looking for real life and real emotion presented credibly.

Ring 3: Possibility
This ring covers the feeling of self-realization. The audience experiences the rise of individuals from ordinary athletes and their humble beginnings to their joining of the company of the world's elite. This identification reinforces belief in their own ability to achieve. This embodiment of possibility gives the viewer a reason he or she can make it through.

Ring 4: Idealism
The Olympics are still viewed by a vast majority in the contexts of purity and honor. They appeal to what is best in us. This area summarizes the viewer's need to integrate the intellectual and the emotional.

Ring 5: Patriotism
Love of country is not just limited to an American viewer's love of the United States. National honor and Olympic tradition seem to go hand in hand. The viewer recognizes the love of his or her own country, but, at the same time, respects the international athletes' love of their nation as well.

NBC's Coverage of the
Games of the XXVI Olympiad

Directing the Remote

Portraying passion and teamwork is key in covering sports.

—Lee Henry, Director

The goal of the event director:
1. Build the viewers' excitement about the event.
2. Reveal relationships and educate the audience about the intricacies of the sport.
3. Catch the ambience and emotion of the event.
4. Communicate the event with clarity.

Types of Sports Action

*(by Harold Hickman, Directing Television,
© 1991, McGraw-Hill, Inc., reproduced with
permission of the McGraw-Hill Companies)*

Whatever the sport, we can divide coverage planning into three variables the director should understand: (1) action flow, (2) team versus individual sports, and (3) horizontal versus vertical versus circular action.

Action Flow

Action flow concerns the continuity of action within the sport. Is there a constant flow, or is the action periodically interrupted by time-outs? In hockey, for example, the action is continuous, with few breaks. The ending of the periods or the stopping for face-offs may be the only interruptions. Soccer is another such game. On the other hand, American football involves very sporadic action. There is a break after every play. Each actual action is condensed into 10 or 15 seconds of intense physical conflict followed by approximately 30 seconds of time out. Golf action is also very slow and sporadic. A shot may last only 5 to 10 seconds, while time spent in walking, club selection, scouting, and preparation add another 5 minutes or more per player. Action flow can thus be divided into two categories: stop-and-go and continuous action.

Stop-and-Go Sports

Stop-and-go sports tend to be rigorous and involve a great deal of physical contact or energy exertion. Golf, perhaps, is the single exception. The chief stop-and-go sports covered by television include football, baseball, tennis, golf, bowling, and track and field. All of these sports involve emotionally intense action followed by some period of inactivity.

Directing Stop-and-Go Action

From a production and directing standpoint, the need to maintain audience interest during time-out periods is the primary challenge. Pauses in action are frequent and sometimes very long (at least from the viewers' standpoint). Replay devices have provided an excellent production value for such periods. The longer the "stop" periods or the more complex the action, the greater the need for replay units to provide isolation of and different angles on the same action.

The use of analysis for such events is also essential to maintain the tempo of the production. To sustain viewer interest, it is wise to include sophisticated analysis of the athletes' performance, such as the following: blocking, running, passing, and all elements of defense in football; hitting and fielding form in baseball; form and agility in tennis; form in golf and bowling.

Tips for Remote Switching

1. *Make sure that every camera operator knows what you want them to do before you begin the program. They should consider themselves "live" all the time. That way, if you mis-switch, you may not look bad. If the operators have a basic game plan, you won't have to keep telling them what to do.*
2. *Study each monitor carefully before you switch to it. Even though the director may be screaming "take camera two" and camera two is out of focus, he or she may be confused and really mean "take camera one."*
3. *Use all your fingers on the switcher keys. It is much faster to cut quickly between cameras if you already have your finger on the button.*
4. *Try to anticipate what the on-camera person may do before you switch. When in doubt, cut to a wider shot. Always have at least one camera on a wide shot at all times.*
5. *Try to develop a switching or cutting cadence to your shots. If the action is speeding up, cut faster between cameras. This establishes a rhythm.*

Adapted from
Ten Steps to a Better Remote Switching

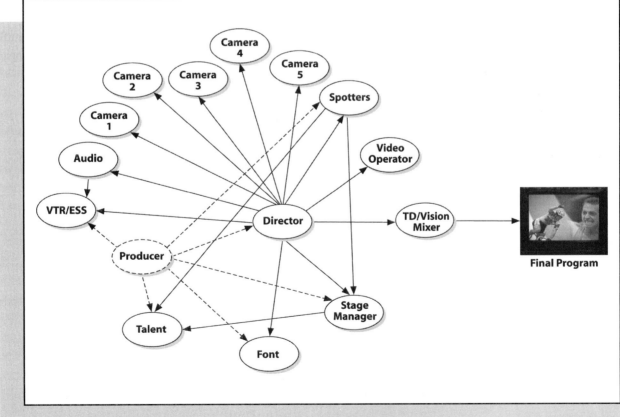

The first time observer of a remote production may perceive that all is chaos. However, you can see the large number of interactions that need to take place for the producer and director in a simple five camera sports production. This chart does not include engineering, logistics, and all of the assistants that many of these positions include.

Directing Emphasis on Scoring

The director must be able to even out the emotional highs and lows of the stop-and-go game. Obviously, the coverage of the action is relatively simple—follow-the-bouncing-ball. This means that the director must frame the action in the physical direction of its flow. Most action in stop-and-go is offensive action—that is, the individual or team on offense is the center of the directing concentration. Normally, the team on offense is the only team that can score. A team may intercept a ball (or puck), but that team is immediately on offense. The concentration is on scoring and, therefore, the director's responsibility is to follow the team that has the greatest opportunity to score.

In baseball we have a single player (the hitter) against an entire team. Coverage of defense is a much larger item than coverage of offense. After all, the whole playing field is filled with defensive players and the hitter is even standing out of bounds while in the batter's box. Yet, despite the fact that the main focus of baseball is defense, most of the coverage is of the offensive play (the hitter against the pitcher).

Tennis may also be considered an exception to the "only the offense can score" situation. Here, either player can score—both are on offense. But the serving player has a marked advantage, since he or she has the first offensive opportunity. Each time the ball passes over the net the offense shifts.

Maneuvering the team or player into position to score is the aim of the play in stop-and-go. This is normally accomplished through a series of "plays." The closer the team or player gets to scoring, the more intense the game. The director can enhance this emotional involvement by warming up the coverage—that is, tightening the shots as the emotional level of the production increases. It also means adding more radical shot angles and increasing the intercutting of shots. The pace of the production needs to pick up as the emotional level of the production increases. This enhancement of the emotional level helps the audience grasp the pressure of the sports performance.

Pumping

To enhance an otherwise dull sport performance,

the director may want to pump the game through the use of additional production values that may be viewed as unethical by some. Any attempt to make a game or contest appear more exciting or tight (in terms of who will win) can be viewed as beyond the presentational responsibilities of the director. Some viewers may want the director merely to provide adequate coverage and let the viewer decide whether the game is exciting or dull.

But the director's goal and responsibility is to make the production interesting and entertaining for the audience, so there is a very basic objective to be met in the use of increased production values toward that end. How far to go with the introduction of additional production values so as to achieve this end must be determined before the production begins. Obviously, it is questionable whether to allow the announcing talent to pump up the closeness of the conflict through false excitement in play-by-play and color presentation (analysis of game strategy or quality of individual performance), and to augment this with exciting, fast-paced production when the score is 50 to 0. The new director may want to observe the techniques of a seasoned television director faced with coverage of a game that is lopsided in score or athletic match or performance.

The addition of more shots of the crowd (including people with painted faces and bizarre masks or sleeping babies) that are not part of the game or contest will help alleviate the boredom of the game without pumping. Interesting activities on the sidelines can also be included— a worried coach or an injured player. Basically, anything of interest that can divert attention from the slow moving game itself will help maintain the attention level of the audience. Stop-and-go sports make this type of coverage even more difficult and essential.

Continuous Action Sports

Unlike stop-and-go sports production, the continuous action contest provides little or no time to interrupt for color analysis. Continuous action sports include basketball, hockey, and soccer. Generally, these sports have not been as popular as stop-and-go performances on American

---

Director's Slang

The following are some of the slang words used by directors:

Effect: Switcher cue term for animation, box or special effect
Fly: A non-switcher effect that is generally created by a digital effects generator (DVE)
Go wide: Zoom out
Go close: Zoom in
Mix: Mix cameras without a full dissolve
Pull Focus/Rack Focus: Change the focus from one subject to another
Push in: Zoom in
Pull out: Zoom out
Transform: Animated graphics
You're hot: Your camera is on

Directing HDTV

HD allows the viewer to see much more of the event, as the shots incorporate much more of the action. The expansive shots make viewers feel "much more a part of the event."

Mike Wells, 17-time Emmy Award-winner

Live sporting events shot in HD tend to have approximately 30% fewer cuts and could sometimes be covered with as few as two cameras.

Jeff Cree, Sony Acquisition System Specialist

Each HD shot seems to offer more to the viewer, the detail in every aspect of the shot holds your attention longer, and thus eliminates the need to switch camera angles to improve ones perspective. With HD, I found that the shot simply lasts longer, offering more to the viewers. The clarity of the image requires the director to watch the total shot as opposed to the action you routinely photograph in standard definition. Close-ups in HD can be too overwhelming and thus distract from what you were hoping to accomplish. It is simply more advisable to photograph things from a reasonable distance, than to potentially overwhelm or bombard the audience with sensory overload.

Brian Douglas, HDTV Director,
2002 Olympic Opening Ceremonies

Directors on Directing Sports

Alexandro DeMartino, Director (Sky), Italy
- *Favorite sport to direct: Football*
- *Quote: "For me directing is like a conductor and an orchestra. Single work of each camera means nothing…together they can make something."*
- *How do you prepare for directing? A good director must understand the rules of the sport and must be physically ready*
- *Advice: Be diplomatic, know finance, audio must be at the same quality level as video. Graphic operators need to not only understand the rules of the sport but must be able to predict what is going to happen in order to have the correct graphics together.*

Gary Milkis, Director (NBC and CBS), United States
- *Favorite sport to direct: Downhill Skiing*
- *Quote: "Directing is telling a story with cameras."*
- *How do you prepare to direct? Design the monitor wall so that it makes sense for the sport.*
- *Advice: Find a balance between pushing the crew and not abusing the crew. Have a little fun on the headset.*
- *Biggest challenge: Locating the best camera positions*

Greg Breckell, Director (CTV, TSN, and ESPN), Canada
- *Favorite sport to direct: Golf*
- *How do you prepare to direct? Complete a detailed survey of the course.*
- *Advice: KNOW the game, not just the rules. Properly motivate the crew member who may not feel that their job is an important as others.*
- *Biggest Challenge: Communication and coordination of game plan. Everyone needs to understand what is going on and why. Simple things are what can really hurt a production.*

Brian Douglas, Director (over 700 NBA games), United States
- *Favorite sport to direct: Basketball*
- *Quote: "Know the sport and the people. How a player dribbles the ball can tell you if he is going for a three pointer."*
- *How do you prepare to direct? Research is key, look at tapes.*
- *Advice: Establish a creative environment to work in. Keep in mind that you are there to make others look good, not you. You are not part of the show.*
- *Biggest challenge: Maintaining control of the situation.*

Bai Li, Director (Shanghai TV Sports), China
- *Favorite sports to direct: Table tennis and basketball*
- *Quote: "Have creative new ideas when covering traditional sports. It is easy to do it the old style."*
- *Advice: Know the sport. Watch a lot of sports.*
- *Biggest challenge: This generation is not used to working as a team. The Chinese director must spend more attention on building teamwork and fostering good communication.*

Mark Wallace, Director (BBC and LiM Africa), United Kingdom
- *Favorite sport to direct: Rugby Union*
- *Quote: "The 5 P's of Sports Television: Prior Preparation Prevents Poor Performance!"*
- *How do you prepare to direct? Go around the crew, introduce myself, talk to each member of the crew and explain what I would like them to do. Then get clearly in my own head what needs to be done and when.*
- *Advice: Try to appear calm and in control of yourself. Have a back-up plan and try to always think one step ahead.*

television, because they do not provide the natural breaks for commercial insertion or for the audience to take a break in their viewing to do something else. The single exception is basketball (both professional and college level). Basketball can be considered a basically continuous action sport. There are no breaks between field goals, although there are more breaks in basketball than hockey or soccer. Action stops in basketball for fouls and team time-outs. During the extended stop for a foul, one or more replays of the foul can be shown and other comments made. These are really semi-stops, because the game does continue and there is little time for commercials or extended replays.

Continuous action sports tend to be very rigorous and are usually limited to a specific, bounded playing area. In the cases of basketball and hockey, these areas are rather small, which increases the emotional potential of the game for a television audience because the crowd is close to the playing area and becomes more emotionally involved with the play.

There are other continuous action sports, minor from a television standpoint, including cross-country or marathon races. The Boston and New York marathons are considered major sporting events, especially by runners and by residents of those cities. But not much television time is given to marathons compared to other continuous action sports events. Track-and-field events generally do not fit into this category, because the various events, considered as a single coverage, involve a great deal of stop-and-go.

The director must take into consideration a number of factors when preparing to cover continuous action sports: (1) rapid camera action, (2) increased shot sizes, and (3) camera changes during action.

Camera Action Tends to Be Rapid

Shot size usually is rather wide angle to give the audience a chance to see the relationship of offense to defense and offensive player to defensive player, and to establish the relationship between the ball, the team on offense, and the goal. Still, to increase the warmth of a game, the camera shot needs to be as close as possible.

The Image

It is not the number of cameras that determines the quality of the picture, it is the quality of the perspective. We can learn a great deal from the old masters such as Leonardo da Vinci, Michelangelo, Goya, Rubens or Rembrandt. Their pictures had a strength of the middle. They have a center of concentration, which catches the eye involuntarily. This strength of the middle is also possible in the moving picture, where the eye is guided to the focus point and can rest quietly. Unfortunately, it is missing in many cases.

Horst Seifard, former director of
Sports Programs at ARD, Germany,
Television in the Olympic Games: The New Era

Increase in Shot Size

As the speed of the action increases, there is a tendency also to increase the size of the shot in order to include all of the action. However, as action speed increases, the director really should attempt to tighten shot size to capture the emotion of the faster pace. In basketball, for example, the intensity of the action increases as the ball is worked closer and closer to the basket. Camera shot size should get closer and closer. This does two things: (1) it increases the warmth of the coverage and the emotional involvement of the audience and (2) it gives the audience a better perspective on the action.

This is especially critical in hockey, where the puck is so small and moves so fast that it is difficult for the audience to see and follow it. As the play moves across the blue line and closer to the goal, the camera coverage should move closer to the play.

Camera Changes During Action

A basic rule in sports coverage is to never change from camera to camera when critical action is taking place in the playing area. In basketball this means the director should not change from camera to camera when a shot is in the air (either a field goal or a free throw). In football this means the camera covering a quarterback who is fading back to throw must cover the flight of the ball until it is caught or incomplete. To change camera angles at these critical times requires that the audience reestablish their relationship to the game from another angle. This only takes a second to do, but becomes critical in the split second involved in the pass or the shot. The same critical point occurs in baseball when a pitcher delivers to a batter.

The director must be careful during continuous action sports not to over-direct the coverage. Often a single shot of a mile run, for example, will satisfy the audience, because they are interested in the continuity of the event. Only when the race comes down to the final 100 yards or so should the director attempt to increase the suspense and emotional involvement of the audience by zooming in on the lead runner (or runners).

Team and Individual Sports

Sports coverage can also be planned from the standpoint of the number of athletes involved. Most television sports are team sports (football, basketball, baseball, hockey), but for a number of years there has been a growing interest in individual sports (tennis and golf).

Team Sports

We are obviously spending too much time covering the line-up, the race, and the results, rather than the emotions of the competitors and taking the viewer behind the scene.

—Alan Pascoe, Managing Director of Fast Track, Great Britain

With team sports there is a built-in interest because of the complexity of the teams working together. Most avid sports fans understand the sophistication of various games and appreciate the role of various team members and their contribution to the team's success (or failure). For example, the offensive line of a football team should be made up of players highly skilled at their specific positions. Fans (and replays) may want to concentrate on the efficiency of these players as they carry out their assignments. This increases the attention factors for the viewer, and thus the excitement of the game. In most team sports, the ability of the team to work together as a well-organized and effective unit provides unusual coverage opportunities. It also, however, increases the demands on the director to understand the game and the complexities and fine points of quality play. Because of these complexities, coverage of team sports is more involved than for individual sports.

Individual Sports

Individual sports, on the other hand, have their advantages. There is a greater opportunity for the director to increase the emotional level of the production by concentrating on close-up production techniques. It is easier for the audience to associate themselves with an individual player than with a team of players. This involvement is inherently greater if the individual is in a contest with another individual (tennis) than if he or she is in a contest with him or herself (golf).

With individual sports, the director has a greater opportunity to warm the production through the use of close-ups and single shots. Examples include tennis, boxing, skiing, track and field, golf, and wrestling (real or exhibition).

The director of an individual sports coverage has a number of considerations: (1) building emotional involvement through tighter coverage, (2) dealing with the dominant player, and (3) limited space for coverage.

Building Emotional Involvement

The director has an opportunity to build the emotional involvement of the audience by increasing the warmth of the production. The director can get inside the personal space of the individual in the shot and draw the audience in. He or she can develop a visual situation in which the audience member can relate to the athlete and feel the pain, pressure, and thrill of victory or agony of defeat.

Dealing with the Dominant Player

If the sport provides a conflict between individuals (such as tennis or boxing), coverage may concentrate on the dominant player. This may not always be the winning player. For example, a loser who is suffering from injury or losing control of a match may be the story the director wants to cover. American audiences have a natural affinity for the underdog and this can be translated into interesting coverage if the underdog is attempting to upset the star. Because the player in these contests usually has fans, the director needs to balance the coverage of each player so the fans will be satisfied. Of course, the director can build audience interest and loyalty by the type of coverage given. It is relatively easy to slant the coverage toward one player or another in an individual sport. But the director should try to avoid this. If the coverage takes more shots or tighter shots or better angles of the favored player, cuts away when the favored one is in trouble, shows the disfavored player when he or she is in trouble, or slants the comments from play-by-play or color commentators, then the production is slanting the coverage unethically.

The director should try to be as journalistic as

Softball Coverage in 1945
It was necessary to shrink diamond dimensions for proper perspective. Two cameras covered the game. One was set up behind home plate, the other at first base looking toward second. A 12-inch (30.5 cm) ball was used instead of the standard ball, again to limit action, to keep flies in close, keep hits from going over the fence.

Television Show Business

Monday Night Football, ABC Sports
The Monday Night Football influence of long lens close-ups, greater quarterback coverage, and increased field level shots have enhanced football by providing mythic images of modern gladiators engaged in both sport and spectacle.

Joseph Maar,
Football And Television—A Perfect Match

possible in these situations. He or she should provide balanced and fair coverage of all contestants. This is often difficult when covering the game for the local high school or college against an arch rival from the next town and even more difficult when covering the United States team in Olympic competition. Balance in camera coverage and the establishment of a strong coverage formula will help reduce the possibility of slanting coverage.

Limited Space for Coverage

Individual sports normally have a very limited space that must be covered. You may argue that golf is not limited at all—as a matter of fact has one of the largest playing fields in sports. But we are talking here about the area in which the athlete must work at any given time, not the total field of play. At any point in the round, the golfer is dealing with a small tee area, a bunker, or a green—not the whole golf course. The marathon runner also is dealing only with that space in which he or she is running at the time—not the entire course. In team sports this area is greatly expanded because the team can take up a great deal of area (field or court).

The bowler deals with only a single alley, the tennis player works with a relatively small court and the vaulter deals with two standards, a bar and a short runway. This provides the director with a great deal of flexibility and opportunity for intensity in coverage. Golf and racing (marathons and auto) are perhaps the exceptions, for the director must be prepared to cover wide areas but concentrate on small play areas at any given time. The portable mini-cam and refined portable microwave units have greatly aided such coverage.

This limited working space provides increased warmth to coverage of the individual sport. Because the director can concentrate more cameras on a smaller area, there is the opportunity to tighten shots and to mix angles for more effect. The director who fails to make use of this opportunity will find the coverage becoming dull and cool. For the individual sport to compete with team sports on television, the drama of the contest and the struggles of the athletes must be portrayed. The director is in-

volved in telling the story of the conflict. Anything that can be done to make sure the audience understands the real story should be done.

Horizontal versus Vertical versus Circular Action

All productions have a horizontal axis. In most sports this axis is critical to the orientation of the audience. With few exceptions, sports coverage can be divided into three types: (1) horizontal action, (2) vertical action, and (3) circular action.

Horizontal Action

Fortunately for television directors, most sports contests are horizontal in nature; that is, the action takes place on a horizontal plane in front of the cameras. Football, for example, is made up of two teams moving up and down the field across the screen. Basketball also is a contest of two teams moving up and down the floor in front of the cameras. Unfortunately for the director, such action violates the z-axis rule—it is better to have action toward and away from the camera than across the screen. But since the orientation of the audience to the game is horizontal, this dictates the type of coverage you must use.

The director can take advantage of the ease of establishing cameras in horizontal games by drawing the imaginary axis down the middle of a football field, from goal post to goal post, and down the middle of the basketball court, from backboard to backboard. If during action all cameras are kept to one side of that line, it will be easy to keep the audience in the game.

Cameras can be located within the end zones or under the backboards in a horizontal contest. But if coverage of play extends beyond those points and crosses the axis, the audience will become disoriented. Cameras can be placed in these locations for color and for some time-out coverage, but they should not be used extensively for coverage of plays. The single exception, noted previously, is their use for reverse-angle replays. In these cases the audience must be reestablished through a statement from the announcing crew or from a graphic on the screen indicating that the replay is from the opposite side of the field of play.

Vertical Action

In horizontal games, such as tennis, the director must treat the action as if it were vertical. The movement of the ball and the action of the players makes it difficult to provide general coverage in the horizontal camera set-up. In these cases the z-axis becomes a major factor. The director attempts to make the movement of the ball function within the z-axis, moving toward and away from the camera. In tennis, for example, cameras set up for coverage from one of the baselines show the ball moving from one player (with his or her back to the cameras) to another across the net (facing the cameras). It makes little difference which baseline is used, since the players exchange sides of the net throughout the match. In this case, although the game is horizontal (across the net from court to court), the coverage is vertical (toward and away from the cameras). Since tennis is a stop-and-go game, sideline cameras can be used for "stop" coverage, with close-ups of players and fans.

Golf, on the other hand, is a purely vertical game. The ball, and action, moves toward and away from the camera. There is no horizontal axis. It is extremely difficult to track the ball horizontally because of the speed, distance, and size of the ball. The axis is very flexible in golf, because no two courses are the same. There is a tee area that leads to a fairway that leads to a green, but no two are alike and few have similar out-of-bounds situations.

The dramatic elements of golf occur on the greens during putting. The golf expression "you drive for show and putt for dough" means that the critical element of the game for the professional is putting. This is where scoring happens. Obviously, the objective of golf is to hit the ball fewer times than your opponents—the lowest score wins. The saving of strokes normally comes on the green during putting. The director must, therefore, concentrate on the putting portion of the game. It is at this point that the camera shots must warm. Here, too, the axis is a minor factor. But the director must make sure the audience is established so they can reference the location of the ball to the hole. Since putting is always in the direction of the hole, once establishment has taken place there is little need to reestablish. One caution, however: During the action portion of golf (striking the ball) it is essential that the audience be able to follow-the-bouncing-ball. When the ball is putted, for example, the audience should be able to see the ball and the hole and be able to follow the ball as it rolls toward the hole. As the ball approaches the hole, the director may want to zoom in on the ball and the hole; but the reference between the two must always be maintained.

Some track-and-field sports may be considered vertical as well: javelin, hammer, and shot put are examples.

Circular Action

Some sports appear to be basically round-axis sports—baseball, boxing, racing, and wrestling are examples. Golf putting may also fit into this general category. Here the action seems to move in a circle (although most of the playing areas are square, such as baseball diamonds and boxing rings). Because of this it is difficult to establish a specific axis. The director may help establishment through the use of boundaries, such as the foul lines in baseball or the ropes of the boxing ring. The audience generally will not mind a loss of orientation in these sports as long as reestablishment is provided periodically.

Combinations

Most sports are a combination of the general types we have just discussed. Football is a team, horizontal, and stop-and-go sport. Baseball is a team, stop-and-go, basically circular sport (although the action of the ball, from the pitcher's delivery to the batter as well as its flight from the bat, is more vertical than circular). Golf is an individual, vertical, stop-and-go sport.

These classifications are important because they provide the basis for the design of coverage. The placement of cameras for proper coverage will depend on the axis of the game. The size of shots used, the lenses needed for those shots and the need to establish and reestablish at specific times will be determined by these factors.

Personalize the Production

I'm a firm believer that more cameras do not make a better director and do not make a better show. I've seen directors take four cameras and make them look like eight and vice versa. Whether the viewing public sees more because cameras are used depends on the ability of the director. My number one priority is the athlete. We try to personalize, thereby enabling the viewer to experience the emotion of the game... My camera (operators) know that when someone scores, I want to see his/her face as well as the faces of the opposing coaches. I've tried to instill in my people a principle I learned years ago ... that the individual is the key to any story.

Chet Forte, Director

Coverage Design
Follow-the-Bouncing-Ball

The single most critical production value in sports coverage is the need to know where the ball is at all times. This is true for all sports with, perhaps, the exception of individual sports, such as boxing and wrestling, where there is no ball to maneuver.

Needs of the Audience

Sports coverage is presentational television. The directing style is normally invisible. The need of the audience to know the status of the contest is primary. The job of the director is to tell the story to the audience.

Orientation. The audience must have clearly in mind the general situation regarding the game. They must know which team/individual has control or has the momentum in the contest. This orientation is different from establishing, which deals with spatial location. Orientation has to do with the emotional status of the contest. It also has to do with the current score. The audience must know which team/individual has scored the most points (or fewest points as in golf). Your first question when arriving late to watch a football game with friends is usually "What's the score?" It is part of orientation.

Orientation also includes time/distance/frame factors. How much time is remaining in the game/quarter/period? How much more distance must the runner cover? What bowling frame (or boxing round) are we in? So, after you have asked what the score is, your next question may be "What quarter are they in, and how much time is left?" It is easy for the director to forget about the orientation needs of the audience. From a position in the remote truck, the director knows the orientation factors, but the audience at home does not. It is a general rule that the audience must be re-oriented after each play in football (where yardage, down, and time are important) and after each hole in golf (who is leading, what hole we are on). These are just examples. It is not just the last two minutes of a football or basketball game in which the audience wants to know the time remaining; they want to know periodically throughout the game.

Direction of Play. The direction the ball and move

to score must be established and maintained. The audience does not need to know if the stadium or playing floor runs north–south or east–west (although almost all outdoor football stadiums run north–south, with camera coverage coming from the west stands because of the afternoon sun). The audience is not concerned about the location of the stadium or arena in the city. They are concerned about the location of the ball and the direction of play within the boundaries, however.

Location of the Ball. The audience must know the location of the ball, especially in games such as football and hockey. The movement of the ball (puck) toward the goal is important. In football the location of the ball with reference to yard markers must be established. The game changes drastically as the ball nears the defensive goal. The audience must reestablish location of the ball between plays, especially after plays that gain high yardage. For variety, a director may want to try some shots of the crowd as it follows a play, but unless the audience has been reestablished before the next play begins, they will be frustrated during the action.

Ball in the Frame. During action sequences, the audience must see the ball in the frame. This is basic to follow-the-bouncing-ball coverage, as has been noted. There is nothing more frustrating to the audience than not knowing where the ball is during action.

Directing Style

Directing style during action elements of a sporting event must be basically invisible. Directors must place themselves psychologically in the position of the audience and then show the audience what they need and want to see.

Directors, especially new directors, should plan to select an action camera that will handle the bulk of the coverage during the action portions of stop-and-go contests. This is especially true of games in which the ball moves quickly or where the action is complex. Other cameras can then be designated to provide coverage during non-action periods.

It is only during the time-out points in stop-and-go that the director may want to show a little creativity or pump up the coverage with production values, such as instant replay, tight

World Cup—Camera 1 Description
Camera one: Main camera positioned at midfield. Camera one is the main coverage camera or master shot. The shot is wide enough to show the flow of play, but not so wide that the ball and players become specks on the screen. The basic philosophy is to show everyone involved in the play, but not anyone who is clearly out of the flow. The camera leads the play in terms of direction of camera movement.

Broadcasters Handbook, XV FIFA World Cup

High Definition Sport Coverage

High definition (HD) really stands out when there's a fast break or long pass down court because you don't have to pan the camera much if at all. One static wide shot can show the entire court. For viewers who like to see plays evolve and follow game strategy, HD provides much more interesting coverage. HD production advice:

- *Loosely frame the majority of shots.*
- *When framing tight on people, be prepared for images that reveal every detail and possible facial flaw.*
- *HD image quality really goes down in areas that aren't well lit.*

Terry Ewert, Head,
Host TV Production, 1996 Olympics

shots, color analysis, or insertion of graphics for additional information. As a general rule, no more than 35% of the show should be taken up with color coverage, unless the contest is so poor it is necessary.

The director must have a sense of the pace of the sport and attempt to match that pace with the style of directing. In many ways the movement of the game and the movement of the athletes in the game are much like directing a musical production, such as a dance or a concert. The movement of the game will rise and fall as the conflict heats and cools. The physical action of a football team must be as precise and rehearsed as that of a ballet group. The quality director will be able to sense this pace and movement and build on it by using a directing style that matches and augments the game.

Facilities and Coverage

How the crew is utilized and how facilities are controlled is sharply different in the coverage of sports—especially in small and medium sized markets. And the role of the director is much different in this situation. In most other situations the director makes every decision regarding camera shots, camera movement, the development of graphics, and the actions of talent. In sports coverage the director becomes the center of a coordinated effort by all talent and crew to provide shots, tape replays, and other input from which the director can select what will be put out on the air. He or she becomes an editor, in this sense, selecting and guiding the production. That is not to say that the director doesn't call for specific shots, coverage, and isolation. But the tempo of the activity in the director's truck is so rapid that the director cannot possibly talk through every shot or sequence with crew and talent.

Directing Cameras
Assigning Cameras

Specific camera placement recommendations for various sports are included later in this chapter. At this point we will outline the general types of camera coverage assignments that can be made for any situation. The camera designations outlined in this section deal with the type of coverage the camera generally provides.

Depending on how many individual camera units you are blessed with for a particular production, each can be generally designated in one of these types. Our concern here is with assignments, not numbers.

Each camera will have a general responsibility: (1) action/game, (2) hero/shag, or (3) iso/special assignment.

Action/Game Camera. The action, or game, camera (or cameras if you have that luxury) is responsible for covering the general action of the sport. This does not mean the director may not use other cameras for this purpose, but the action camera has that specific assignment. If, for example, a football team moves the ball to the one-yard line, you may want to increase warmth by using a utility camera behind the goal post to get a different view of the impending battle at the line. But for general assignment, the action camera has that specific responsibility.

Hero/Shag Camera. The hero, or shag, camera takes close-ups following a particularly outstanding athletic effort, thus the "hero" designation. This camera can also be used to follow the action to highlight important points in the context— hence the "shag" designation. (The term comes from the concept of shagging fly balls in the outfield during baseball practice. This camera is chasing down various shots like an outfielder shags fly balls.) The camera operator must be able to sense the drama and emotion of the contest and give the director shots that show that drama. For example, even though the basketball game continues following a driving lay-up by a guard on the team, the hero-camera operator will give the director a shot of the guard. If the shot the guard attempts is blocked by the big center, the hero camera will focus on the center. The person who makes the play gets the camera shot.

On the other hand, if a football linebacker makes a particularly bruising tackle and injures the runner, the hero camera will focus on the injured player (as long as the injury is not terribly serious), while another camera takes shots of the linebacker. Similarly, the hero camera (with instruction from the director) may concentrate on the tennis player who seems to be losing the momentum in the match. If the player who seemed to have control of the match is beginning to slip, the hero camera will concentrate there. That is where the story is. If, on the other hand, the opponent is making a great comeback and is playing better tennis, that may be the story. The hero/shag camera also covers referees during penalty situations. That's part of the shag responsibility. It is the job of the hero or shag camera(s) to fill in the emotions of the game and to give the director shots that help the production do that.

Iso Cameras/Special-Assignment Cameras. Iso cameras cover specific (isolated) anticipated action points that can be tape recorded for later playback. The iso camera operator's responsibility is to understand the sport well enough to determine when specific actions in the game can be expected. For example, third-and-long yardage situations in football generally mean the team will throw a pass. In addition, the iso camera operator should know (from pre-production meetings) what style of game a particular team (or individual) normally plays. This information will give the iso camera operator a chance to feed the tape assistant director or operator a shot that may be usable when play slows or stops.

The director may have time to cue the iso cameras regarding particular anticipated actions, but then the iso cameras are on their own to provide the shots. The director will not have time to talk them through such coverage.

Special-assignment cameras are designated for specific coverage during the game. Sideline cameras in football or basketball may have the assignment of providing coverage of the bench or the coach. They may shoot sideline talent for special reports. Other such cameras may cover talent in the booth or provide shots of a clock. Most coverage situations in smaller markets and non-network feeds don't have the luxury of many such units, and iso cameras can fill both responsibilities.

Camera Initiative

In pre-production meetings the specific assignments for each camera are reviewed. The camera operators must know what part of the coverage is their responsibility. Specific game situations should be reviewed—"what if" situations. "What do we do if the War Chiefs get

inside the 10-yard line?" "Who gets shots of Coach Johnson?"

Before game time, the camera operators experiment with their cameras to see what kinds of shots they can get within their specific assignment, then they may experiment to see what other shots they can get to add to the repertoire of shots from which the director can select.

During the game, all camera operators should provide the director with a broadcast table shot almost all the time, and they should tell the director (via intercom) when they think they've got a shot the director can use for some effect—in a way they try to sell the director on their shot or potential shot.

Sometimes the camera operator may take the initiative to begin to get a particular shot and the director accidentally cuts to that camera in the middle of the move to get to the shot. As a director works with a crew on coverage, however, each will get to know how the other works, so such glitches will occur rarely. The director should be able to watch the monitors of all cameras. Such a cut is the director's mistake, not the camera operator's (unless the director has called for a specific shot on that camera and the operator is out freelancing on his or her own).

When the action of the contest is taking place, the director may be locked to an action camera. The other camera operators, however, must have their heads into the game and should be looking for shots so that when the action stops or slows they can help tell the story and support the style, mood, pace, and rate of the project.

Directing Replays

A replay always breaks the viewers' connection with the reality of the line event. Therefore there must be a strong motivation for a replay—only then does it enhance the coverage. Unnecessary replays annoy the viewer.

—Kalevi Uusivuori and Tapani Parm, Producers, YLE, Finland

This same kind of teamwork occurs with tape operators and tape assistant directors. The director usually does not have time to call all the replay set-ups, or assign a particular camera to a particular VTR. Nor can he or she tell each iso camera what part of the action to cover. The tape AD or the operator will select (using a simple routing switcher at the VTR) which camera to record on which iso machine. When the director needs a replay, slo-mo, or iso of any kind, the tape AD can tell the director what is available—on which machine—and sell the director a particular cut. The director can then decide which replay to use. Normal coverage in a small market will have two or three replay machines capable of playback at regular and slow-motion speeds.

Directing Graphics

Primarily, sports coverage is a numbers game. There are scores, player numbers, and statistics to be organized and presented in a dynamic view on demand. Multichannel character generators and fast operators are a must. Success here often depends on careful pre-game or pre-game-date assembly and storage of names and player stats. CG and tape are the most heavily involved elements during the pre-game production where ten-things-at-once displays are made to happen with the push of a button during the game. A recent addition to the already heavy graphic load in sports has been the introduction of real-time relay and display. In football, this would include hang time of a kickoff presented as a running stopwatch. In baseball, the speed of the pitch and the speed of the batted ball can be shown as a dynamic cell in a corner bug where the ball/strike count and base runner graphic is often included.
—Bennett Liles, Production

In sport production, directors have the same type of relationship with graphics as they do with tape ADs and camera operators. A font coordinator coordinates the loading of graphic material into the electronic character generator equipment (sometimes called Chyron after one of the most popular systems in the field) coordinating the work of the character generator operator with the needs of the producer/director of the production. Pre-existing information is typed into the equipment before the game begins in addition to formatting pages used to input statistical material gathered during the course of the game. This "in game" information can

Replays

Replays are shown whenever the director considers a particular action noteworthy. As a general rule, replays do not cut into live action when the sport is in play. The director may overlap some important replays over live action but only if the live action does not involve interesting play. There must never be a danger of losing important action. The order and length of the replay is the directors call.

Replays generally enter and leave by a digital effect so that the audience knows that it is a replay and not live action. Many times replays end with a freeze frame.

The International Amateur Athletic Federation Television Guidelines state that cameras should also focus on what happens after the finish for some time, before going into slow motion replays. Reaction of the competitors is more important than slow motion. Slow motion shots should have an editorial basis and should not be an automatic decision. It is advisable to have a variety of options available by isolating several cameras in the stadium.

Figure 7.1: Competitor identification: graphic used to show the sport, event, athlete's name, and country.

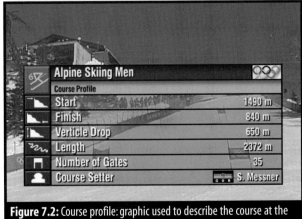

Figure 7.2: Course profile: graphic used to describe the course at the beginning of each event.

be manually inputted during the game or it can be delivered automatically to the device during the competition by a sport data interface. Before the event begins, individual statistics that producers and/or directors anticipate using will be some statistical material during the contest (score, yardage, fouls, field goals, records) that will be entered for immediate display on the screen. Some sports productions (although it is a rarity) will use two character generators—one for retrieval of pre-produced graphics and one for graphics entered during the production.

Since the graphic area is one of the most hectic areas during a sports event, the crew and all of the graphic equipment are sometimes out boarded to a separate trailer, room or truck. This would generally only happen for very high profile events that are very graphic intensive. It has been estimated that graphics get out boarded roughly 10% of the time.

The Camera

It is not the total number of cameras which is important, as much as their positioning. The principle should be that it should be possible to show the whole of one performance with one camera.

> —*International Amateur Athletic, Federation Television Guidelines*

A sports production will utilize a variety of camera types (*see figure 7.3*), unique point-of-view shots, extremely long telephoto lenses and different kinds of camera mounts. However, the best equipment is useless in the hands of an unskilled camera operator. One of the keys to being a good camera operator is the ability to listen to the director and to anticipate where the action is going and the type of shot the director wants to include. The following section outlines the various shots, camera moves, composition often used, and touches on basic care of a video camera.

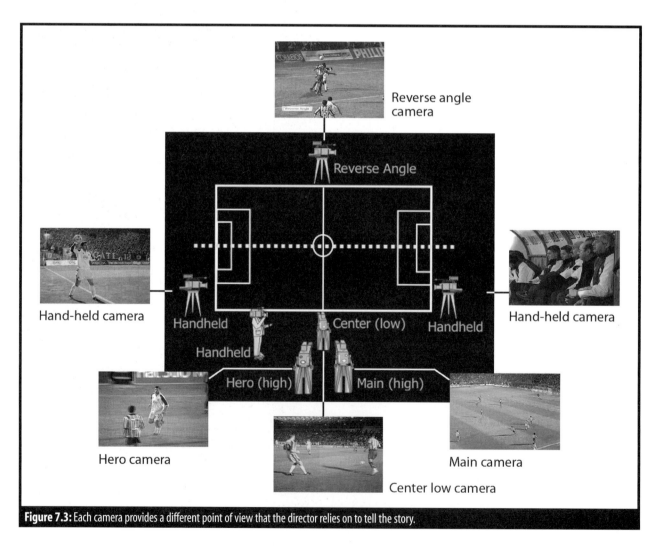

Figure 7.3: Each camera provides a different point of view that the director relies on to tell the story.

Figure 7.4: Extreme Long Shot (XLS).

Figure 7.5: Long Shot (LS).

Camera Shots

Camera shots are relative to what you are shooting and must be defined by the director. Camera shot categories are loosely defined. A long shot for one director in a stadium may be a medium shot for a studio director. See figures 7.4–7.8 for illustrations of the general shot composition categories.

The long shot (LS) establishes the scene. This shot shows the audience and director the overall context in which the action is taking place. The distance from the camera to the subject is relative to what you are shooting. For example, a long shot of a person would show the entire person from head to toe. A long shot of the field of play may show the entire field of play.

The extreme long shot (XLS or ELS) is further away than the long shot. Using the examples under long shot, an XLS shot of a person would show the person and their immediate surroundings. An extreme long shot of the field of play may be a blimp shot capturing the entire stadium.

The medium shot (MS) generally tells the story. This is the main shot that shows the subject as well as some of the context. A medium shot of a person may capture them from the waist up. A medium shot at a stadium may include the whole person or even a couple of people.

The close-up shot (CU) adds drama. It is a close shot of the subject being discussed in the program or a person's face. In a large stadium, the close-up may be a shot of a person from the waist up.

The extreme close-up shot (XCU or ECU) intensifies the drama by showing the viewer details of the object being discussed or capturing the

Figure 7.6: Medium Shot (MS).

Figure 7.7: Close-up (CU).

Figure 7.8: Extreme Close-up (XCU).

Figure 7.9: Parts of a hard camera.

Figure 7.10: Parts of a hand-held camcorder.

emotion on a person's face. ECUs dramatically increase the communication of the emotion.

Camera Movement

In the planning chapter we discussed a variety of moving cameras, such as a rail camera, boat-cam, helicopter, Steadicam, and crane. It is the director's responsibility to decide if a specialty camera should be used. Generally, specialty cameras are used when they contribute to the viewer's understanding of an event. The following are the primary reasons why camera movement is used during an event:

- It gives a unique perspective of the action that can't be seen any other way. For example: a helicopter or blimp shot puts the field of play into perspective geographically. A camera mounted on a motorcycle allows the director to stay with the leader throughout a marathon.
- It provides the viewer a feel for the motion of the action. A tracking camera can move alongside sprinters enhancing the viewer's perception of their pace, or a dive camera can drop with a diver capturing impact into the water and the speed of descent.
- Camera movement can pull the spectator into the event. A crane shot can continuously move from a wide shot, with the camera showing the audience, to a close-up of action occurring on the field of play. A Steadicam, moving with an athlete from the locker room to the field of play gives the viewer an intimate view of the athlete's perspective of an event. *(See figure 7.11.)*

Camera/Lens Moves

A variety of camera and lens moves are used by camera operators to capture the desired coverage. *(See figure 7.11.)*

Zoom. A variable focal length lens. This lens has the ability to continuously go from wide angle to close-up. Directors will sometimes use the word "tighten" to zoom in and "loosen" to zoom out to a wide shot.

Pan. Refers to moving the camera left or right on the camera support's axis, for example, pan right, pan left.

Tilt. Refers to moving the camera up or down on the camera support's axis, for example, tilt up, tilt down.

Figure 7.11: Camera moves.

Hand-held HDTV Cameras

With hand-held cameras, plan on a constant follow focus world when moving into and out of shots. Most operators aren't used to focusing when they're zoomed out, yet in HD you need to.

Starting Here, Starting Now

Your focus is 1000 times more critical in HD, you can see how light affects each blade of grass. You can really tell if your focus is off just a bit.

Eye on the Game: Cameras in Sports

Camera Blocking Notes from Fox Sports Baseball

Camera 1: Low Third Base

- On left handed (LH) batters shoot waist-shots for stats, after tally goes out zoom back for head-to-toe shot
- If LH batter bunts, give batter more looking room on the left side of screen and go with ball
- Right handed (RH) pitchers
- Both dugouts
- If you have a batter and there are two men on base, take the back up runner after the ball is put into play
- If you do not have a batter, you have the lead runner
- If bases are loaded and you have the lead runner you score lead runner and then pick up runner that was on first trying to advance
- Low cameras runner responsibilities will cascade as runners cross the plate
- If you don't have a batter or lead runner, shoot the pitcher. After pitcher goes into wind-up, go shag the entire field
- Cover plays at first base, after play bring player into third base dugout; if batter was on other team look for infield hero shot
- On-deck circles
- When following runners always shoot head-to-toe

Camera 2: High Home

- Follow the ball; play-by-play
- Cover appeals with first and third base umpires
- Infield and outfield defense: Put home plate in lower-right corner as a reference and then pan left to right—sweep bases same as defensive shot (if gap in Left Center or Right Center, include home-plate in corner of shot)
- Two-shot runners at first and second or second and third
- If you have a runner at second base, please include runner on your battery shot
- Always include the outfielders in the picture when the ball is hit to the outfield; show where the ball is going and who's going to catch it
- We will stay on camera 2 for all plays at home plate

Camera 3: High First Base

- Shag infield and outfield
- Defensive pull across: get catch of ball through the throw to a base
- Go for infield or outfield hero shot after play

- If the drama is at first base where the out is made, keep a look-out for the first baseman, runner/umpire reaction
- Two-shot of runners at first and second
- Pick-offs at first base
- If runner steals go with runner
- If ball is overthrown at first or second base, go with ball
- Pitcher-runner shot at third base
- Triangle shot (pitcher/home plate/third base): show the whole thing when there is a chance of a squeeze bunt or sacrifice play at home
- If there are runners at the corner, you may be asked to cover the potential pick-off play at first base
- Dugout shots
- On-deck circles
- Third base coach for signs
- Players/managers in dugout

Camera 4: Center Field

- Pitcher-batter-umpire shot
- Go with ball on passed balls, wild pitches, pop-ups behind the plate and steals of second base
- Go with ball if its on the ground between second base and shortstop
- If ball is in the air, wait until your tally light goes out and then go for the shag/defense
- On a routine out or great play, stay with player for hero shot
- If ball is still in play, follow ball until play is dead
- Don't worry about pick-offs at first base
- Do worry about pick-offs at third base
- Base on balls: follow runner to first base, head-to-toe
- If pitcher strikes out batter to end the inning follow off pitcher
- If pitcher strikes out batter and its only out 1 or 2, follow batter to dugout
- Dugout reaction shots
- Follow on-deck batter to batters box
- On home runs, listen to the announcers you have three options:
1. Follow the batter after swing, push in tight for reaction
2. Pause, then go for ball—looking for diving catch, player climbing the wall to steal a home run, etc.
3. Zoom to pitcher for reaction shot as ball is being launched

Figure 7.12: Camera blocking notes from baseball. (courtesy Director James Angio, Joseph Maar and Television Broadcast) *continued next page.*

Camera 5: Low First Base

- Right Handed (RH) batters: waist-shot for stats; after tally goes out, zoom back for head-to-toe
- If RH batter bunts, give the batter more looking room on the right side of screen and go with ball
- LH pitchers
- If you have a batter and there are two men on base, take the backup runner after the ball is put into play
- If you do not have a batter you will have the lead runner
- If the bases are loaded and you have the lead runner, you score lead runner and then pick up runner that was on first trying to advance
- Low cameras runner responsibilities will cascade (or alternate) as runners cross the plate
- If you don't have a batter or lead runner shoot the pitcher, after pitcher goes into his wind-up shag the entire field
- Cover plays at first base
- If its a routine out at first base, follow the player back to the dugout
- After play look for infield hero shot
- Both dugouts
- On-deck circles
- When following runners, always shoot head-to-toe

Camera 6: Low Home

- Tight shot of pitcher
- Pitcher-batter shot
- On LH batters you need to move to your left
- On RH batters you need to move to your right
- Follow ball when your tally light goes out
- Look out for behind-the-plate action
- Cover shots
- Runners with good speed: cover the runner at first base; if he steals go with runner
- If ball is hit up-the-middle and a runner crosses in your path, then pick up runner trying to score. What really looks good here is the third base coach trying to hold up runner or giving him the advance sign to home plate

Camera 7: High Third Base

- Pitchers
- Plays at first base
- Dugouts
- On-deck circles
- Pitcher-runner shot
- If runner steals go with runner
- Two-shots of runners at second and third

- Runners at first and third
- Help on passed ball and wild pitches
- If you have a runner, stay with him
- If no runner responsibilities: go with ball for defense shag CF to RF
- Beauty shots
- Congrats in dugout after scoring play
- Sometimes shoot LH batters to show his stance
- Players/managers in dugout
- If you're on the pitcher-runner shot and the pitcher throws over first, don't move. We can cover the man stealing and also see if there had been a balk by staying on your pitcher-runner shot

Camera 8: Concourse Level, Third Base Side—shooting down first base line

- Include batter, catcher, pitcher, first baseman
- Ball looks great hooking down the right field line
- Great diving play by first baseman
- Shag from CF to RF
- Bunts by both RH and LH batters
- If there's a good runner at first base, include catcher and runner—this looks great for pick-offs at first base
- Suicide squeeze at home
- Dugouts
- On-deck circles

Camera 9: Center Field

- Frequently directors use a second camera as a tight ISO.

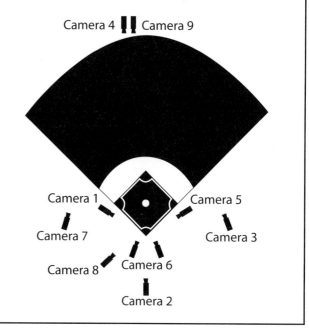

Arc. Refers to the movement of a camera on a curved path. Arcs can occur on a dolly track, hand-held or Steadicam, for example, arc left or arc right.

Truck. A camera and mount movement to the left or right, for example, truck left or truck right.

Dolly. A camera support that allows a camera to move in different directions. It can also refer to an actual camera move (dolly-in or dolly-out). Dolly-in refers to moving the camera and support forward. Dolly-out is when the camera and support moves backwards.

Crane up/Pedestal up. A crane/pedestal movement is when the camera is moved up or down utilizing a crane or pedestal. Cranes have become an accepted and even expected part of sports coverage. The crane allows continuous movement from a close-up to a high, wide angle giving an entirely different perspective of the event.

Shooting Sports

The field cameras had only sports sights consisting of a wire frame at the front and a peep-sight at the back. The cameraman had no control over focus, which was adjusted from the control truck by remote control, and the field seen in the crude sports-sight was, I'd have to assume, fairly inaccurate.

—Art Smith, Sports camera operator, 1939

As we mentioned earlier, the director will assign the crew to specific cameras and also dictate the type of shot that the camera operators must capture. The camera's viewfinder may not display exactly what the director is seeing in the truck. It is not uncommon for a camera operator to find that centered for their camera may not be centered in the truck. The director will instruct the camera operator on composition. The camera operator should stick with the director's instruction, even if it looks a little off on the camera.

The wider a camera shot, the easier it is to follow the action. However, the wider the shot, the less exciting the image is. Many times directors will ask camera operators to start tight and then widen the shot as the action proceeds. It is important to remember not to get too tight making it impossible to follow the play.

Another advantage of the wide shot is that it is easier to shoot steady handheld images. Telephoto lenses amplify camera movement; movement is less noticeable with a wide shot. Hand-held camera operators should get as close to the action as possible while still using the wide angle shot. Of course, in sports, it is not always possible to get close to the action. For this reason, cameras are equipped with long lenses and always placed on heavy-duty tripods to ensure steadiness.

A tripod substantially increases the stability of the camera and allows more accessibility to the camera's remote controls, even on an ENG-type camera. Without a tripod, it is difficult to focus, zoom, tilt, and pan at the same time.

For beginners, keeping the subject in focus can be incredibly difficult. However, with experience, it becomes second nature. There are primarily two methods of focusing in sports—follow focusing and zone focusing.

Follow Focus. Follow focus, also known as critical focus or tracking focus, means that the camera operator is continually adjusting the focus in order to keep the subject in focus. This is particularly critical when using a telephoto lens.

Zone Focus. The zone method of focusing means that the camera operator prefocuses on the field of play, knowing that anything that comes into a specific area will be in focus. There are a number of variables that determine the effectiveness of zone focusing. First of all, if a wide angle lens is being used on a bright day, the zone of focus, or depth of field, may be from 1.2 m to infinity. The longer the lens, the less depth of field it can cover. Many times there are not enough cameras to allow cameras to focus only on one zone.

Composition

Anticipation is the key to composing shots for sports. The camera operator must anticipate where the competitors are going next in order to capture an image that means something to the viewer. Although good composition is relative to a person's perspective, there are certain composition standards. Good shot composition allows the viewer to have a better understanding of what is going on, makes the viewing experience more enjoyable and can significantly improve the entire production quality. *(See figure 7.14.)*

Composition for Action Shots
- Make sure that there is enough headroom.
- Always keep the subject in the frame (with fast moving action, this can sometimes be incredibly difficult).
- Keep the competitors centered in the frame. However, when the player or team is in motion, always shoot with lead room.
- Watch the background. Ensure that it adds context to the shot.
- Make sure that the horizon is straight for all cameras. This can especially be a problem for handheld cameras.

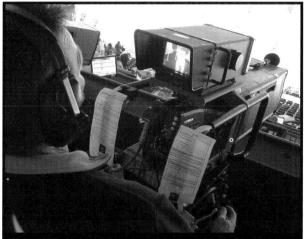

Figure 7.13: Camera operators sometimes attach team lists to their camera in order to quickly identify a player being asked for by the director.

Composition for Interviews
- Make sure there is enough headroom.
- When needed, compose for graphics. A graphic may need to be inserted below or beside the head.
- Always watch the background. Look for elements that appear to pop out of the talent's head (flags, trees, etc.).
- Whenever possible, interviews should be shot in context. The background should add something to the interview. It should tell you something about the person being interviewed or the event being covered.
- Do not show too much profile.
- Make sure that there is lead room, space for the talent to look toward.

Caring for the Camera

Cameras are very fragile and it is essential to treat them with the utmost care. When working remotes, camera operators and assistants must be especially mindful of the following conditions which could damage the equipment.

Weather. Cameras must be protected from extreme heat, rain, and snow. Extremely cold temperatures reduce the life of equipment and batteries. Condensation can form when moving equipment from cold temperatures into a warm room, rendering the equipment useless.

Water. Cameras cannot be submerged in water without the appropriate underwater gear. If a camera does become submerged, it is generally irreparable.

Composed for Graphics

Context

Head Room

Lead Room

Level Horizon

Dust/Sand. Dusty situations wreak havoc on equipment, especially record/playback heads. When the heads become dirty, recording and playback is impossible. It is generally impossible to repair a lens or camera that has been dropped into sand.

Drops/Vibrations. Equipment must be carefully packed in shock absorbent material (foam or a padded case) when travelling. Airplanes, cars, and all other types of transportation will vibrate the camera, often loosening boards and screws. Cameras cannot handle the jolts from being dropped, which can cause video/audio heads and CCDs to go out of alignment.

Magnetic Fields. Videotapes must be kept away from magnetic fields. This can erase or deteriorate the image on the tape.

Shading

It is essential to have all cameras properly adjusted for optimal image quality. Video operators (VO), sometimes known as shaders, are responsible for shading or adjusting the cameras. Cameras need constant attention, especially when shooting outdoors. As the weather changes or as the sun and/or clouds move across the sky, the lighting can change drastically on the same field of play. Video operators work in the video control area of the mobile unit, using the camera control unit (CCU) or remote control unit (RCU) to adjust the various components of the cameras. Generally an RCU is used to control the CCU.

Video operators adjust cameras for correct color, white balance, and contrast. VOs use master black (pedestal) and the white level (iris) for camera adjustments. They use an oscilloscope and wave form monitor to enable them to create the best quality video image.

Audio for Remotes

I learned my craft in a recording studio and my goal has been to paint a picture with the sound, not just cover the action. Theater of the mind, just close your eyes and feel the boxer's pain with each punch. Experience the thundering sound as you hit 200 miles per hour in a Formula 1 car. Good sound accentuates the soundtracks of life.
—Dennis Baxter,
Senior Audio, four Olympics

The types of microphones being used and microphone placement is determined during the planning phase. Microphones are cabled and placed during the set-up phase. Therefore, at production time the A-1 or senior audio person should be ready to mix the event. Audio inputs come from a variety of sources which may or may not include:
- Multiple talent
- Public address system
- Field-of-play microphones (including camera mics)
- Ambience microphones
- Crowd microphones
- CD
- Player/coach/referee wireless mic
- Multiple VTRs or other type of playback equipment

The A-1 is responsible for mixing all of these audio signals into a clear representation of what is actually occurring at the event.

The A-1 must concentrate on which camera is being called for by the director as well as know

Field Hockey Audio

Hockey is a sport where good sound effects will significantly heighten television coverage and the viewers experience of the game. Play action will constantly be moving up and down the field, and sound will be generated by the players when they strike the ball with the stick. The players tend to be vocal and exchange commands during a match to set up and coordinate field positions.

1996 Atlanta Olympic Broadcasting
Venue Technical Manual

Figure 7.15: Audio area in a small truck.

which talent is going to speak. Then, he or she can "pot up" the corresponding microphone in order to provide the audience with the sound from the proper source.

During the production, the A-2 or audio assistant's responsibilities include hand holding microphones, making sure that wireless mics have good batteries, changing batteries, keeping the appropriate mic flag on the microphone, and troubleshooting any problems with the microphones and cables. Sometimes a microphone or cable may need to be changed during the broadcast.

Audio Guidelines

1. Always test the microphones before the production begins.
2. Run microphone cables perpendicular to electrical cords, not parallel.
3. Limit the distance between the talent and the mic to reduce ambient noise.

Pregame, post-game, and half-time productions offer a myriad of challenges for audio. There are a number of areas that require quality sound, making it almost impossible to only go with "live" sound. Prerecorded audio is often used to supplement and sometimes completely replace live sound. The following is a list of some of the reasons prerecorded audio was used during the 1992 Barcelona Olympic Games Opening Ceremony. At this event, prerecorded audio was used for every aspect of the ceremony—from the roar of airplanes crossing the sky, to opera singers, to the applause of the spectators.

1. Prerecorded sound allows for near perfect synchronization of the technical aspects of the spectacle, offering the ability to link sound, lights, camera movement, and other enhancements.
2. Prerecorded sound ensures optimal quality for television, allowing for stereophonic sound (stadium spectators only hear monophonic sound), as well as mixed enhancements.
3. Prerecorded sound allows a better experience or sense of proximity to the event for television viewers. For both television and stadium spectators prerecorded sound also can direct attention to specific events happening in a very large stadium in a way that live sound can not.

4. Unforeseen weather conditions, such as the rain or the wind, do not affect the prerecording but can affect live music leading to irreparable distortions in a live broadcast.
5. Unforeseen noises, such as friction between the microphone and the actors' clothes, movements of the announcers in respect to the microphone or various feedback effects, can be avoided.
6. The use of prerecorded sound can be more comfortable for the performers in the stadium, especially for the opera singers, some of who, in fact, preferred that their music be prerecorded.
7. There were also several microphones strategically placed in the stadium in order to pick up spontaneous sound during the event, in the form of applause, booing, and cheering.

Graphics

As a director, I always assume that the audience is watching from a noisy bar, or contending with the children, and ultimately unable to hear the commentators. Hence I always place a huge emphasis on the value of graphics and consequently the amount of time devoted to inserting the graphical information on the screen so that the audience has sufficient time to digest the information.

—Brian Douglas, Head,
Host TV Production,
2002 and 2006 Olympics

Graphics were initially introduced to enhance the dialogue of the commentators, but in many situations they have evolved and the industry has changed to a point where they have almost replaced the audio track as the primary means of communication for information and statistics.

Television graphics can be divided into two basic types—text graphics and illustrative graphics. Both these types of graphics contain some of the same elements but they are generally produced for separate purposes, often by separate types of operators and sometimes by separate departments.

Text Graphics are usually composed in either 2D or 3D character generators. They can be static or they can be animated. They usually contain a dense amount of information—in fact their whole purpose is to communicate as much information as possible. The screen can contain some graphic elements but the whole focus is the information not the pretty background or the design elements which usually come out of the standard library for the particular look or show. The person composing this type of graphic is generally called a character generator operator.

Illustrative Graphics are much less predictable on a day-to-day basis. This type of graphic must also adhere to the design concepts defined as being correct for the look or show but the type of requests depend on the needs of that day's stories. This type of graphic can include over-the-shoulder graphics to illustrate the story being talked about by the person on the screen, static or animated backgrounds for text from the CG, maps that illustrate story locations, animations to illustrate what happened in the story being covered, logo designs, promotional material for print or air, introductions to a show or segment, and bumpers in and out of the show. Illustrative graphics can be composed in many different systems. These systems can range anywhere from a simple and inexpensive system where a PC runs a paint program to the large and hugely expensive systems where masses of extremely high end UNIX computers are running 3D real time animation programs. The person composing this type of graphic varies from place to place, in general they are designated as a composer, animator or graphic artist.

Television Graphics Goals
Design for design's sake is useless. We haven't reached our objectives if viewers only talked about our new set. We want people to appreciate the scenery and graphics as part of a more pleasurable way to see the whole...information package that we present.
　　—Noubar Stone, Creative Director, ESPN

1. Convey information clearly and directly.
2. Establish the show's overall mood and tone through the graphic style.
3. Present facts, concepts or processes visually so the viewer will understand the program content.
4. Prepare for maximum communications impact.

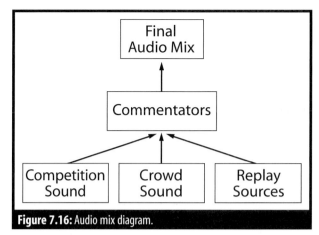

Figure 7.16: Audio mix diagram.

HDTV Audio

HDTV brings more than just better pictures. There are 5.1 channels of audio versus two in an analog feed. I now hear the referee's microphone on one channel, the announcer's on another, the crowd in another, and the sideline reporters have their own. As if I can't keep all of that straight, one channel plays music. With two channels of audio (analog feed), the crowd, the referee, and the announcers share the same channel and a lot of audio information is muffled.

Norm Samet, ABC Sports,
The Guide to Digital Television

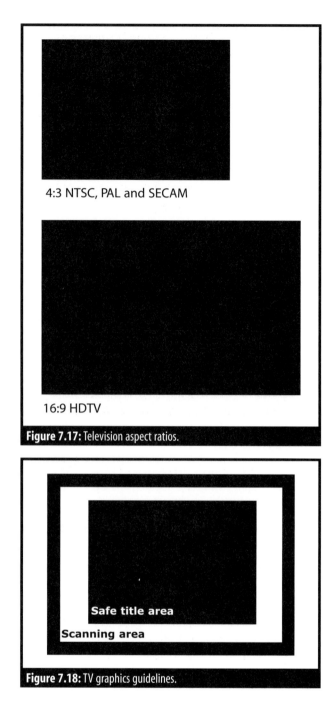

4:3 NTSC, PAL and SECAM

16:9 HDTV

Figure 7.17: Television aspect ratios.

Safe title area

Scanning area

Figure 7.18: TV graphics guidelines.

The design process begins, of course, with the need for a particular graphic. The needs vary, but basically the graphic is to impart information—identification, results, statistics, time or speed, position, titles, etc. Once the need is known, the graphic artist goes to work on the design concept, then a graphic operator converts the design to a digital format. A digital format allows the image to be manipulated into a number of variations. The image might be titled, reversed, flipped, zoomed, squeezed, folded and, using colors, the image can be provided in a 3D effect.

—Olympics Television Production

Television as a format has an aspect ratio that is defined as the ratio of the proportions of the height to the width of the television image. NTSC, PAL, and SECAM televisions have an aspect ratio of 4:3 while HDTV has an aspect ratio of 16:9. It is important to understand the ratios so that graphics can be designed to fit the format of the production. Graphics created for 4:3 should be different than those created for 16:9. *(See figure 7.17.)* The scanning area is the image seen in the camera viewfinder or in the graphics or on-air monitor.

In many cases home televisions do not have the same scanning area as the production equipment. As a result, the graphic should not fill the scanning area as it may not be seen on home television sets. For this reason a safe title area has been created that allows a graphic designer or operator to create graphics within a set area that has been designed to be seen, roughly the center 80% of the scanning area, is where all graphics should be placed to ensure the goals for television graphics are met. *(See figure 7.18.)*

Most companies or events have created their own graphic look for events. Stations and networks have created graphic standards that identify specific colors, font styles, sizing, presentation, and specific animations that are to be used for programming. These graphics are used to create a television brand. The idea is that whenever anyone sees the combination of font, color, and presentation, they will immediately know what event, network or station they are watching.

HDTV graphics bring new challenges to the

graphic designer. Unlike television images of the past, the high quality of the HDTV image allows every detail of the graphic to be scrutinized. That means that every bit of design has to be specifically created or it will look like a mistake.

According to the International Amateur Athletic Federation Television Guidelines, graphics must be bold and clear, because satellite transmissions will cause a down-grading of quality. For full screen graphics "freezing" the background helps marginally, but even more effective is to put the graphics against a clear background (e.g., grass rather than crowd); increase the size of the lettering; and add a drop shadow to prevent bleeding. In addition, brighten the colors. A defocused, soft background gives greater texture to the superimposed image and greatly improves legibility.

Where time allows, all competitors need to be identified, including name, number, country, and vital biographical information.

A variety of equipment is used to create the different graphic looks that are seen on television. Stand-alone systems (character generator/paint boxes) are slowly giving way to graphic production software that can run in almost any high-end desktop computer. (See figure 7.19.)

In most cases the actual design of the graphics has been determined months or even years before the sport event. Depending on the rules of that particular graphics package, the operator will have either little or no input into which graphics are used and in what manner. The use of these "shells" should be laid out in the package rulebook, or outlined by the font coordinator if that position exists in the crew and the person has worked with the package before. In all cases, preparation time consists of inputting data and statistics that will be used during the game, locating and documenting locations and usage of formats that will be updated with statistics during the game as well as making backup copies of everything that could be needed. There will be no time during the game to stop and look it up and no chance to rebuild something that was accidentally erased. There may be some circumstances when an operator is required to create or modify a shell because

Preparing for an Event as a Graphics Operator

1. *Develop a deep understanding of the sport or event. The more you know about the official rules and participants, the more valuable you are to the production team.*
2. *Gain a very deep knowledge of your graphics package. You contribute greatly if you know the capabilities of the system and can recall specific items with minimum use of reference material. Reacting quickly, accurately, and decisively to the needs of the production at hand is of the utmost importance.*
3. *Organization actually impacts everything and is the key that allows everything to be used to its full potential.*
4. *Gain knowledge of the hardware. It helps with communication and teamwork between coordinator and operator. Knowledge is power.*
5. *Know your support services. Learn to recognize system problems. Know alternative information sources and keep handy the reference that gives emergency procedures and contact methods for support personnel.*
6. *Think teamwork. When everyone works together as a cohesive unit the capability of the unit becomes something greater than anyone would think possible.*

Maria Persechino-Romero, Manager, Host Graphics, 2002 and 2004 Olympic Games

Sports Data for Graphics

Character generators can be connected to an official scoring/data system. This type of interface has significantly improved the accuracy of the broadcast graphics, allowing for automatic changes updated by the official system.

In the case of a system using a sports data interface, rules for usage and the "do" and "don't" of the system should be well documented. This includes any warnings or standard procedures that must be followed. All interfaces should be tested to see that they are working correctly well before the event begins. It should be noted that in many data interface systems, things like page numbers and content of pages are strictly defined by the system. Usually pages cannot be deleted, modified or moved without causing problems with the system. Pages added by the operator may or may not be supported by the data interface system. Safe record locations for operator-defined pages should also be documented.

Graphics at the Olympics

You are probably so used to seeing graphics on Olympic coverage that you assume they are created by the network over which you are viewing the Games. In some cases this is true however, in reality, the graphics that will be shown on most networks are the responsibility of Host Olympic Broadcaster Organization (OBO).

Rights Holding Broadcasters will use the OBO graphics in different ways. Some rights holders do create their own graphic packages so they can have a unique look and feel for their specific show usages, but even of those, most also take the host provided graphics for other uses. In some cases the host graphics are used as they are, with little or no changes, and in other cases the rights holder compliments the information provided in the host production with supplementary or interpretive graphics designed to be as indistinguishable as possible from the host provided sport competition information. In a few cases they will translate the entire look into their own language or duplicate it to allow for animation or other effects not used in the host feed.

The OBO believes that graphics exist "to help explain what is happening on screen, not to replace or detract from what is being seen. The graphics must accent the action on the screen, not overwhelm the competition." Given the breadth of the audience, they must be as simple and as easy to understand as possible. Designers need to take into account the various differences in technology that Rights Holding Broadcasters will use around the world as well as the cultural differences that exist in the countries where they are broadcast. "Our duty is to inform clearly and concisely."

Since English is the most popular second language, English is used. Designers keep the English as simple and basic as possible to allow for best comprehension by all segments of the worldwide television audience. For this reason also, illustrations such as flags, icons, and pictograms are used often to communicate. Once the graphics have been designed, style specifications are locked to provide a consistency across all of the venues at the Games.

There are basically three different types of graphics the OBO uses in production of the Host Broadcast:

Timing and Scoring Graphics: These take information and data from the field of play with no calculations. This includes, judges marks, start information, running time, interval or split point information, and speed and distance measurements.

Result Graphics: These are any graphics that require stored information or a calculation. This means no running clock but does mean such things as start lists, result lists, and judges scores with sport rules applied to weed out the highest or lowest or worst score.

Support Graphics: These include a pretty substantial list that includes:

- *Slates, used prior to an event but not seen by viewers (just for "traffic", production or engineering proposes).*
- *Advisories, which have a similar usage but can be seen by viewers if necessary.*
- *Technical graphics, such as overlays that go over color bars or the resolution chart to ensure proper technical adjustment and key level.*
- *Manual graphics (medal presenters or opening and closing graphics).*
- *Bumpers for highlights (identification with texts and flags in the intermissions).*
- *Final montage (text).*
- *DVE boxes (camera replays).*
- *Animations (sport and venue introductions).*
- *Any needed backgrounds for the production.*

Designers create basic concepts, which are then interpreted for each sport and for each format. Each sport essentially has its own distinct and individual graphics package. All in all, over 65,000 pages of data driven sports graphics are estimated to be available from the various venues. Every graphic must be checked in each format to see that contrast, luminance, color, alignment, and other factors are all correct according to both the design philosophy and the various world video engineering standards.

no available formats fit the usage. In this case the package rulebook should include guidelines on how to do this while still following the format.

Tips on Making Great TV Graphics

Effective graphics take time to create. The graphic artist needs to think through a number of stages in the process. Al Tompkins, from The Poynter Institute, has the following suggestions about creating great television graphics. We have adapted them a bit to fit our context:

1. *What is the context of the graphic?* Is the information something that is important to the viewer? How does this statistic relate to others? Does it help the viewer understand the game better?
2. *Think clearly about the purpose of the graphic.* Ask yourself, what exactly do I want the viewer to learn from this graphic?
3. *Does an image convey the message better than words or numbers?* Consider the Olympics where pictograms are used to illustrate sports instead of words.
4. *Movement is good but don't overuse it.* Don't overwhelm the viewer with a constant variety of movement.
5. *When creating a new graphic design, get someone else to look at it.* Let them tell you what the graphic conveys to them.

The Crew

The producer and director are responsible for ensuring the needs of their crew are met. This care includes good lodging, good food, and protection from the elements. If the crew cannot leave during a production, catering will need to be provided. If the crew's needs are neglected, attitudes can deteriorate. Low morale in the crew can impact the overall quality of the entire project.

The crew must be prepared for any type of weather when shooting an outdoor remote. During warm weather, they should wear sun protection, light collared clothes, and be prepared for sudden weather changes, such as rain or temperature drops. Cold weather shoots require layered clothing so that as the temperature fluctuates they can dress accordingly.

Figure 7.19: Graphics area in a HDTV truck.

ATHENS 2004 Olympic Broadcasting Facts

34	Venues
2	Periscope cameras
1	Mobycam
2	Wirecams
7	Steadicams
64	Super slow motion cameras
18	Tracking cameras
2	ENG cameras
28	Cranes
122	POV cameras
230	Hand-held cameras
225	Hard cameras
52	Mobile units/OB vans
64	Character generators
3500	Games-time staff

Figure 7.20: Virtual graphics can be used to electronically insert finish lines on the field of play that can only be seen by the television audience.

CHAPTER 8
Sports Announcing

Sport should be fun, and I want viewers to share in the enjoyment I get from the games. But I also owe it to those same viewers to be thoroughly prepared and to know what I am talking about.

Chris Berman, Commentator, ESPN

This chapter is not meant to be a primer for those interested in being professional talent. Instead, it is meant to help the production crew understand the talent's role and responsibilities.

The talent needs to know their specific role in the production and understand the vision of the director and producer. The play-by-play person should have the "ability to call a sporting event with a concise description of the action, while maintaining a natural delivery. The role of the color commentator or analyst is to enhance the broadcast by adding specific and important information, while interacting with the play-by-play announcer." (from *Play-by-Play Sportscaster Training*)

Play-by-Play Sportscast Training
Many times, former athletes or coaches are chosen for the role of analyst since an in-depth knowledge of the sport is required. While the play-by-play person describes who the athletes are and what they are doing, the analyst is responsible for explaining to the viewer why the athletes did what they did.

Research
With the competing television channels, newspapers, magazines, and Internet, television commentators have the difficult task of being

Olympic Research
A small group of dedicated (research) people…will have worked two years to complete nearly 4500 pages of information pertinent to the summer Games. The information in several volumes will be distributed…to the commentators for their use on air. In addition, every page, every word of the biographies, every rule, and every record is entered in the research computer so that the information may be kept up-to-date and rapidly accessed to fill an immediate need.

James Hay, 1984 Olympics

Figure 8.1: Sideline or field-of-play stand-ups provide context to commentary.

Table of Contents

General Information

Figure 8.2: Table of contents of NBC Sports' Games of the XXVI Olympiad, Research Manual Volume 1.

Television Announcer Sports Cliches

- *Sportscasters rarely argue—on the contrary, they go out of their way to compliment each other for saying the most mundane things. The cliché response to a broadcast partner's cliché statement is: "I couldn't agree with you more."*
- *Announcers really struggle with past, present, and future: "He'll smack that ball into the gap for a base hit." He will? Didn't we just see it? Or are you making a prediction about the next guy up? And when analyzing an instant replay, they never switch to the past tense: "If he makes that catch, we've got a whole new ballgame." How about: "If he MADE that catch we'd have a whole new ballgame?"*
- *The highest expression of disbelief for an announcer is the ubiquitous "Unbelievable!", but may soon be replaced by "Are you kiddin' me?!"*
- *If an announcer is hyping-up a team in the pre-game show, for example: "The Chiefs are capable of putting a lot of points on the board", the cliché response is, "Well, the Broncos might have something to say about that."*
- *Often you'll see a slow motion replay of a coach arguing with an umpire, referee or official. One of the announcers is guaranteed to say: "I hope the kids watching at home can't read lips!"*

Mike Hasselbeck

The Commentator in 1945

The television announcer must learn the value of silence, must learn to pace his comments. He can make a dull fight interesting by covering lack of action with colorful comments just as he can talk too much when the boys are mixing it up.

WRGB Announcer Techniques for Boxing,
Television Show Business, 1945

innovative every time they are on the air. The audience tires of listening to the same information and the same statistics. Research is the commentator's weapon in being able to comment on the really important issues and describe the images provided to the audience with the maximum drama.
—*Kostas Kapatais,*
Coordinating Producer, Greece

The talent is responsible for being thoroughly familiar with the event, which involves a tremendous amount of research. Of course, the extent of the research required varies based on the size of the event. See figure 8.2 for two pages of the table of contents from NBC Sports' Games of the XXVI Olympiad, Research Manual Volume 1 showing the first 160 out of 558 items researched for this event.

To prepare for a production, talent should:

- Study the teams and players (know numbers and names so that they can be easily identified).
- Study team and player strategies.
- Study supplemental information from team publicity offices, contacts, and press clippings. Read newspapers, Internet sites, and articles, talk to and/or interview coaches and team members.

Announcer Techniques

The announce booth is designed to give announcers immediate access to information about the event and athletes. *(See figure 8.3.)*

Before going on the air it is imperative that all equipment is checked to make sure that it is working properly. While this may happen

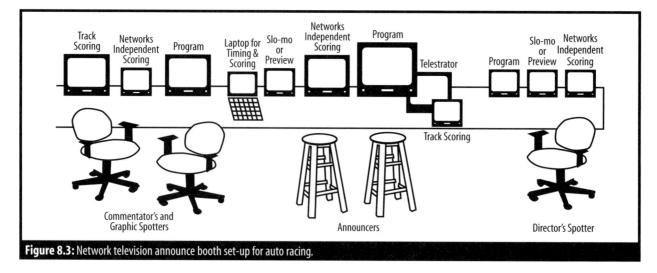

Figure 8.3: Network television announce booth set-up for auto racing.

during the facilities check (FAX), microphones, intercoms, and monitors should be double checked right before air.

The play-by-play person is almost always in the lead with the color commentator playing a supportive role. Commentators generally work out a signal to let each other know when they want to step into the broadcast. However, the play-by-play person usually determines who will talk.

Talent input should complement the visual component. Don't state the obvious. As former ABC commentator Keith Jackson liked to say the role of the sportscaster is to amplify, clarify, and punctuate. Sometimes there are moments when it is important not to talk allowing the event to speak for itself.

Sportscaster James Brown stated that the influx of ex-athletes and coaches (to television) can be a plus. They "have a wonderful way of telling riveting stories and they, more than anyone, understand what the athletes on the field are going through. But unquestionably, the successful ones are those who know they have to put in the time, that they have to work as hard in television as they did (as athletes)."

Announcers must keep one eye on the field and the other on the air monitor in the booth. The game is actually called from the monitor. *(See figure 8.6.)* Most booths also include an additional monitor that shows the announcer the slow motion footage. The challenge commentators face is the numerous tasks that they must do at once—they must watch the field, watch the monitor, listen to the director and/or producer and still make sense to the viewing audience.

Interviews

The key to good interviewing is to find the things that aren't so obvious. Interviewers should strive to get responses that tell us something we don't know or something that adds a level of depth to the scene.

—Ken Colemen and Brad Schultz

The secret is to know (the athlete), if not personally then at least by having read about him or her, to know what their interests are and

Figure 8.4: Venue officials generally must approve, in advance, shooting locations that are not in the normal broadcast area.

Figure 8.5: Commentators are sometimes able to stand up in their broadcast booth and turn around in order to appear on camera.

Figure 8.6: Announcers must watch the field and monitor when broadcasting a game.

Delivering Information

First and foremost, I try to deliver information, especially information that the audience might not have been previously aware of or has to be reminded of from time to time. Information is first and foremost in any of the categories as host of an anthology program, as play-by-play man, or doing the NFL wraparound and post-game shows.

Brent Musburger, Commentator, ABC
Live TV: An Inside Look at Directing and Producing

Figure 8.7: Some broadcast booths are equipped with POV cameras in order to show the commentators without pulling a camera operator away from the game.

Figure 8.8: On-camera commentators need to know the amount of time allocated for their talk.

Figure 8.9: This commentator prepared a photo page to identify players.

what they like to talk about. Get them going on what is familiar, easy ground for them and you have the makings of a good interview. Interviews are another essential part of sports broadcasting. There are a number of basic rules that need to be kept in mind when conducting an interview:

- Guests needs to know the amount of time allocated for the interview. They usually range from 20 seconds to a few minutes.
- Commentators need to communicate their goals for the interview to the guest.
- The commentator should let the guest know how they plan to close the interview.
- Unless using separate microphones, the commentator should always control the microphone so they can decide who will speak. Commentators determine who will speak by aiming the microphone at the talent or at themselves.
- In order to obtain a good response from the athlete, commentators should always ask questions that require more than a yes/no answer.

Go Beyond the Obvious

Asking the right questions when doing interviewing is key to obtaining great story coverage. However, it is sometimes tough to know how far to push or just how to elicit the information that you need. Joe Gisondi has the following suggestions to think about as an interviewer:

- Athletes are people, and people make mistakes. Don't shy away from asking a player or a coach what his/her rational was behind a bad play. You can present a different side other than critiquing how wrong that call/ play was.
- Bring a fresh perspective. Think about what other angles there are or find fresh sources.
- Talk about the big plays, but don't forget to discuss what led up to them. Who were the playmakers?
- Know the terminology of the sports you are covering.
- The coaches and players know more than you do. Use them as a resource

- Go to practices and establish relationships. Let them see that you are going to portray them in the most accurate light possible.
- Don't create heroes/villains, state what is there.
- Talk to multiple people. The more perspective you have the more educated you will be to decipher a player's strengths/weaknesses and what they need to improve.

Spotters

Spotters are often used in the announce booth or in various positions around the field of play to help announcers and the director identify various players and to point out significant developments during the competition. The stage manager is generally responsible for the broadcast booth, including assisting the commentator and giving them requested information.

Anchor

Chronologically, anchoring is the very last thing a sports broadcaster does with his show. It comes after the research and legwork, after the planning and preparation, and after all the shooting, producing, and writing, but anchoring is probably the single most important element of the entire process. Certainly, the other elements are important, but it takes good anchoring and good delivery to bring out the best in the writing and photography. A good sports anchor ties all the other elements together and communicates them in an interesting and entertaining way. It is five or so minutes that will make or break your entire sportscast and in some cases an entire career.

Brad Schultz, Sports Broadcasting

What Sportscasters Collect

1. *Key statistics*
2. *Games stories*
3. *Anecdotes*
4. *Highlights*
5. *Coach's comments*
6. *Player development and/or injuries*
7. *Card files on individual players and teams*
8. *Statistics of every game, if possible*

Play-by-Play Sportscast Training

Figure 8.10: The key to interviewing is to know the athlete as well as possible.

CHAPTER 9
Post-production

*P*ost-production gives a producer an opportunity to improve and enhance the original production or correct a mistake. Often it is said, "Don't worry, we'll fix it in post."

Gary Milkis, Director Eight Olympics

At its most basic level, post-production is the process of combining individual shots in a desired order. It can have several purposes:

- To assemble material in a sequential fashion. The competition may have been shot over a number of days and then assembled into one program.
- To correct mistakes by cutting them out or by covering them with other material. The on-camera talent may have made a mistake, but an editor can remove those few seconds or cover them with another shot so that the performance appears to flow flawlessly.
- To create (often re-create), enhance, embellish, and bring to life images and events that were once captured live. Tools such as visual effects, sound effects, and music can give the story more drama, thus more impact on the audience. Slower portions of the competition are often edited out, allowing the production's pacing to move along. Features are added to give the viewer a more in-depth knowledge of a participant or part of the event. The various segments of the event are then assembled into a cohesive production.

The producer supervises the entire editing process with primary concern for keeping the program within the network or station's production guidelines or look. The producer also needs to keep the project on time and on budget. The editor is responsible for operating the editing equipment and combining the various shots in the desired order based on information from the producer. The production assistant (PA) assists the editor by logging footage, keeping track of administrative details, and organizing footage for the edit session. The PA may also be responsible for overseeing the creation of the graphics. The sound editor operates the sound editing equipment, provides edited dialogue, voiceovers, sound effects, and music tracks for the final edit.

It is imperative to maintain post-production continuity. Continuity means that when the production is edited, the viewer should perceive it as a continuous flow and should not be aware that it was assembled from a series of segments that were shot out of order. For example, the opening and some of the features may have been shot the day before the event.

Live productions require very little post-production work other than elements such as opening animations, sound bites or personality features that need to be produced prior to the broadcast. When the production is shot there may be some production reports to complete and, possibly, a post-production meeting to discuss the various aspects of the production with those involved. The post-pro-

Figure 9.1: Non-linear editors digitize the footage for manipulation by a computer.

Figure 9.2: Digital linear editing laptops are popular for sports news.

Figure 9.3: Linear editors are slowly being phased out of the production process.

duction meeting gives the producer an opportunity to evaluate the production by listening to crew feedback. They can use the information learned in this meeting to improve future productions.

Live-to-tape productions require extensive post-production work. After the event, the director or producer may want to shoot interviews with some of the outstanding athletes in the event. These will usually be shot with an ENG camera. The tapes are then taken to a post-production facility for editing.

Before the editing can begin, the program footage needs to be logged. This requires someone, often a production assistant, to review all the footage and write down the tape identification number, a description of the footage, any appropriate notes (great shot, bad audio), and the location, generally in time code, where the footage can be found on the tape. It is important to effectively and concisely translate the visuals into descriptive words. Most editors require the in point or beginning point of each new shot and the out point or ending point of the shot. A log can be as simple as a list on a plain piece of paper, a printed log sheet, or the log could be generated using computer software. Logging saves time in the edit suite if the appropriate shots have been selected and the time code location noted. See figure 9.4 for an example of a logging sheet used to document the contents of a videotape.

After shooting the 2000 Women's Series NorAm Cup to tape, NBC Sports spent approximately three and a half days in post-production which included:

Day 1: Digitize program into non-linear editor (midafternoon, day of shoot)

The digitization process is when the program content, generally recorded onto tape during the live event, is played (digitized) into the computer of a non-linear editor. This process is time-consuming, done in real time. However, once the program is in the computer, the content can be easily edited and manipulated.

Day 2: Edit tease, features, ski segments, and bumpers.

The tease is a short package used to promote the upcoming broadcast event. It is usually edited in a dramatic way to grab attention and convince the viewer to tune in.

Features are video packages that highlight

<table>
<tr><td>Athens Olympic Broadcasting
350 Messoghion Avenue
Athens – Greece
153 41

AOB
AΘHNA 2004

Tel: +30 210 659 6600
Fax: +30 210 659 6682</td><td>**AOB**
Log Sheet

Athens 2004
Olympic Summer Games
13–29 August, 2004</td><td>Sport*   Tape Number

Date ___/____/___ (____)
     DD   MM   YY   Day of Week

Page: ____ of _____</td></tr>
</table>

Sport* _____   Event _____   Phase _____

Venue _____   Camera Op. _____   Logger _____

Time Code	Video and Audio Description	Rating

* Please use following sport abbreviations:

AR Archery	**CF** Canoe Kayak Flatwater Racing	**EQ** Equestrian	**HB** Handball	**SH** Shooting	**TE** Tennis
AT Athletics	**CS** Canoe Kayak Slalom Racing	**FE** Fencing	**HO** Hockey	**SO** Softball	**TR** Triathlon
BD Badminton	**CM** Cycling Mountain Bike	**FB** Football	**JU** Judo	**SW** Swimming	**VO** Volleyball
BB Baseball	**CR** Cycling Road Race	**GA** Gymnastic Artistic	**MP** Modern Pentathlon	**SY** Synch Swimming	**WP** Water Polo
BK Basketball	**CT** Cycling Track	**GR** Gymnastics Rhythmic	**RO** Rowing	**TT** Table Tennis	**WL** Weightlifting
BV Beach Volleyball	**DV** Diving	**GT** Gymnastics Trampoline	**SA** Sailing	**TK** Taekwondo	**WR** Wrestling
BX Boxing					

Figure 9.4: Logging sheet used to document the contents of a videotape.

someone or something that is related to the sports event. A feature may be an up close and personal view of an athlete or a behind the scenes look at some part of the event. Features are generally short packages that are edited into the final production in order to hold the audience's attention.

Ski segments refer to the ski portions of the competition being broadcast.

Bumpers are generally dramatic shots, often high angle, low angle or spectacular scenery shots, used as transitions between the show segments and commercials.

Day 3. Composite show and create graphics.

Compositing is the editing of the video when visual and sound effects are overlaid and graphics added.

Graphics may be created from scratch or may be typed into a pre-produced template or graphic shell.

Day 4. Record talent voice-overs, mix audio, and complete show.

Since the live-to-tape production is generally shortened, keeping primarily the highlights in the program, the original talent's commentary may not be used. This means that a voice-over will need to take place in a recording studio. The talent must attempt to match the voice energy to the type of energy they would have if they were at the event so that the voice-over sounds like the real thing.

The audio is then mixed, adding the new voice-over track with real venue sound sweetened with sound effects to add realism.

The audio and video components are then edited together to create the final program.

If the show was entirely shot by multiple ENG cameras, the very time-consuming process of cutting an entire show from separate cameras will take place during post-production. Live-to-tape productions also require production reports and possibly post-production meetings.

Editing Guidelines

Post-production is like falling into a mud puddle and coming up with a fish in your pocket. It is the process of forging a glorious result from a seemingly untameable beast.

—Stephen Fleming,
Coordinating Producer,
Athens Olympic Broadcasting

- A change of time, slow motion shot or reverse angle shot is indicated by a dissolve, wipe or digital video effect (DVE).
- A change of geographical location is often indicated by a dissolve, wipe or DVE, and a new establishing shot.
- A program intended to be sequential avoids jump cuts, meaning cutting between two shots that are so similar that the subject appears to jump on screen. The use of a cutaway in between the two shots helps to avoid the jump.
- In general, programs avoid cutting from a camera shot that is in motion—that is, in the middle of a pan, tilt or zoom—to a still camera shot since this is jarring to the viewer. It is better to move from a shot in motion to another shot in motion, and to move from one still shot to another. If you need to get from a shot that is in motion to one that is still, ideally you wait until the moving shot has completed its move. In other words, wait until it is a still shot and then cut to the still shot.
- Cuts should occur during subject movement rather than before or after it. For instance, if a person is about to stand up from the bench, the best place to cut from the medium shot of the person on the bench to the long shot is when the person is in the middle of standing up.
- Cuts should not occur without motivation. The viewer shouldn't notice the edit and wonder why it occurred. In general, it is time to make an edit when:
(a) The current shot has been on screen long enough for the audience to take in all the pertinent information. This could be as short as one second for a very simple shot or much longer for a shot in motion. The issue of pacing is more an art form than a science.
(b) Another shot would help to develop the story, advancing the plot and maintaining good pacing. If an athlete scores, it would make sense to cut quickly to the reaction of teammates or the crowd. This will help move the story forward.

(Kathy Bruner contributed to this chapter.)

CHAPTER 10
Television, Computers and Sports

Viewer enhancement tools . . . provide television stations with an innovative tool to upgrade their sports programs . . . and will become standard for major sports events in the near future.

Hartmut Hiestermann, Global Sportsnet, Germany

Roone Arledge, innovative television sports pioneer, said that television tools such as instant replays, slow motion and even superimposing the names of the players on the screen after a good play, were called gimmicks when they were introduced. The computer invasion into television production that began years ago with the character generator, continues to grow. As directors and producers continue to look for tools and techniques that will lead to a more informed viewer, they are increasingly turning to computer based, viewer enhancement tools.

Computer driven techniques cover a wide range of possibilities. Some of them have been successful, some not. Just as computer graphics were considered gimmicks at one point, some of these technologies will be normal in the future. Below is a review of some of the past technologies as well as some of the newest ones.

The FoxTrax

One of the original technological enhancements to television sports was the glowing hockey puck created by Fox Sports called the FoxTrax. "The goal was simple. Make the televised image of a hockey puck glow so it's easier for the viewer to spot, and, when it's going really fast, put a tail on it showing its path. The company hoped the system could overcome the main

complaint about televised hockey: the trouble that casual views have in following the fast-moving puck on television screens. To track the puck, a number of parameters had to be fed into a computer system and updated continually. First, the system had to know exactly where the broadcast cameras were focused. It also had to have some idea of how each camera lens distorts the image; different brands of lenses vary. It then had to figure out which camera's feed was being displayed to viewers at any moment. Meanwhile, the system had to know where the puck was and how fast it was traveling, and then it had to create a graphic based on that data and overlay it onto the video image 60 times a second. All of these things had to be exactly synchronized, as the cameras were zooming and panning and the puck was traveling at up to 160 km an hour. Making it work required putting infrared transmitters into each hockey puck *(see figures 10.1 and 10.2)*. Technically, the project was a success. But serious hockey fans hated it. After three years, pro-hockey broadcasts in the United States switched networks, and the system died a quiet death. *(Sportvision)* The FoxTrax system's technology has now been adapted and is used to highlight racecars during a motor sports events. The glow technology

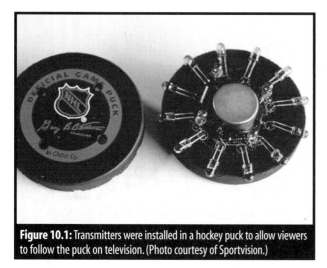

Figure 10.1: Transmitters were installed in a hockey puck to allow viewers to follow the puck on television. (Photo courtesy of Sportvision.)

Figure 10.2: The transmitters in the hockey puck, shown in Figure 10.1, created a comet tail on the puck for television viewers. (Photo courtesy of Sportvision.)

allows a commentator to illustrate a specific car's place on the track when it is amid other cars.

Virtual Information Graphics

A number of companies have now created virtual lines on the field of play of different sports and they have become almost the norm. The virtual line on the field of play was more difficult to develop than the hockey puck since the line needed to be perfectly straight (which is difficult with the variety of lenses used), had to look realistic when located on rough ground next to the actual field lines and must appear under the players. This technology was almost immediately accepted by the viewers in sports like American football, football/soccer, and cricket. *(See figure 10.3.)*

RACEf/x

Global Positioning System (GPS) technology is now used in race cars in conjunction with computer graphics to give the viewer detailed information about the driver's name, car's position on the course, speed, brake status, and tachometer. *(See figure 10.4.)*

"Matrix" Style

"Matrix" style computer/camera systems now give the viewer a look at the action from multiple vantage points. Although there are multiple systems using different technology, they both have systems that potentially provide a 360-degree view of a sports image. Robotically controlled cameras, placed 5–12 degrees apart, are used to capture the images. Some of the systems have software that fills in some of the missing information between the camera's images, actually providing moving images as well as still images. A server channel records each individual camera, allowing the system's operator to provide a replay and cut between the multiple digital disc recorders. This provides the capability to rotate the viewer perspective around an image of a play before resuming action. A camera operator will control one of the cameras as a master camera. The other cameras will synchronize, following the

Figure 10.3: Virtual field of play lines allows the production personnel to communicate more information to the viewer. (Photos courtesy of Sportvision and Orad.)

Figure 10.4: Global positions system (GPS) technology allows more data to be transmitted to the viewer. (Courtesy of Sportvision.)

cue of the master camera, focusing on the same action, such as a golfer. *(See figure 10.5.)* Each camera interacts with the master camera, constantly adjusting its zoom and focus to keep the image of the golfer the same size as in the images of all the other cameras. "This shared center of focus is what creates the illusion that the player can be seen in three dimensions," said Takeo Kanade, director of the Robotics Institute and a computer vision expert. When images taken at the same time by each camera are viewed sequentially, the effects is of walking or flying around the player. The system has been used for all types of sports. Larry Barbatsoulis, CBS Technical Director, said, "In individual sports, like gymnastics, I could do a 360 around someone doing a rings routine, or the long jump, or a pole vault. Imagine freezing a guy who's going backwards over the high jump, then revolving around him to show his form." (compiled from BUF Technology, The Wire, Newsday.com, Post-Gazette, Berkely.edu/mhonarc, Cahners Business Information)

Transposition Replay Systems

SimulCam transposes a live athlete's performance with the previous or record holder's performance. This simultaneous broadcast of the two performances looked so real that unknowing viewers during the 2002 Winter Olympics voiced concern that the two athletes should not be skiing so close together. *(See figure 10.6.)* This computer transposition system allows the audience the opportunity to compare two performances, allowing them to observe the minute differences in the athletes' movements. This technology can be used with any sports that included individual performances within certain constraints on the field of play.

Another transposition technology, Cyber-Sport, creates a virtual runner that moves at a world record pace around an athletics track as a race unfolds. Like SimilCam above, the virtual runner adds to the drama of the race, allowing the viewer to understand how the current race compares to others.

StroMotion

StroMotion was first used by ABC Sports to

Figure 10.5: Cameras positioned around the athlete portray a "matrix" style of coverage. (Courtesy of Visage-HD.)

allow the viewer to analyze the quadruple jump in figure skating. The technology shows individual video frames of the athlete's performance within one visible frame. Since some sports occur so rapidly that the viewer cannot see the detailed action, StroMotion can break the action down to show key frames, compiling them into one frame, allowing the viewer to analyze the athlete's action. *(See figure 10.7.)*

Virtual Ads

A number of companies provide virtual ad services. These services generally use a type of "green screen" or chroma-key technology to place the ads on the screen. The systems electronically replace existing advertising signs and banners or insert graphics right on the field of play with advertising that has been sold to television program sponsors. The images can also be inserted into the natural landscape of the field or on a race track. While the virtual ads are not seen if you are at the venue, they are added to the broadcast output for the viewing audience. *(See figure 10.8.)*

Internet/Interactive Television

Internet sites and television continue to partner together to attract viewers and provide interactive experiences for sports fans. One Internet application called PitCommand, allows paid subscribers to watch a virtual aerial view of the race and view the track and data for any car they select, run instant replays at will, and change track perspective. Another company

Figure 10.6: Transposition systems allow the viewer to compare athletes. (Courtesy of Dartfish/Sportvision.)

Figure 10.7: StroMotion is used to analyze the athlete's movements. (Courtesy of Dartfish/Sportvision.)

has created sports webcasting technologies that allow sports fans to "watch and play" live or delayed sports events on their computers. Their player and ball automatic tracking methods, combined with Intel's web 3D environment generates live or delayed 3D graphical simulations of live soccer action. Fans get to enjoy a graphical visualization of the match with the added functionality of choosing their viewpoint (for example, viewing the entire match through the eyes of one player). (Virtual TV Becomes Reality) RACEf/x, is developing interactive television games that will allow viewers to insert their own virtual race car onto the screen and allow them to race against the professional drivers during an race.

Technology Summary

The biggest challenge with new technology is to overuse them. At the end of the show you want them to remember the game ... not the technology. The difference between using new technology as "electronic toys" and using them responsibly is when they are selected on the basis of whether they contribute to the viewer's understanding and enjoyment of the sport being covered.

... this is about content ... it's factually easy to become mesmerized by new technology for its own sake. But technology is only a means to an end—and the end is great content.
          —*Michael Grade, Chairman, BBC,*
                          United Kingdom

Figure 10.8: Virtual ads have become commonplace on many networks.

Figure 10.9: Sports analysts have used technological tools, such as this Telestrator, to illustrate what the athlete's strategies since the 60's. While it may look like a normal television monitor, the Telestrator's monitor is touch-sensitive and can be used to draw circles, lines, arrows or pre-loaded graphics directly over the video.

PART 4:
History of Sports Television

CHAPTER 11: Milestones in Sports Broadcasting

CHAPTER 11
Milestones in Sports Broadcasting

Figure 11.1: July 1922: H. Gernsback published, in *Science and Invention* magazine, detailed drawings of how sports will be covered in the future. While numerous experiments had been completed up to this point, television is not really considered invented until 1926.

Television, What's in a Name?
In the early 1920s it was called visual listening, audiovision, telectroscopy, telephonoscope, raduo, electric vision, and radiovision. Finally, television seemed to be the name everyone accepted. The name television comes from "tele" (far off) and "vision" (to see).

July 12, 1928: Although some sources list tennis as being televised as the first sport on television, they were actually only images of a tennis player hitting a ball. It was not really a sports event.

Figure 11.2: Photo etching of the first closed-circuit telecast of a sporting event. (*Television News*, November-December 1931)

February 17, 1931: The first closed-circuit telecast of a sporting event was a baseball game played by the Waseda University baseball club. The images were not seen by the public and were transmitted directly to the Electrical Laboratory at Waseda University in Tokyo. (*See figure 11.2.*)

Figure 11.3: The entire vehicle shown above was the camera used to cover the first broadcast sports event. (Courtesty *Radio News*, March 1932 and Tom Genova)

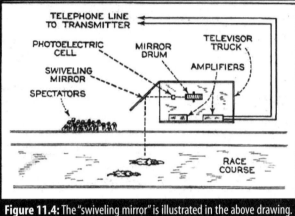

Figure 11.4: The "swiveling mirror" is illustrated in the above drawing. It utilized a moving mirror in order to follow the running horses. (Courtesy *Radio News*, March 1932 and Tom Genova)

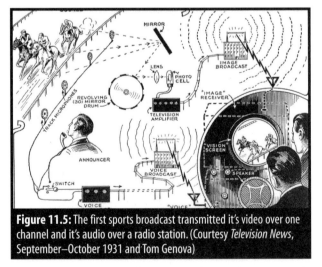

Figure 11.5: The first sports broadcast transmitted it's video over one channel and it's audio over a radio station. (Courtesy *Television News*, September–October 1931 and Tom Genova)

June 2, 1931: The earliest true broadcast (available to the public) of an outdoor sporting event was the BBC's coverage of The Derby (horse race) at Epsom in Great Britain. The production's mechanical television equipment utilized one camera. A movable mirror was used to focus the images of the horses into a large wagon,

which contained the camera apparatus. Thus spectators were able to view the entire race from start to finish. The audio and video images were transmitted separately to the home viewer. *(See figures 11.3, 11.4, and 11.5.)*

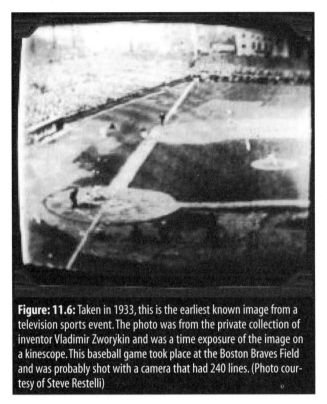

Figure: 11.6: Taken in 1933, this is the earliest known image from a television sports event. The photo was from the private collection of inventor Vladimir Zworykin and was a time exposure of the image on a kinescope. This baseball game took place at the Boston Braves Field and was probably shot with a camera that had 240 lines. (Photo courtesy of Steve Restelli)

1936: The first live television coverage of a sports event, utilizing electronic equipment, was the 1936 Berlin Olympics. RCA and Farnsworth cameras were used for the coverage.

1936: Leni Riefenstahl filmed the 1936 Olympics for the documentary *Olympia*. Her innovative use of dramatic film techniques on a sports event changed the world of film and television sports. The use of tracking dollys, underwater cameras, cameras on hot air balloons, dive cameras, low/high angles had never been attempted before on sports coverage. Broadcasting the Olympics, an International Olympic Committee publication, states that "The shooting techniques used by Leni Riefenstahl have become the standards for Olympic filmmaking and television coverage ever since." See page 42 for more information.

1937: First tennis tournament on television: Wimbledon

February 4, 1937: The first time that sports commentary was heard on television. The BBC hired Herry Mallin to comment on an England versus Ireland amateur boxing contest from the Alexandra Palace.

September 16, 1937: The first football (soccer) match to be filmed live on television was between the Arsenal and the Arsenal Reserves in Highbury, England.

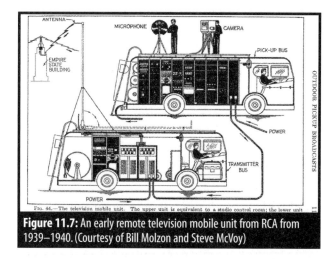

Figure 11.7: An early remote television mobile unit from RCA from 1939–1940. (Courtesy of Bill Molzon and Steve McVoy)

May 15–21, 1939: The first telecast of a bicycle race was broadcast by the National Broadcasting Company. The six-day race featured twelve teams, eight of which finished the 2388 miles event. Yankee baseball player, Joe DiMaggio fired the starting gun.

June 1, 1939: First heavyweight boxing match televised, Max Baer versus Lou Nova, from Yankee Stadium

August 26, 1939: First major league baseball game telecast, a double-header between the Cincin-nati Reds and the Brooklyn Dodgers at Ebbets Field, Brooklyn, announcer Walter L. "Red" Barber or Bill Stern (sources differ), on W2XBS.

September 30, 1939: First televised college football (American style) game, Fordham versus Waynesburg, at Randall's Island, New York, on W2XBS. (*See figure 11.8.*)

October 22, 1939: First NFL game is televised by W2XBS: Brooklyn Dodgers versus Philadelphia Eagles at Ebbetts Field in Brooklyn. Play-by-play announcer was Allen (Skip) Walz.

February 25, 1940: First hockey game televised, Rangers versus Canadians, on W2XBS, from Madison Square Garden.

March 2, 1940: First televised track event, from Madison Square Madison

October 5, 1940: WPTZ-TV was the first in the country to carry a complete football (American style) schedule—all home games. With only 700 television sets scattered throughout the Philadelphia area, Philco broadcast the University of Pennsylvania's Quakers 51–0 victory over the University of Maryland at Franklin Field.

June 19, 1946: First televised heavyweight title fight (Joe Louis versus Billy Conn), broadcast from Yankee Stadium, was seen by the largest television audience to see a fight (141,000).

September 30, 1947: The first World Series game to be telecast was between the New York Yankees and the Brooklyn Dodgers at Yankee Stadium. The game was carried by WABD, WCBS-TV, and WNBT in New York, and was also telecast in Philadelphia, Schenectady, and Washington. The 1947 World Series brought in television's first mass audience, and was seen by an estimated 3.9 million people, mostly in bars [Tim Brooks].

July 14, 1951: The first "color" sports event was the $15,000 Molly Pitcher Handicap held at the Monmouth Park Jockey Club in Oceanport, New Jersey. This event was broadcast using the CBS Color Television System, which was pre-NTSC.

Figure 11.8: First televised college American football game on September 30, 1939. (Courtesy of David Sarnoff Library)

September 22, 1951: First live sporting event seen coast-to-coast in the United States: a college football game between Duke and the University of Pittsburgh, at Pittsburgh (NBC-TV).

1955: Helivision anti-vibration helicopter camera mount was invented by French director/cinematographer Albert Lamorisse.

November 1, 1959: WLWT-TV televised the first indoor sports event in television history in color. The Cincinnati Royals pro basketball game from the Cincinnati Gardens. It was fed to NBC.

April 1960: Ampex introduces the Intersync accessory, which makes it possible to cut to or from videotape without rolls or discontinuity and to do dissolves and some special effects.

Figure 11.9: In the 1960s this camera was responsible for the infield, outfield, and graphics. (Courtesy of Lytle Hoover)

May 16, 1960: WLWT-TV (USA) televised the first night major league baseball game in television history in color from Crosley Field. Three RCA TK-41 color cameras equipped with low light tubes were used.

August 25, 1960: The opening of the 17th Olympic Games in Rome is transmitted live via the Eurovision link. Video tape was used by broadcasters for the first time at an Olympics.

March 17, 1962: ABC Sports (USA) used special rerun equipment to replay portions of a boxing match.

October 10, 1964: First live color satellite broadcast in history was the opening ceremonies of the 1964 Summer Olympics in Tokyo.

August 1965: MVR video disc machine is built to CBS specifications and is used for instant replays of football games.

April 1967: Ampex introduces the first battery-powered portable high-band color tape recorder. Weighing 35 pounds, it could record for 20 minutes. The accompanying camera weighed 13 pounds.

April 1967: Ampex announces high-band color video disc machine, HS-100, for instant replays. ABC uses it for slow-motion playback of downhill skiing at the World Series of Skiing—an early, if not first, use of slow motion instant replay in sporting events.

1968: NHK in Japan begins work on high definition television (HDTV).

1968: Ampex HS-100 video disc recorder with slow motion and stop-action facilities is used for first time by ABC during Olympic Games.

1969: Development of first handheld video camera.

1969: First exhibition of HDTV at STRL open house (Japan).

1976: Steadicam camera mount, devised by Garrett Brown, is introduced.

1984: Olympic Games were broadcast in stereo.

June 3, 1989: Japan begins regular high definition television transmissions by satellite.

October 1, 1998: Major League Baseball began streaming video on the Internet of post-game conferences, playoff game highlights shortly after each game and the greatest moments in baseball.

December 1, 2000: Digital satellite broadcasting began in Japan.

2001: Major League Baseball streams real-time video of games over the Internet.

May 31, 2003: The Women's National Basketball Association (WNBA) featured the first-ever live video webcast of a game in women's professional sports history.

November 2003: MobiTV becomes the first streaming television content service that delivers live television programming to mobile phones.

August 2004: Broadcasters at the Athens Olympics streamed video and highlight clips of the Olympic Games through mobile phone handsets and via the Internet. The BBC called the Athens Olympics the "Interactive Olympics."

February 2006: Torino Olympics is the first all HD Olympics by NBC.

(Compiled with input from Iain Baird, earlytelevision.org, Ed Reitan's Color Television History, Philo T. Farnsworth Archives, Lytle Hoover, terramedia.co.uk, Alexander B. Magoun, David Sarnoff Library, SportandTechology.com, WLWT, Temple University Urban Archives, TV Acres, tvhistory.tv, oldradio.com, and Tom Genova.)

The Inventors of Television

It is very difficult to say exactly who really "invented" television, so many individuals were working around the world on the project. The "inventor" title is based on how you define television. However, there are two individuals who seem to have had the most impact at the beginning of television.

John Logie Baird, of Scotland and later England, was the inventor of mechanical television in 1926. He was the first person who was able to create a visual transmission of a television image. While his mechanical system was defunct in a few years, he continued to experiment and was the first person to ever televise a sports event (see the description of the first sports broadcast from the Derby). His later work included color television, high definition television, and some of the foundation for television as it is today.

Philo T. Farnsworth is credited as being the inventor of electronic television in 1927. While his methodology was significantly different from Baird's, his early television tube was the foundation for electronic television. Farnsworth also created the first television camera and was able to sell his technology to organizations all over the world. In fact, Fernseh, the television production company who televised the Olympics in 1936, used some of Farnsworth's cameras in their coverage.

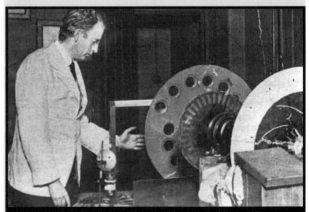

John Logie Baird (Courtesy tvhistory.tv)

Philo T. Farnsworth (Courtesy the Philo T. Farnsworth Archives)

APPENDIX I:
Truck Diagrams

A series of television production truck diagrams are included to show the variety of trucks and the types of equipment available in each truck.

Mountain Mobile Television -- MMT 1

50' Long, 13' High, 8'6" Wide

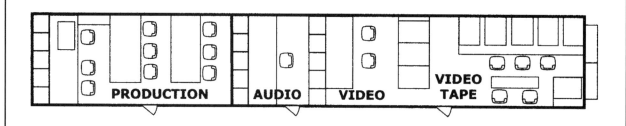

Control:

- Sony 7350 36-input, 3-M/E switcher
- Sony DME-7000 DVE (dual channel) and single channel Abekas A-53D
- 5-rack monitor wall with 40 - 9" black & white monitors, 8 - 9" color monitors and 3 - 13" color monitors.
- Chyron Infinit
  - o 060 processor, 128 MB Expanded Memory, third channel mix, Transform, 1.1GB hard drive, 230 MB Bernoulli drive, 2 GB Jaz drive, 250 Mb Zip drive, Intelligent Interface and video capture
- Dual channel Abekas A42 still store (600 fields)
-

Cameras:

- Sony chip cameras
  - o Hard cameras (BVP-375) 5O/55:8.5 lenses
  - o Handheld cameras (BVP-90) 18x 8.5 lenses
  - o Up to 10 total cameras available on request
- 2 clock cameras

Tape:

- Up to 6 BVW 75 VCRs available on request (with slo-mo controllers)
- BVW-65 playback only VCR
- EVS 4-channel slow-motion disk recorder (available on request)
- 1 BVH-3100 1" VTR
- 2 VHS VCRs
- Master time code generator

Audio:

- Soundcraft Europa audio mixer 40+8/8/2
- Digicart II with 220 keyboard, Sony Minidisc, CD player, audio cassette
- 11 DBX compressor/limiters, 2 Telos and 2 QKT telephone interfaces
- Microphones: 5 Senneheiser ME-66s, 2 - 816s 8 Sony lavalieres, 5 RE 50s, 5 EV 635s, 4 Sportscaster headsets and 3 talk-back boxes

Communications:

- RTS communications system, 12 channel system, 802 master stations, all dual listen
- RTS 4000 series IFB system (12 channels)
- 6 camera ISO system, 20 RTS belt packs, 9 RTS IFB boxes
- 8-Line Panasonic telephone system

Engineering, Cable and Miscellaneous:

- 32 x 32 DataTek router - breakaway
- Redundant sync generators, w/ auto changeover
- GVG processing amp (patchable), external tallies
- 2 frame synchronizers (more available on request)
- 4,000 feet of triax, 2,000 feet of coax, 1,500 feet of DT-12 audio mults, 2,500 feet of 4 pair audio mults (More cable available on request)
- 2 - 13" portable color monitors, 7 - 9" portable color monitors
- 1 lighting kit
- Power: 208VAC, single-phase, 150 amps

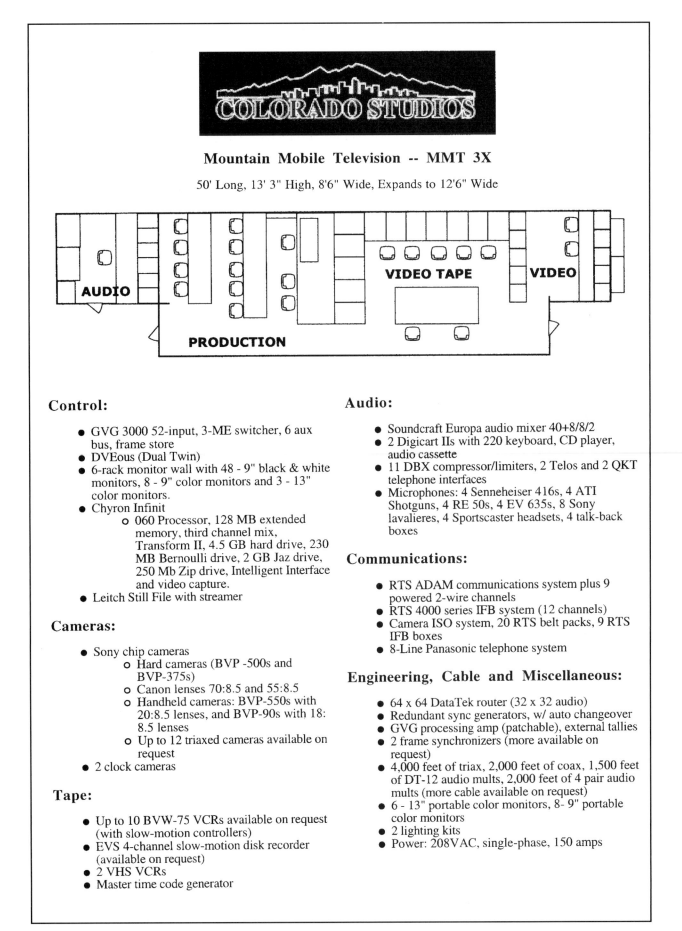

COLORADO STUDIOS

Mountain Mobile Television -- MMT 3X

50' Long, 13' 3" High, 8'6" Wide, Expands to 12'6" Wide

AUDIO

PRODUCTION

VIDEO TAPE

VIDEO

Control:

- GVG 3000 52-input, 3-ME switcher, 6 aux bus, frame store
- DVEous (Dual Twin)
- 6-rack monitor wall with 48 - 9" black & white monitors, 8 - 9" color monitors and 3 - 13" color monitors.
- Chyron Infinit
  - o 060 Processor, 128 MB extended memory, third channel mix, Transform II, 4.5 GB hard drive, 230 MB Bernoulli drive, 2 GB Jaz drive, 250 Mb Zip drive, Intelligent Interface and video capture.
- Leitch Still File with streamer

Cameras:

- Sony chip cameras
  - o Hard cameras (BVP -500s and BVP-375s)
  - o Canon lenses 70:8.5 and 55:8.5
  - o Handheld cameras: BVP-550s with 20:8.5 lenses, and BVP-90s with 18: 8.5 lenses
  - o Up to 12 triaxed cameras available on request
- 2 clock cameras

Tape:

- Up to 10 BVW-75 VCRs available on request (with slow-motion controllers)
- EVS 4-channel slow-motion disk recorder (available on request)
- 2 VHS VCRs
- Master time code generator

Audio:

- Soundcraft Europa audio mixer 40+8/8/2
- 2 Digicart IIs with 220 keyboard, CD player, audio cassette
- 11 DBX compressor/limiters, 2 Telos and 2 QKT telephone interfaces
- Microphones: 4 Senneheiser 416s, 4 ATI Shotguns, 4 RE 50s, 4 EV 635s, 8 Sony lavalieres, 4 Sportscaster headsets, 4 talk-back boxes

Communications:

- RTS ADAM communications system plus 9 powered 2-wire channels
- RTS 4000 series IFB system (12 channels)
- Camera ISO system, 20 RTS belt packs, 9 RTS IFB boxes
- 8-Line Panasonic telephone system

Engineering, Cable and Miscellaneous:

- 64 x 64 DataTek router (32 x 32 audio)
- Redundant sync generators, w/ auto changeover
- GVG processing amp (patchable), external tallies
- 2 frame synchronizers (more available on request)
- 4,000 feet of triax, 2,000 feet of coax, 1,500 feet of DT-12 audio mults, 2,000 feet of 4 pair audio mults (more cable available on request)
- 6 - 13" portable color monitors, 8- 9" portable color monitors
- 2 lighting kits
- Power: 208VAC, single-phase, 150 amps

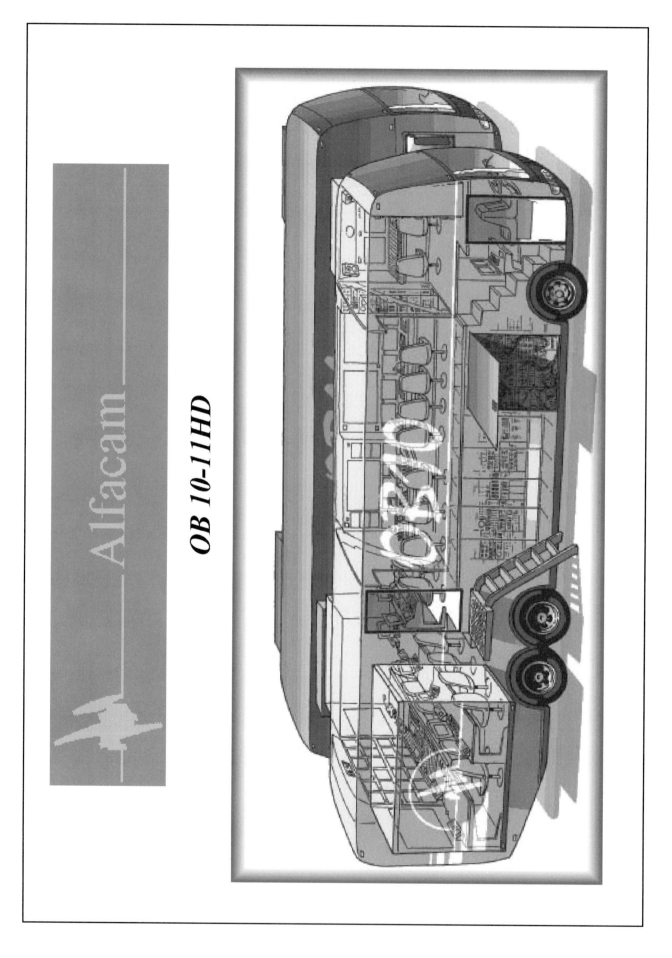

Alfacam

OB 10-11HD

VEHICLE

- VAN HOOL T 927 - 2 level coach, super hi-end finishing
- Special custom made body with 5 areas
- length over all: 13,7 m, width after extension 4,50 m, height 4 m
- 2 levels, ca 68m² workspace in total!
- complete with 6 separate air conditioning units, air suspension, automatic leveling system, mains transformer, power stabilisers, ...
- 460 HP MAN motor
- OB10-11HD can operate in 3x170V, 3x190V, 3x380V (63A) in 50hz or 60hz

VIDEO

FULL DIGITAL 16:9-4:3 switchable
FULL HDTV 1080/50i or 60i switchable up to 30 cameras

- Serial Digital Production Switcher PHILIPS DD 35
  SDI mainframe 62 inputs - 3ME+PP
  HDTV mainfram SERAPH 32 inputs - PP
- 4 mixing panels in this truck (absolutely UNIQUE)
  -35/3 with 24 access on 3 MES on main desk
  -24/2 with 24 access on 2 MES on second desk
  -extended satelite panel 16 access on desk where wanted
  -small satelite panel on desk where wanted
- built in FX panel permits
  -4x8 sec RAM recording of clips
  -2 channel built in DVE

SDI MODE

- up to 30 SDI - cameras BTS LDK 100-200 with 8x to 86x lenses
- 6 cameras on FRAME STORES (f.i. steadycam or unlocked)
- 6 SUPERSLOMO cameras BTS LDK 23 available
- 10 LSMs: 4/2-3/1-2/2 and superslomo LSMs (cabled for 10)
- 15 VTR capacity
- different legs and heads (HAWK, VARIPEDS, CRANES, HEAVYLEGS, ...)
- editor BVE 2000
- SDI matrix 96x224
- over 150 viewing monitors:
  BARCO ADVM14, BARCO I-studio multisplitters 5 PLASMAWALLS, 10 BARCO
  CBM 5049 with 10 Vivaldi quadsplits, 6 hi-end computer LCDs with quadsplits...

HDTV MODE

- up to 30 cameras BTS LDK 6000 with 8x to 86x lenses (today Alphacam owns 48 cameras)
- integration of any NON-HDTV signal is possible
- at present all slomos through Panasonic D5HDTV recorders
- 15 VTR capacity
- different legs and heads (HAWK, VARIPEDS, CRANES, HEAVYLEGS, ...)
- over 20 viewing monitors in HDTV
- in HDTV MODE, OB10-11 can work in both 50 fields-60 fields, this means that all HD sources are in this cases available in rest. PAL-SDI/50 and 1080i/50 or in NTSC-SDI/60 and 1080i/60

DIGITAL SURROUND AUDIO

- Audio desk SOUNDTRACKS DPCII - 80 faders - 112 inputs FULL DIGITAL surround 5.1 audio desk
- CD, DAT, ...
- many different audio effects
- Matrix Plus III intercom system 72-72

OPTICAL VIDEO AND AUDIO

- different coders, decoders (PAL, SDI, audio...) on OPTICAL cables
- AUDIO frame with 56 sources can be set inside the venue and connected optically on 1 optical MADI-FIBRE!!

CONTROL

- All crucial equipment is dedoubled on many different computers, and worked out redundantly

APPENDIX II:

Olympic Broadcast Planning Document

The following is a small part of the television planning documentation from an Olympic broadcast. This documentation illustrates the level of pre-planning that is required for a large sports event.

'E' Center

Venue Quick Facts

GENERAL VENUE	
Commentary Positions	70
Observer Seats	80
Parking (Total Spaces)	120
ISB	20
Rights Holders	100
Compound Location/Size	Located on the Northwest side of the venue, in the parking area. (46,500 sq.ft.)

KEY DATES	
Set Up	Feb. 5 – Feb. 7
Final Fax	Feb. 7
Rehearsal	Feb. 8
Training	TBD
Air	TBD
Strike	TBD

EQUIPMENT	
Cameras	18
Videotape Recorders	10
Microphones	33
Specialty Equipment	13
Graphics & Timing	
Character Generator(s)	1
Timing Generator(s)	1
Mobile Unit(s)	Two (Mountain Mobile 3X and one Type C)

CREW	
Total	63
Freelance	36
University Level	20
Vendors	7
Total	63
ISB Local	31
ISB Non-local	32

'E' Center

1.1 The Venue

Sport(s)	Hockey: Two events
Location	'E' Center 3200 S. Decker Lake Dr. West Valley City, UT 84119
Temperature	Average February: 2.9° C (average for Salt Lake area)
Snowfall	Average February: 24.9 cm (average for Salt Lake area) Average annual: 163.3 cm (average for Salt Lake area)
Altitude	Base: 1,305m
Competition Days	Men's hockey: TBD (pending schedule approval) Women's hockey: TBD (pending schedule approval)
Seating Capacity	10,000
Distance from IBC	Located southwest of Salt Lake City, approximately 14km/ 12 minutes from the Salt Palace – IBC
Directions	Take I-15 south and exit at 2100 South. Head westbound on 2100 South and take exit 16 (Redwood Road). Turn left onto Redwood Road and continue to 3100 South. Turn right on 3100 South and travel ½ mile to Decker Lake Dr., turn left.
Current Status/History	Site has been determined and venue exists
SLOC Venue Designer	
ISB Venue Ops Timeline	Included on following pages
ISB Exclusive Use Start Date	January 25, 2002
SLOC Exclusive Use Start Date	February 1, 2002

ISB RECOMMENDATIONS/REQUESTS

SLOC Venue Operations Timeline
- ISB has received a preliminary venue fit-up schedule, but is awaiting a full venue operations timeline from SLOC. This timeline may affect ISB's current plan.

'E' Center

1.2 Sports

Ice Hockey

Events/Disciplines	Men's Tournament Women's Tournament
Competition Dates	TBD – Final schedule is currently under consideration by SLOC and the IIHF.
Number of Athletes/Teams	Men's Teams: 14 Women's Teams: 8
Training Site	Men's – Acord Ice Center Women's – Murray Arena
Competition Format	**Men** *Preliminary round:* Eight teams, divided into two groups, will compete in round-robin play within each group. The winners of each group will move to the final round. The team that ranks higher at the Olympic qualifying round will be known as Qualifying 1 and the other team as Qualifying 2. Three relegation games will be played to determine the ranking of the remaining teams. *Final round:* Six prequalified teams join the competition, and along with the Qualifying 1 and Qualifying 2 teams, will form two groups and compete in round-robin play within each group. *Playoff round:* Following the final round, each team will compete in a quarterfinal game against one team from the other group. The four winning teams will compete in the semifinals. *Medal round:* The losing teams from the semifinals will compete for the bronze medal, while the two winning semifinalists will meet for the gold. Each game will consist of three 20-minute periods with two 15-minute intermissions between periods. In preliminary round play, all ties will be counted to determine a team's record. A special criteria will be used to break ties for teams qualifying for medal round play. A tie at the end of regulation play in the bronze medal game will result in a 10-minute sudden death period followed by a shootout, if necessary.

'E' Center

1.2 Sports (continued)

Ice Hockey

Competition Format (continued)	**Women** *Preliminary round:* Eight teams, divided into two groups, will compete in round-robin play within each group. The top two teams from each group will move to the playoff round. The remaining two teams from each group will move to the relegation round. *Semi-final round:* Following the preliminary round, the top two teams will compete in a semi-final game against one team from the other group. *Medal round:* The losing teams from the semi-finals will compete for the bronze medal while the two winning semi-finalists will meet for the gold medal. *Relegation round:* The losing teams from the preliminary round will compete in a relegation round. Schedule TBD. Each game will consist of three 20-minute periods with two 15-minute intermissions between periods. In preliminary round play, all ties will be counted to determine a team's record. A tie at the end of regulation play in the bronze medal game will result in a 10-minute sudden death period followed by a shootout, if necessary. A tie at the end of regulation play in the gold medal game will result in a 20-minute sudden death period followed by a shootout, if necessary.

Sports Contacts	**SLOC**
	 Sports Competition Manager: Tel.:
	                                               Fax:
	                               E-mail: _____
	
	 Sports Competition Manager: Tel:
	                                               Fax:
	                               E-mail: _____
	
	 International Federation
	 International Ice Hockey Federation (IIHF)
	 President IIHF:
	 Secretaire General:
	
	                                          Tel.:
	                                          Fax.:
	                               Internet: _____

'E' Center

1.4.1 Production – Venue Review

Ice Hockey

Coverage	ISB will utilize 18 cameras to broadcast ice hockey at the 'E' Center. Coverage will focus on the speed and action of the game. Replays will illustrate offensive strategy and the defensive battles around the goals. Passing and goaltending nuances will be captured in super slow motion. Cameras will be mounted above, behind and inside the goals. Creative audio techniques will be employed to introduce a more exciting and intimate sound presentation of the broadcasts.
Cameras (Total)	18
Fixed	3 (No. 1, No. 3, No. 10)
Hand-held	4 (No. 4, No. 6, No. 7, No. 11)
Mini	7 (No. 12, No. 13, No. 14, No. 15, No. 16, No. 17, No. 18)
Lipstick	2 (No. 8-RF, No. 9-RF)
Super Slow Motion (SSM)	2 (No. 2 – fixed, No. 5 – hand-held)
Videotape Recorders (Total)	10
Super Slow Motion (SSM)	2
Slow motion isolation	6
Backup PGM record	2
Specialty Equipment	13
Robotic lipstick	(No. 8, No. 9)
Robotic mini	(No. 14, No. 15, No. 16, No. 17, No. 18)
Robotic hand-held	(No. 6, No. 7)
Mini cam w/fixed mount	(No. 12, No. 13)
SSM	(No. 2 – fixed, No. 5 – hand-held)
Graphics & Timing	
Character Generator(s)	1
Timing Generator(s)	1

'E' Center

1.4.2 Production – Cameras

Ice Hockey

No.	Type	Lens	Mount	Location	Coverage
1	Fixed	55x1	Tripod	High mid-ice	Game camera
2	Fixed (SSM)	70x1	Tripod	High mid-ice	Tight camera
3	Fixed	55x1	Tripod	High, northwest end zone	Action
4	Hand-held	18x1	Sticks	Northwest corner	Ice level action
5	Hand-held (SSM)	18x1	Sticks	Southwest corner	Ice level action
6	Hand-held	18x1	Type II	Above north goal judge	Action (replay)
7	Hand-held	18x1	Type II	Above south goal judge	Action (replay)
8	Lipstick (RF)	TBD	Type IV	Inside north goal	Action
9	Lipstick (RF)	TBD	Type IV	Inside south goal	Action
10	Fixed	70x1	Tripod	High mid-ice, opposite main camera side	Reverse angle (replay)
11	Hand-held	18x1	Sticks	Player benches	Bench shots/pre & post
12	Mini	TBD	Fixed mount	Over goal – north	Disputed call (replay)
13	Mini	TBD	Fixed mount	Over goal – south	Disputed call (replay)
14	Mini	TBD	Type III	Exit from locker rooms; exit/entry between periods	Athletes leaving the ice
15	Mini	TBD	Type III	Exit to locker room post-game	Athletes leaving the ice
16	Mini	TBD	Type III	High end zone, southwest side	Interior beauty shot
17	Mini	TBD	Type III	Secured to glass in penalty box	Penalty box
18	Mini	TBD	Type III	Secured to glass in penalty box	Penalty box

ISB RECOMMENDATIONS/REQUESTS
- ISB would like to make SLOC aware of the addition of the two mini cams in the penalty boxes.

- ISB feels it is necessary to note that safety concerns exist regarding the cameras and mics in the penalty boxes.

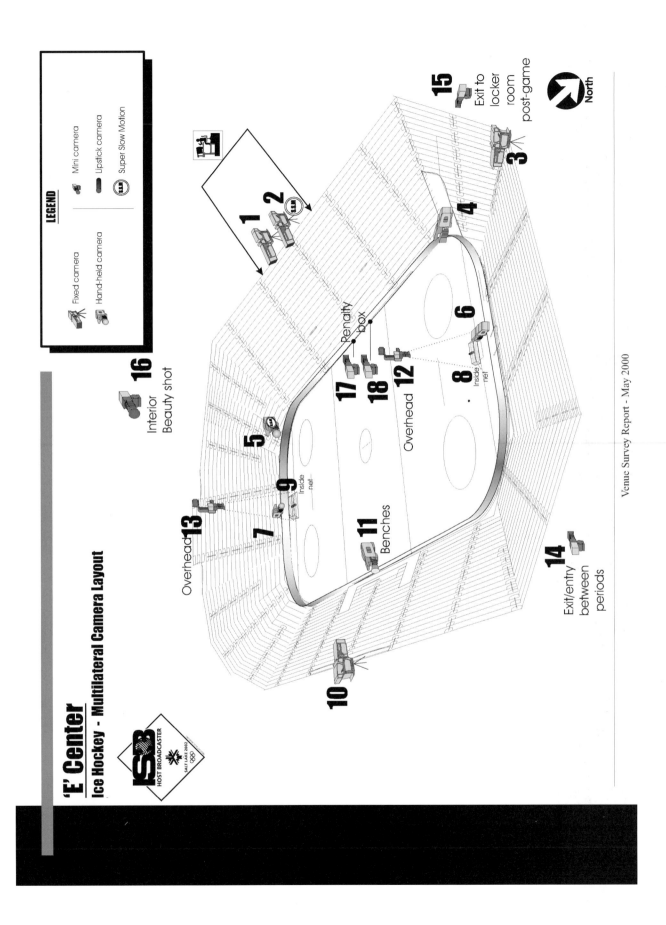

'E' Center
Ice Hockey - Multilateral Camera Layout

LEGEND

Fixed camera
Hand-held camera
Mini camera
Lipstick camera
Super Slow Motion

16 Interior Beauty shot

13 Overhead
5
9 Inside net
7
11 Benches
10 Exit/entry between periods

17 Penalty box
18
12 Overhead
8 Inside net
6
4
3 Exit to locker room post-game
15

1
2

North

Venue Survey Report - May 2000

'E' Center

1.4.4 Production - Specialty Equipment Requirements

Ice Hockey

No.	Description	Source	Mount Type	Source	Reference
SP1	Fixed (SSM)	TBD	Tripod	TBD	IH2
SP2	Hand-held (SSM)	TBD	Sticks	TBD	IH5
SP3	Hand-held	Truck	Type II-robotics	TBD	IH6
SP4	Hand-held	Truck	Type II-robotics	TBD	IH7
SP5	Lipstick (RF)	TBD	Type IV-robotic	TBD	IH8
SP6	Lipstick (RF)	TBD	Type IV-robotic	TBD	IH9
SP7	Mini	TBD	Fixed mount	TBD	IH12
SP8	Mini	TBD	Fixed mount	TBD	IH13
SP9	Mini	TBD	Type III-robotics	TBD	IH14
SP10	Mini	TBD	Type III-robotics	TBD	IH15
SP11	Mini	TBD	Type III-robotics	TBD	IH16
SP12	Mini	TBD	Type III-robotics	TBD	IH17
SP13	Mini	TBD	Type III-robotics	TBD	IH18

'E' Center

1.4.5 Production – Graphics

ISB GRAPHICS INSERTS

As Host Broadcaster, ISB is responsible for the graphic inserts that will be used during the transmission of the International Signal for the 2002 Olympic Winter Games.

In developing these inserts, ISB's goal is to integrate design elements with data and to ensure that the graphics will be readable for the worldwide television audience. Emphasis will be placed on presenting the IOC graphic design in a manner that will clearly identify the coverage as being specific to the Olympic Games. Minimal movement and animations will ensure that the sport is presented without undue distractions.

Graphics will be dissolved on and off. In most cases, ISB will not wipe or use digital effects to insert any graphics. In some cases, cutting to graphics will be acceptable only after discussions with senior graphics personnel.

GRAPHIC INSERT EXAMPLES – 'E' CENTER

The pages that follow this section contain examples of ISB's graphic layout plan for ice hockey.

GRAPHIC EQUIPMENT

For standard graphics at all events, ISB will use a Chyron character generator. The standard graphics include presentations of the venue and events, start lists, individual identifications and result lists. The Chyron character generator will be interfaced directly with the on-venue results system to allow instant access to results information.

For timing graphics, ISB will use a character generator constructed especially for conversion and display of timing data.

GRAPHIC EQUIPMENT – 'E' CENTER

The following equipment will be used at the 'E' Center venue:
- One (1) Chyron character generator for results
- One (1) timing generator

OPENING AND CLOSING ANIMATIONS

ISB will design an opening and closing animation that will run prior to the feed and close every transmission. It will identify the venue, the sport and will incorporate various pictograms.

REPLAYS

ISB intends to trigger all TV action replays with a DVE type Olympic Ring transition sequence, similar to what will be used in Sydney during the Summer Games.

ON-SCREEN CREDITS

The on-screen credits for Seiko, the official Timing and Scoring sponsor for the 2002 Olympic Winter Games, will be inserted by the timing generator. The timing sponsor logo will be associated with the timing graphic, and will be positioned directly below the running clock in the lower right-hand corner.

Other requirements for sponsor credit obligations have not yet been determined.

'E' Center

Venue Location

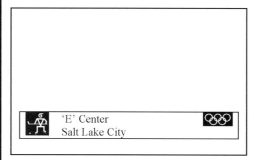

'E' Center
Salt Lake City

Event Identification

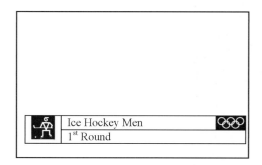

Ice Hockey Men
1st Round

Game Presentation

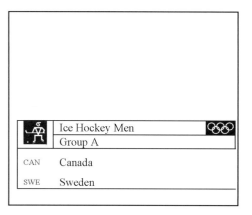

	Ice Hockey Men	
	Group A	
CAN	Canada	
SWE	Sweden	

Team Record (preliminaries)

CAN	Canada		
Wins 0	Ties 0	Losses 1	
SUI	2 – 8	Switzerland	

Team results (Final Round Game 2)

CAN	Canada		
SUI	2 – 8	Switzerland	Preliminary
NOR	3 – 1	Norway	Preliminary
DEN	2 – 2	Denmark	Preliminary
GER	1-2	Germany	Final Round

Team results (Medal Round)

CAN	Canada		
SUI	2 – 8	Switzerland	Preliminary
NOR	3 – 1	Norway	Preliminary
DEN	2 – 2	Denmark	Preliminary
GER	3-2	Germany	Final Round
RUS	2-1	Russia	Final Round
FIN	2-2	Finland	Final Round
GER	3-2	Germany	¼ Final
FIN	2-1	Finland	Semifinal

'E' Center

Score

	Ice Hockey Men	OOO
	End of 1st period	
CAN	Canada	0
SWE	Sweden	0

Mini-Score

CAN	0
SWE	1
10:00	1st

Line Score

	Ice Hockey Men					OOO
	1	2	3	[OT]	Total	
CAN	1	1	[ ]	[ ]	2	
SWE	0	2	[ ]	[ ]	2	

Scorer Identification

SWE	2	Tomas Jonsson	F	OOO
	at 13:00			

Penalty Identification

USA	3	Mark Astley	D	OOO
Hooking (2:00) at 5:44		[2nd penalty]		

Power Play Scoring Ratio

CAN	Power play	OOO
OLYMPICS	9 / 42	

'E' Center

1.4.6 Production – Results & Timing

RESULTS AND TIMING VENDORS

SLOC's Information Services Department is responsible for supplying and managing athlete-related information such as start lists, standings and results. SLOC will team with SEMA Group, Seiko Timing and WIGE-MIC to provide the complete results service for the Games.

SEMA Group is a major IOC sponsor with the responsibility for the central results and information diffusion. SEMA Group will be supervising the integration between Seiko, the official timing sponsor, and WIGE-MIC, the on-venue results contractor. SEMA Group is also responsible for development of all Games-wide data systems, such as the Commentary Information System, Info 2002, accreditation and other Games management systems.

Seiko Timing will be responsible for providing all timing data to WIGE-MIC and to ISB. Timing data will be converted to video information in the ISB compound and will be inserted into the feed for each sport at the venue.

SLOC has selected WIGE-MIC to provide on-venue results services for the 2002 Olympic Winter Games. WIGE-MIC will implement results systems for each sport that will maintain a two-way data link with the ISB graphic generator to ensure accurate and near-instant updates of all sport information. WIGE-MIC will also drive all scoreboards and print output at each venue.

VENUE RESULTS OPERATIONS

To display results information, ISB will implement a Chyron graphics character generator that will accept data input from the on-venue results system (WIGE-MIC). The interface with the results system will provide all athlete information required for the sport, such as the accurate spelling of the athlete's name, bib number, age, height and weight. The start lists, intermediate standings and results will be available in less than one second after approval in the results system.

An interface program will reside on a computer located in the SLOC results area. This interface will be responsible for converting the results data to a Chyron data format. The interface program will respond to data requests issued by the Chyron character generator.

The graphics operation positions will be located in or near the ISB production truck. When appropriate, WIGE-MIC will be responsible for providing assistance to maintain the interface integrity, as well as provide any assistance required by the ISB graphics team. The engineer in charge of each mobile unit will oversee maintenance of the Chyron character generator.

A headset communication link will be established between the graphics operation position and the SLOC results control room. This will help to maintain coordination between the results operation and the broadcast graphics operation, and will help to manage any problems that may arise.

Each graphics operation position will have a font operator, a font coordinator and a data interface coordinator. The font coordinator is responsible for instructing the font operator to call up the correct graphics on the character generator. The data interface coordinator will assist in monitoring the data feeds and informing the font coordinator as to the availability of updated results and timing data.

VENUE TIMING OPERATIONS

To display timing data, ISB will implement a graphics character generator that will accept data input from the on-venue timing system (Seiko Timing). An interface program will reside on the computer portion of the timing generator. This interface will be responsible for converting abbreviated data to a display format (i.e. the timing systems may send an athlete's bib number, which the interface will convert to a full name).

Engineers from the timing generator vendor will be located on a regional basis and available to support the hardware. A software engineer from the timing character generator company will be located at the IBC, and will be available on short notice to fix any programming problems with the timing data interface.

'E' Center

1.4.7 Production – Transmission (Runups)

Ice Hockey (Preliminary round, Final round, Quarterfinals, Semifinals)

	Start of International Signal		
Time	*Contents*	*Graphic*	*Duration*
-60:00	Pre-unilaterals or wide shot of venue with ID	G	40:00
-20:00	Live picture of venue		10:00
-10:00	Beauty shots		4:30
-5:30	Countdown clock	G	:27
-5:03	Black		:03
	Start of Transmission		
-5:00	Opening animation		:30
-4:30	Wide/aerial shot of venue with venue & event ID	G	:25
-4:05	Atmosphere at venue		:20
-3:45	Match-up/team statistics	G	:15
-3:30	Group standing	G	:15
-3:15	Atmosphere at venue		:15
-3:00	Athletes introduction/rosters	G	1:00
-2:00	Goalkeepers	G	:30
-1:30	Head coaches	G	:30
-1:00	List of officials	G	:15
-0:45	Athletes preparing for start/venue atmosphere	G	:45
0:00	*Start of competition*		

	Intermission		
Time	*Contents*	*Graphic*	*Duration*
	End of period		
-15:00	Lower 1/3 scoreboard	G	:30
-14:30	Athletes leaving ice/venue atmosphere		:30
-14:00	Full page game score	G	:30
-13:30	Beauty shot		7:30
-6:00	Lower 1/3 scoreboard	G	:30
-5:30	Score summary	G	:30
-5:00	Game statistics	G	:30
-4:30	Game highlights	G	1:00
-3:30	Full page game score	G	:30
-3:00	Atmosphere at venue		1:00
-2:00	Athletes with statistics	G	2:00
0:00	*Competition resumes*		

'E' Center

1.5.1 Technical Operations – Compound

The compound will accommodate ISB technical production and transmission facilities, along with Rights Holding Broadcasters' vehicles. Inside the compound, ISB will include space for mobile units; additional technical vehicles and trailers; and support facilities. Further details regarding space allocated within the compound may be found on the following page. Rights Holding Broadcasters who wish to further personalize their coverage will have the opportunity to book additional space and facilities through ISB's Booking Office.

The compound will come under the control of the ISB Broadcast Venue Manager.

'E' CENTER COMPOUND

Main Location	Located on the northwest side of the venue, in the parking area.
Size	46,500 sq. ft. (4185 m²)
Access Personnel/Equipment Pickup & Delivery	Staff will enter the compound through the designated accredited broadcast staff entrance. Non-accredited individuals who need access to the compound must request a "Day Pass," which will be available through the Venue Accreditation Center.
Vehicles	Accredited vehicles with a permanent compound vehicle pass will be granted access through a designated entrance. Non-accredited vehicles requiring access to the compound must request a "Day Pass" from the Venue Accreditation Center. All deliveries to the broadcast compound will be set up in advance and approved by the Broadcast Venue Manager.
Conditions	Level space with access to adequate power, fenced for security and access. External compound lighting, along with safety/security lighting, will be required.
Unilateral Requests	No unilateral requests at the current time

'E' Center

1.5.1 Technical Operations - Compound

Broadcast Compound Space Allocation

No. [1]	User	Type	Size W	Size L	Footprint W^2	Footprint L^3	Area / Unit
	**ISB Mobile Units**						
1	ISB	Mountain Mobile 3X	10	65	18	75	1,350
2	ISB	Mobile Unit (Type C)	10	45	18	55	990
	**ISB Trailers**						
3	ISB	TOC / Tech Manager	12	60	20	70	1,400
4	ISB	Broadcast Venue Mgmt / Logistics [4]	12	60	28	70	1,960
5	ISB	Production / Information	12	60	20	70	1,400
6	ISB	Catering / Crew	12	60	20	70	1,400
7	ISB	Catering Kitchen	20	40	28	50	1,400
23	ISB	Technical Storage	12	60	20	70	1,400
	**Unilateral Mobile Units**						
8	Unilateral	Mobile Unit (Type B)	10	65	18	75	1,350
9	Unilateral	Mobile Unit (HDTV)	10	65	18	75	1,350
10	Unilateral	Flash Unit	10	40	18	50	900
11	Unilateral	Flash Unit	10	40	18	50	900
	**Unilateral Trailers**						
12	Unilateral	Trailer	12	60	20	70	1,400
13	Unilateral	Trailer	12	60	20	70	1,400
14	Unilateral	Trailer	12	60	20	70	1,400
15	Unilateral	Trailer	12	60	20	70	1,400
16	Unilateral	Trailer	12	60	20	70	1,400
17	Unilateral	Trailer	12	60	20	70	1,400
18	Unilateral	Trailer	12	60	20	70	1,400
19	Unilateral	Trailer	12	60	20	70	1,400
	**Generators**						
20	SLOC	Dual Generator Package [5]	10	45	18	55	990
21	Unilateral	Dual Generator Package	10	45	18	55	990
22	Unilateral	Dual Generator Package	10	45	18	55	990
	**Other**						
	SLOC	Portable Restroom Facilities	15	40			600
	ISB	Miscellaneous [6]					5,230
	SLOC	Fire Lane / Access [7]					10,700
					Total Area Compound (rounded up)		**46,500**

[1] Refers to the number assigned to the trailer on the Compound CAD

[2] Footprint Width = Size Width + 8 ft for stairs

[3] Footprint Length = Size Length + 10 ft for tongue and access

[4] Handicap access is required for this trailer, Footprint width = Size width + 16 feet for ramp

[5] SLOC provide generator for ISB use

[6] Allocations have been increased due to existing structures, obstructions in compound area, or unique shape of the compound.

[7] Assuming units can be parked on either side of Fire Lane

'E' Center

1.5.2 Technical Operations – Trailers

A variety of trailers within the venue compound will serve different functions. These trailers will provide ISB with office and catering space. Offices contained within the trailers include Broadcast Venue Management & Logistics and Production & Information, while one trailer will be reserved for technical storage.

An additional 12' x 60' trailer will house the TOC and the tech manager. The TOC will serve as the technical nerve center for all venue operations. All incoming and outgoing venue signals will be checked for quality in the TOC and sent to their respective destinations. All required camera and audio splits will also be accessible at the TOC. A general trailer layout can be found on the following page.

'E' CENTER TRAILERS

Type	Size (W/L)		Footprint (W^1 /L^2)		Area/unit
TOC/Tech Manager	12	60	20	70	1,400
Broadcast Venue Mgmt/Logistics[3]	12	60	28	70	1,960
Production/Information	12	60	20	70	1,400
Catering/Crew	12	60	20	70	1,400
Catering Kitchen	20	40	28	50	1,400
Technical Storage	12	60	20	70	1,400
TOTAL AREA					**8,960**

[1] Footprint width = Size width + 8' for stairs and access.

[2] Footprint length = Size length + 10' for tongue and access.

[3] Handicap access is required for this trailer, footprint width = size width + 16 feet for ramp

'E' Center

1.5.3 Technical Operations – Mobile Units (continued)

EQUIPMENT LIST – MMT 3X

Control
- GVG 3000 52 –Input, 3 M/E switcher, 6 aux bus, frame store
- Abekas DVEous (Dual twin on request)
- 6-rack monitor wall w/ 48-9"black & white monitors, 8-9" color monitors & 3-13" color monitors
- Leitch Still File w/Streamer

Audio
- Soundcraft Europa Audio Mixer 40+8/8/2
- Digicart II w/ 220 keyboard, Sony Minidisc, CD Player, Audio Cassette
- 11 DBX Compressor/Limiters, 2 Telos & 2 QKT Telephone Interface
- Microphones: 4 Senneheiser 416s, 4 ATI Shotguns, 4 RE 50s, 4 EV 635s, 8 Sony Lavaliere, 4 Sportscaster headsets & 4 Talk-back boxes

Communications
- RTS ADAM Communications system plus 9 powered 2-wire channels
- RTS 4000 Series IFB System (12 channel)
- Camera ISO system, 20 RTS Belt packs, 9 RTS IFB boxes
- 8-Line Panasonic Telephone System

Camera
- Sony Chip Cameras, Hard Cameras (BVP-500s & BVP-375s), Canon Lenses 70:8.5 & 55:8.5, Handheld Cameras: BVP-550s w/20:8.5 lenses, and BVP-90s w/ 18x8.5 Lenses, Up to 12 total cameras available on request
- 2 Clock Cameras

Tape
- Up to 10 BVW 75 VCRs available on request (w/slo-mo controllers)
- EVS 4-channel slow-motion disk recorder (available on request)
- 1 VHS VCR
- Master Time Code Generator

Engineering, Cable, & Miscellaneous
- 64x64 Data Tek Router (32x32 Audio)
- Redundant sync generators w/ auto changeover
- GVG Processing Amp (patchable), External Tallies
- 2 Frame Synchronizers (more available on request)
- 4,000 feet of Traix, 2,000 feet of Coax, 1,500 feet of DT-12 audio mults, 2,000 feet of 4 pair audio mults (More cable available on request)
- 6-13" Portable Color monitors 8-9" Portable color monitors
- 1 Lighting kit
- Power: 208V AC, Single-Phase, 150 Amps

'E' Center
Ice Hockey - Camera Technical Drawing

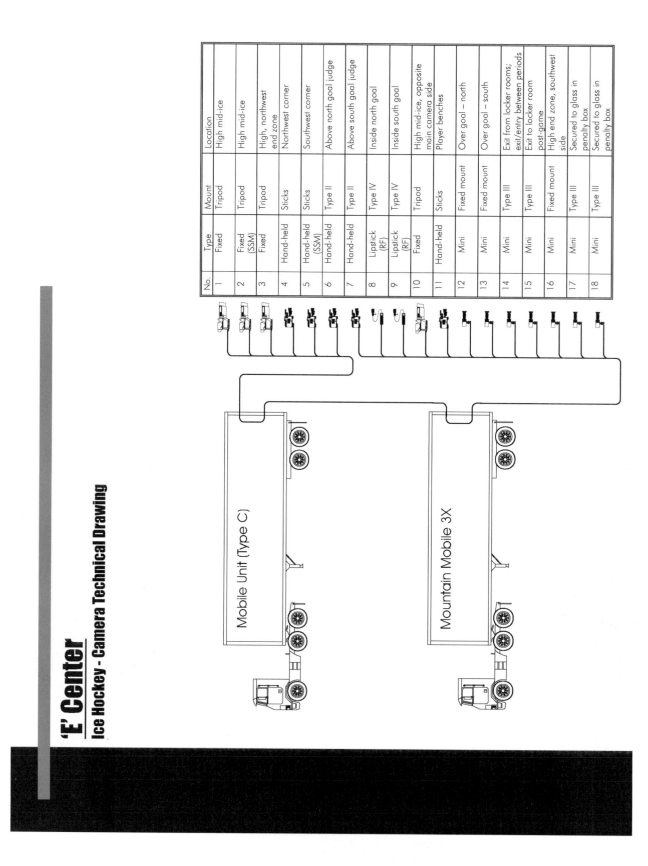

No.	Type	Mount	Location
1	Fixed	Tripod	High mid-ice
2	Fixed (SSM)	Tripod	High mid-ice
3	Fixed	Tripod	High, northwest end zone
4	Hand-held	Sticks	Northwest corner
5	Hand-held (SSM)	Sticks	Southwest corner
6	Hand-held	Type II	Above north goal judge
7	Hand-held	Type II	Above south goal judge
8	Lipstick (RF)	Type IV	Inside north goal
9	Lipstick (RF)	Type IV	Inside south goal
10	Fixed	Tripod	High mid-ice, opposite main camera side
11	Hand-held	Sticks	Player benches
12	Mini	Fixed mount	Over goal – north
13	Mini	Fixed mount	Over goal – south
14	Mini	Type III	Exit from locker rooms; exit/entry between periods
15	Mini	Type III	Exit to locker room post-game
16	Mini	Fixed mount	High end zone, southwest side
17	Mini	Type III	Secured to glass in penalty box
18	Mini	Type III	Secured to glass in penalty box

Mobile Unit (Type C)

Mountain Mobile 3X

'E' Center

1.5.6 Technical Operations – Lighting

IOC Broadcasting Guide, chapter IV, section f:

"The lighting at each stadium and competition site must be of the highest quality for television and photographic coverage. The technical specifications for lighting should be established by the OCOG in consultation with the OBO and Press Operations. In general, the lighting level should not be less than 1400 lux measured in the direction of main television cameras. Special care must be taken to match colour temperature in the case of venues where there is a mix of artificial light and daylight. Additionally, at indoor venues where windows and translucent roofs may cause daylight interference, this problem must be addressed to prevent negative effects.

Back-up generators capable of providing at least 50% of the power necessary for lighting will be installed and able to take over at anytime."

Typically, the ISB Production Plan uses more than one "main" camera. ISB's lighting recommendations specify the lighting requirements for each of these "main" cameras. Generally, unless otherwise noted, ISB requires the following:

- ratio of average horizontal to average vertical not to exceed 2:1
- minimum of 1400 vertical lux
- maximum to minimum ratio not to exceed 1.5:1
- minimum ratio of 4:1 vertical between the field of play and audience areas

'E' CENTER LIGHTING EVALUATION

The building is designed and has a lighting system for IHL hockey. The existing system does not reach Olympic light levels or cover international size ice.

RECOMMENDED SOLUTIONS

Supplemental lighting is required to raise the levels to 1400 vertical lux and to extend the coverage area to include international size ice. All of the instruments will need to be cleaned and relamped prior to competition. All supplemental lighting must match the color temperature of any existing lighting used in the arena.

MIXED ZONE

A minimum of 1,000 vertical lux toward the camera is required from multiple sources or an amount not less than the vertical average of the background (such as the Field of Play at 1400 minimum vertical lux) whichever is greater.

'E' Center

1.5.7 Technical Operations – Power

The power source to operate all of the facilities will be provided by generators and power utility companies. SLOC will consult with ISB in determining the power configuration. Two types of power will be furnished to the compound: domestic and technical.

Domestic power will be used for trailer office heating/air-conditioning; utility lighting, including catering; concessions; and various ancillary services.

Technical power will be provided to all broadcast operations that require the utmost in reliability (i.e., all mobile units, broadcast equipment racks in the TOC trailer, flash units and uplink equipment, CCR, etc.). Full-time backup of technical power will be provided during all transmissions from the compound. These specifications are subject to change.

The specific power source (utility or generator) to be designated the primary and the backup will be determined on a venue-by-venue basis.

Transfer switches will be required to transfer the load from primary to backup source of power.

POWER DISTRIBUTION

Power distribution will be provided to all facilities requiring AC power. Breakout panels and disconnects will be located throughout the compound to facilitate the installation of power to trailers and mobile units.

Disconnect panels will be provided for all mobile units and for installation or removal of power without disrupting other units within the compound.

Fifty percent of the field-of-play lighting at the venues will require generator backup power.

A chart depicting the venue broadcast electrical loads may be found on the following page, as well as the venue broadcast electrical power diagrams.

'E' Center

1.5.7 Technical Operations - Power

#ckts	Description	Domestic Load Volts	Amps	Phase	KVA/KW	Total KVA/KW	Technical Load Volts	Amps	Phase	KVA/KW	Total KVA/KW
					BROADCAST COMPOUND LOADS						
1	Mountain Mobile 3X						208	200	3	72.1	
3	Mobile Units						208	200	3	216.2	
2	Flash Units						208	100	3	72.1	
1	TOC / Tech Manager	208	100	1	20.8						
8	TOC / Tech Power						120	20	1	19.2	
3	TOC / Tech Demarc						120	30	1	10.8	
1	Broadcast Venue Mgmt / Logistics[1]	208	100	1	20.8						
1	Production / Information	208	100	1	20.8						
8	12X60 Trailers	208	100	1	166.4						
1	Technical Storage[1]	208	100	1	20.8						
1	Catering / Crew	208	100	1	20.8						
1	Catering Kitchen	208	100	3	36.0						
1	Spare	208	100	3	36.0						
	Totals				342.5					390.3	
	Compound Totals (rounded)					**342**					**390**

[1] Trailer, heat & lighting provided by SLOC

Additional facilities... compound lighting, security checkpoints (lights, equipment), miscellaneous auxiliary power, etc. not included. SLOC to evaluate.

#ckts	Description	Domestic Load Volts	Amps	Phase	KVA/KW	Total KVA/KW	Technical Load Volts	Amps	Phase	KVA/KW	Total KVA/KW
					Venue Commentary Position Loads						
70	Commentary Positions	120	20	1	168						
70	CIS & Lighting for Comm. Pos. [2]										
10	Positions w/ supp. power	120	20	1	24.0						
	Totals				192.0					0.0	
	Commentary Position Totals (rounded)					**192.0**					**0.0**

#ckts	Description	Domestic Load Volts	Amps	Phase	KVA/KW	Total KVA/KW	Technical Load Volts	Amps	Phase	KVA/KW	Total KVA/KW
					Venue Commentary Control Room Loads						
1	Commentary Control Room [2]										
	Lighting, Heat & Utility power [2]										
1	CCR / Tech Power						120	140	1	16.8	
3	CCR / Tech Demarc						120	30	1	10.8	
1	Supp. air conditioning as needed										
	Totals									27.6	
	Commentary Control Room Totals (rounded)										**28**

[2] Load not included, to be provided by SLOC

Air and Load provided by SLOC as needed

'E' Center

1.5.9 Technical Operations - Radio Frequency Requirements

Ice Hockey

Microwave (above 1Ghz)

No.	Description	Ref.	Path-TX	Path-RX	Notes
RF1	Lipstick	1	In the south goal	Top of judges' platform	Camera 8
RF2	Lipstick	1	In the north goal	Top of judges' platform	Camera 9
RF3	Cable cam	1	Top of dasher	TBD	Camera 19
RF4	Cable cam	1	Top of dasher	TBD	Camera 20

Non-Microwave (below 1Ghz)

No.	Description	Ref.	Path-TX	Path-RX	Notes
RF5	2-Way Simplex	2	Mobile	Mobile	Audio channel
RF6	2-Way Simplex	2	Mobile	Mobile	Video channel
RF7	2-Way Simplex	2	Mobile	Mobile	RF Co-ord channel
RF8	2-Way Simplex	2	Mobile	Mobile	Assignable
RF9	Camera PL Constant Key	3	Commentary	RF Camera PL (listen)	To all RF cameras
RF10	Camera PL Simplex	2	Camera positions	Commentary (talk)	All RF cameras
RF11	RF1 Camera data	4	In the south goal	Top of judges' platform	Camera 8
RF12	RF2 Camera data	4	In the north goal	Top of judges' platform	Camera 9
RF13	RF Lav	5	In the south goal	Top of judges' platform	Mic with cam 8
RF14	RF Lav	5	In the north goal	Top of judges' platform	Mic with cam 9
RF15	RF4 Camera data	4	Top of dasher	TBD	Camera 19
RF16	RF5 Camera data	4	Top of dasher	TBD	Camera 20

'E' Center

1.5.10 Technical Operations – Audio Plan

MICROPHONE REQUIREMENTS

Video
All speaker systems and poles must be placed so as not to obstruct camera angles.

Audio
The natural sound effects created by the athletes while competing are an integral part of the television coverage. Sound systems designed without due consideration of television production requirements, can easily mask these natural sound effects, seriously impairing the quality of the production.

Commentary audio is added over a bed of these natural sound effects. Sound systems designed to provide a high level in the commentary area can mask the commentators' voices before they even reach their microphones. Either direct or indirect audio from the sound systems in the commentary area should be kept to a minimum.

Treating highly reverberant arenas with absorptive material is often the best solution. This will not only increase the intelligibility of the sound system allowing lower sound pressure levels, but also make our directional microphones more effective.

General
All frequencies for wireless microphones have to be frequency coordinated and approved by OGRUC.

Frequency bands will be extremely full. The WAVES system in the spread spectrum requires frequency coordination and approval by OGRUC. The reliable use of this system in Olympic conditions may be difficult to achieve.

'E' Center
•   Audio should be reduced in commentary areas, and over the field of play.

See the following pages for microphone placement narratives. A CAD drawing of the microphone locations may be found on the accompanying compact disc.

'E' Center

1.5.10 Technical Operations - Audio Plan (Microphone Placement)

Ice Hockey

No.	Type	Location	Function	Remarks
1	Senn 416	Cam 1	Specific crowd	
2	Senn 416	Cam 2	Specific crowd	
3	Senn 416	Cam 3	Specific crowd	
4	Senn 816	Cam 4	Ice action	
5	Senn 816	Cam 5	Ice action	
6	Senn 816	Cam 6	North goal effects	
7	Senn 816	Cam 7	South goal effects	
8	RF Lav	In north goal	North goal effects	With cam 8
9	RF Lav	In south goal	South goal effects	With cam 9
10	Senn 416	Cam 10	Specific crowd	
11	Senn 816	Cam 11	Bench reaction	
12	PCC 160	North goal judge	Ice action	On glass above judge
13	PCC 160	Northeast corner	Ice action	On glass
14	PCC 160	Northwest corner	Ice action	On glass
15	PCC 160	North far blue line	Ice action	On glass
16	PCC 160	North near blue line	Ice action	On glass
17	PCC 160	Far center ice	Ice action	On glass
18	PCC 160	Near center ice	Ice action	On glass
19	PCC 160	South far blue line	Ice action	On glass
20	PCC 160	South near blue line	Ice action	On glass
21	PCC 160	Southeast corner	Ice action	On glass
22	PCC 160	Southwest corner	Ice action	On glass
23	PCC 160	South goal judge	Ice action	On glass above judge
24	PCC 160	Cam 14	Athlete reactions	On or near camera
25	PCC 160	Cam 15	Athlete reactions	On or near camera
26	Crown SASS-P	North end	Crowd	Suspend from roof
27	Crown SASS-P	East stand left	Crowd	Suspend from roof
28	Crown SASS-P	East stand right	Crowd	Suspend from roof
29	Crown SASS-P	Stand south end	Crowd	Suspend from roof
30	RF Lav	Spare	Spare for mic 8	Same frequency as mic 8
31	RF Lav	Spare	Spare for mic 9	Same frequency as mic 9
32	PCC 160	Cam 17	Athlete reactions (penalty box)	On or near camera
33	PCC 160	Cam 18	Athlete reactions (penalty box)	On or near camera

'E' Center

1.7 Technology Requirements

	ISB	Rights Holders/ Unilaterals
Telephones	**11**	**TBD**
Mobile units	4 (2 per truck)	
TOC/Tech Mgr	2*	
Broadcast Venue Mgmt/Logistics	2*	
Production/Information	2*	
CCR	1	
Fax Machines/Phone Lines	**2/2**	**TBD**
Broadcast Venue Mgmt/Logistics	1/1	
Production/Information	1/1	
Computers/Printers/Modems	**5/3/3**	**TBD**
TOC/Tech Mgr	1/1/1	
Broadcast Venue Mgmt/Logistics	2/1/1	
Production/Information	2/1/1	
Cell Phones	**5**	**TBD**
BVM	1	
Tech Mgr	1	
Information Mgr	1	
Runners	2	
Pagers	**TBD**	**TBD**
Copiers	**2**	**TBD**
Broadcast Venue Mgmt/Logistics	1	
Production/Information	1	
Radios	**TBD**	**TBD**
Data	**1**	**TBD**
Timing	**1**	**TBD**
Info 2002/Printers	**4/4**	**1/1**
Mobile units	2/2 (one each per truck)	
Broadcast Venue Mgmt/Logistics	1/1	
Production/Information	1/1	
CIS	**5**	**74**
Mobile units	2 (one per truck)	4
Production/Information	1	
Graphics stations	1	
CCR	1	
Commentary positions		70
4-wire (Intercom)	**5**	**38**
Production to Quality Control	1	
TOC to Master Control	1	
BVM to Operations Center	1	
CCR to CSC	1	
Mixed zone to Broadcaster Master Control	1	
VandA	**2+1**	**6**
Analog	1+1	3
SDI	0	1
HDTV/Other	1	0
Return	0	2
ISDN	**1**	**10**
TV Monitors (Broadcast CATV)	**9**	**58**
Compound	8	0
CCR	1	0
Commentary Positions		58

* One line each with roll over capabilities.

'E' Center

1.8 Logistics

Personnel (Total)	63
ISB Non-local	32
ISB Local	31
Accommodations	31 rooms at the Hawthorn Inn & Suites – West Valley City *Note: Additional rooms still needed*
Accreditation	63 – ISB-B
Food Service	Feb – 9: L/D/S Feb – 14: L/D/S Feb – 19: L/D/S Feb – 10: L/D/S Feb – 15: L/D/S Feb – 20: L/D/S Feb – 11: L/D/S Feb – 16: L/D/S Feb – 22: L/D/S Feb – 12: L/D/S Feb – 17: L/D/S Feb – 23: L/D/S Feb – 13: L/D/S Feb – 18: L/D/S Feb – 24: L/D/S L: Lunch D: Dinner S: Snacks
Beverage Service	To be supplied in the compound and for each of the commentary positions. To be provided by SLOC
Uniforms	Heavyweight jacket Pants Fleece vest Turtleneck (2) Gloves Hat
Sanitation	
Commentary Positions	To be provided by SLOC
Compound	To be provided by SLOC
Snow Removal	To be provided by SLOC
Security	24-hour security will be required once the first piece of equipment (technical or non-technical) is placed in the compound. To be provided by SLOC
ENG Drop-off	Located on the southwest side of the venue, near the media parking area.
Transportation (Total vehicles)	4
AWD Mini vans (seven passenger)	2
4x4 Sport Utility Vehicles	2
Parking (Total Spaces)	120 <u>ISB</u> <u>Rights Holders</u> 20 100
Intra-venue Transportation	TBD

'E' Center

1.8.1 Logistics – Accommodations

Accommodations for this venue will be located at the Hawthorn Inn & Suites – West Valley City.

ISB will reserve 31 units for host broadcast personnel at the Hawthorn Inn & Suites. Directions from Salt Lake City are as follows: take I-215, and exit at 3500 South, turn left. The second light will be 2200 West, turn right. The hotel will be on the right side.

> Hawthorn Inn & Suites
> 3540 South 2200 West
> West Valley City, UT 84119
> (801) 954-9292

1.8.2 Logistics – Accreditation

Accreditation Badges
Accreditation badges will be issued in a yet to be determined site. All accreditation badges will contain specific venue privilege markings. These markings will clearly identify: 1) which venue (not necessarily a sports venue) or venue cluster the accredited personnel may enter; and 2) the areas or "zones" within the venue the cardholder may circulate. Accreditation zones specific to a competition venue may be classified as any of the following: all areas; field of play; media areas; Rights Holding Broadcaster areas; Olympic Family areas; etc.

Rights Holder Access
All Rights Holding Broadcaster personnel will have predetermined credential categories for the venues and IBC. Access for individual broadcast constituencies (senior personnel, production, IBC, etc.) will be determined at a later date.

ISB Access
All ISB personnel will also have predetermined credential categories for the venues and IBC. Access for separate ISB constituencies (senior personnel, production, IBC, etc.) will be determined at a later date. However, it will be necessary for the ISB crew to have access to certain athlete areas, due to the fact that some of the cable paths will exist in athlete zoned areas.

'E' Center Venue Access Points
Rights Holding Broadcaster and ISB venue access points will be determined at a later date.

'E' Center Venue Accreditation Location
Rights Holding Broadcaster and ISB venue accreditation location will be determined at a later date.

1.8.3 Logistics – Food Service

The venue meal and craft services schedule will vary each day based on the ISB crew schedule. Inside the broadcast compound, bottled water and vending machines will be available (pending agreement with SLOC).

1.8.4 Logistics – Security

SLOC is responsible for supplying all necessary security and personnel at each of the competition and non-competition venues. Security will be responsible for enforcing all rules and regulations at the venue perimeter. Access and the monitoring of accreditation will be enforced by event services. Sanitization dates have yet to be determined.

Security locations (Command Post, Mobile Police, Fire, EMS Command Post, etc.) will be forthcoming.

'E' Center

1.8.5 Logistics – Transportation

RIGHTS HOLDER TRANSPORTATION

Information regarding Rights Holder transportation will be forthcoming (schedule, etc.)

ISB TRANSPORTATION

An ISB logistics manager will be assigned a fleet of vehicles to manage and, depending on assignment, certain individuals at each venue may be assigned to or will drive a pool car or van. To be assigned to a vehicle, an employee must have a valid U.S. or international driver's license and a clean driving record (no moving violations or accidents within one year from contract date).

The vehicles assigned to the 'E' Center venue will include two seven-passenger mini AWD vans and two 4x4 sport utility vehicles.

A dedicated bus transportation system for the ISB production crew is currently under consideration by SLOC Transportation Department.

1.8.6 Logistics – Venue Logistical Support & Supplies

Information regarding the venue logistical support and supplies will be forthcoming.

APPENDIX III:

Camera Diagrams and Plans

The following camera diagrams and descriptions are actual documents used by networks and production companies to produce television coverage of events. Most of the diagrams are from the winter or summer Olympic Games. Since camera descriptions are included, the camera diagrams can be adapted to smaller events.

Alpine Skiing (Downhill – Men's)

No.	Type	Mount	Location[1]	Coverage
1	Hand-held	Sticks	Warm-up area	Athletes prior to race
2	LPS	Fixed mount	Start house	Shooting start clock
3	Mini	Type III	Start house	Prior to start
4	Hand-held	Sticks	Front of start house	Athlete's face
5	Fixed	Tripod	Edge of rock island	Start house, action
6	Fixed	Tripod	Trail sign, above keyhole	Action
7	Hand-held	Sticks	On course, below entrance to Diamond Bowl at 1st jump	Action
8	Fixed (SSM)	Tripod	Bottom of Diamond Bowl	Action (replay)
9	Hand-held	Crane (Medium)	At Hydrant MD-10 (skier left)	Action
10	Hand-held	Sticks	At Hydrant MD-12 (skier left)	Action
11	Fixed	Tripod	At top of A-Net 3 on V-Tower Platform	Action
12	Fixed	Tripod	Above A-Net 4 (skier left)	Action
13	Hand-held	Sticks	Near top of face, above A-Net 5	Action
14	Specialty	Come & go	At A-Net 5, on gate	Come
15	Specialty	Come & go	At A-Net 5, on gate	Go
16	Fixed	Tripod	Opposite A-Net 6, at Aspen tree with blue marker	Action
17	Fixed	Tripod	On road, before final face	Action
18	Fixed	Tripod	At end of A-Net at final face	Action
19	Hand-held (SSM) (Build-up)	Tripod (studio config.)	At end of A-Net at final face	Action (replay)
20	Fixed	Tripod	At pine tree on finish face	Action
21	Fixed	Tripod	Back of corral, finish area	Finish
22	Hand-held (RF)	Sticks	Finish area	Athletes' faces
23	Hand-held	Sticks	Mixed zone	Current leader
24	Hand-held	Crane (Medium)	Finish stadium	Crowd
25	Fixed (RF)	Tripod	Valley cam	Scenic/action
26	Hand-held (RF)	Type I	Top of mountain	Scenic
27	Specialty (RF)	Stabilized in helicopter	Above venue	Scenic

[1] All cameras to be placed on skier's right side, unless otherwise indicated.

Alpine Skiing

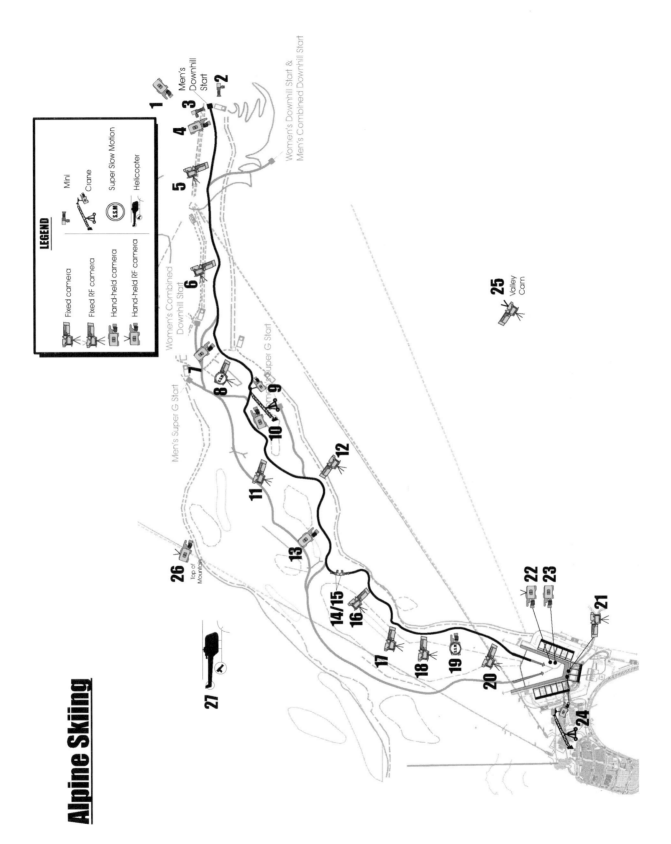

LEGEND

Fixed camera	Mini
Fixed RF camera	Crane
Hand-held camera	Super Slow Motion
Hand-held RF camera	Helicopter

Men's Downhill Start

Women's Downhill Start &
Men's Combined Downhill Start

Women's Combined Downhill Start

Men's Super G Start

Women's Super G Start

Top of Mountain

Valley Cam

Production – Cameras

Aquatics – Swimming

No.	Type	Mount	Location	Coverage
1	Fixed	Tripod	High start/finish	Main follow
2	Fixed	Hi hat	Low start/finish	Close ups
3	Fixed	Tracking dolly	Length of 50m pool	Action
4	Fixed	Hi hat	Low turn	Action/50m start
5	Fixed	Tripod	Mid turn	Master turn/50m start
6	Hand-held (RF)	Steadicam	On deck start/finish	Pool exits
7	Hand-held (RF)	Steadicam	On deck start/finish	Pool exits
8	Hand-held	Sticks	On deck start/finish	Close ups/ceremonies
9	Specialty	Rails – underwater	Bottom of pool running the length to within 2m end walls	Underwater tracking
10	Specialty	Trackcam	80m of track below roof over center lane	Overhead tracking
11	Fixed	Tripod w/wheels	Turn end gantry	Interior beauty shot/action
12	Hand-held	Crane	Poolside on the deck at turn end	Isolation/ceremonies
13	Hand-held	Type II	Suspended on pole over diving pole	Venue wide shot
14	Specialty	Type III (underwater housing)	Pool floor, 3m off camera left start/finish	Flip turn
15	Specialty	Type III (underwater housing)	Pool floor, 3m off camera left start/finish	Flip turn
16	Specialty	Periscope camera mount	Pool wall, 12m from starting block	Underwater coverage from blocks to 15m mark
17	Mini	Fixed mount	In the entry block of lane four	Lane four entry & turn/ swimmers close up
18	Mini	Fixed mount	In the entry block of lane five	Lane five entry & turn/ swimmers close up
19	Specialty	Polecam system	Poolside	Turn end coverage
20	Fixed (SSM)	Tripod	Mid start/finish	Isolation
21	Fixed (SSM)	Tripod	On deck at turn end of pool	Head on isolation
22	Mini	Type III	In athlete's callroom	Callroom isolation

Aquatics - Swimming

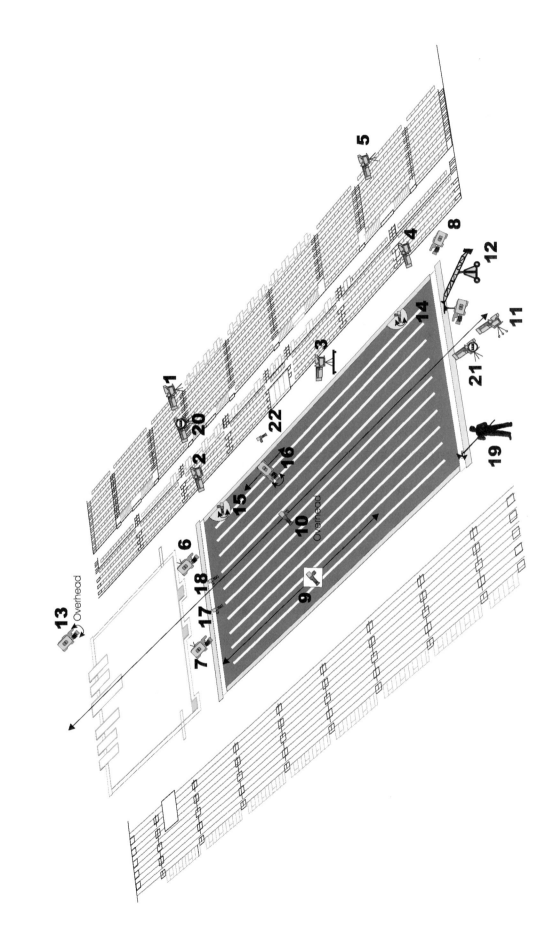

Production – Cameras

Athletics – Track

No.	Type	Mount	Location	Coverage
A-1	Fixed	Tripod	Finish line	Main finish
A-2	Fixed	Tripod	Finish line	Close up finish
A-3	Fixed (SSM)	Tripod	Finish line	Main finish/low angle
A-4	Fixed	Tripod	Head on, run out	Main finish
A-5	Fixed	Tripod	Head on, run out	Isolation finish
A-6	Fixed (SSM)	Tripod	Head on, run out	Isolation finish
A-7	Hand-held (RF)	Steadicam	Head on, run out	Competitor reaction
A-8	Fixed	Tripod	Finish line/roving	Isolation relays/venue wide shot
A-9	Hand-held	Crane	On outside of track at turn	Starts 400/800m, isolation, high jumps
A-10	Hand-held	Crane	On outside of track at turn	Isolation 200m, 500m, steeplechase
A-11	Fixed	Tripod	Turn 4	Master 200m, 500m, steeplechase
A-12	Fixed	Tripod	100m/110m start	High starts, relay final leg
A-13	Hand-held	Sticks	100m/110m start	Low starts, relay isolation
A-14	Hand-held	Steadicam	Roving	Close ups
A-15	Hand-held	Steadicam	Roving	Close ups
A-16	Specialty	Trackcam Rails	Along outside of the frontstretch 100m track	Frontstretch tracking
A-17	Fixed	Tripod	Head on backstraight	Various backstraight
A-18	Mini	Type III	Overhead beginning backstraight	Relay changeover
A-19	Mini	Type III	Overhead end of backstraight	Relay changeover
A-20	Mini	Type III	Overhead beginning home straight	Relay changeover

Athletics - Track

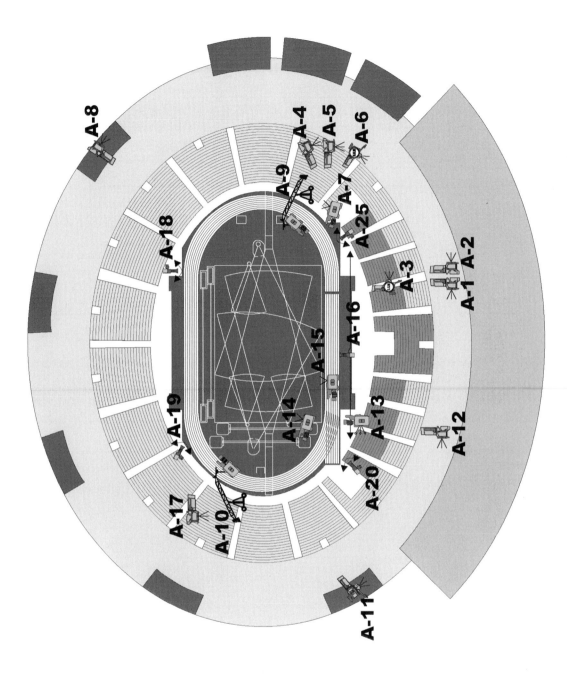

Production – Cameras

Baseball

No.	Type	Mount	Location	Coverage
1	Fixed	Tripod	High home	Main follow
2	Fixed	Tripod	High first	Ball flight & baserunners
3	Fixed	Tripod	Low first, dugout	RH batters, runners on second and third, introductions
4	Fixed	Tripod	Low third, dugout	LH batters, runners on first, introductions
5	Fixed	Tripod w/wheels	Low center field	Batter, catcher
6	Fixed	Tripod w/wheels	Low center field	Pitcher, batter, catcher
7	Fixed	Tripod w/wheels	Low home	Pitcher close up, pitch rotation
8	Fixed	Tripod	Low left field foul line	First – second steals, first base dugout
9	Hand-held	Sticks	Third base dugout	Isolation, third base dugout, pre & post
10	Hand-held	Sticks	High third baseline	Beauty shot
11	Mini	Fixed mount	First base	Runner retreating on pick off
12	Mini	Fixed mount	Second base	Runner approaches
13	Fixed	Tripod w/wheels	Low home	Low action replays, finals only

* A typical five-camera set-up for baseball would include cameras 1 – 5. See detailed baseball camera notes on pages 98 – 99.

Baseball

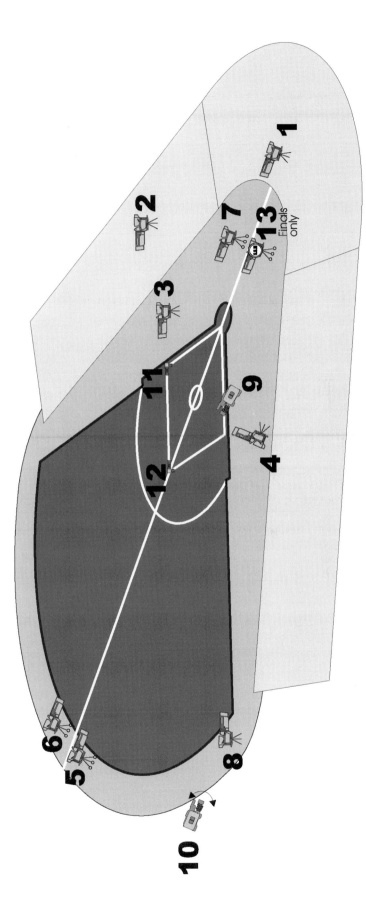

Production – Cameras

Basketball

No.	Type	Mount	Location	Coverage
1	Fixed	Tripod	High midcourt	Main follow
2	Fixed	Tripod	High midcourt	Close ups
3	Fixed	Tripod	Mid left ¾	Isolation
4	Fixed	Tripod	Mid right ¾	Isolation
5	Hand-held	Sticks	Left baseline	Isolation & action
6	Hand-held	Sticks	Right baseline	Isolation & action
7	Hand-held (SSM)	Sticks	Midcourt on floor	Isolation & low action
8	Hand-held	Sticks	Midcourt on floor, far side	Isolation & benches
9	Mini	Type III	Overhead	Overhead isolation
10	Mini	Type III	Behind left backboard	Isolation
11	Mini	Type III	Behind right backboard	Isolation
12	Mini	Fixed mount	¾ high near right corner roof	Venue wide shot
13	Hand-held (RF)	Sticks	Midcourt on floor, roving	Crowd
14	Hand-held	Crane	Far side left corner	Action, crowd

* A typical five-camera set-up for basketball would include cameras 1, 2, 3, 5 and 6.

Basketball

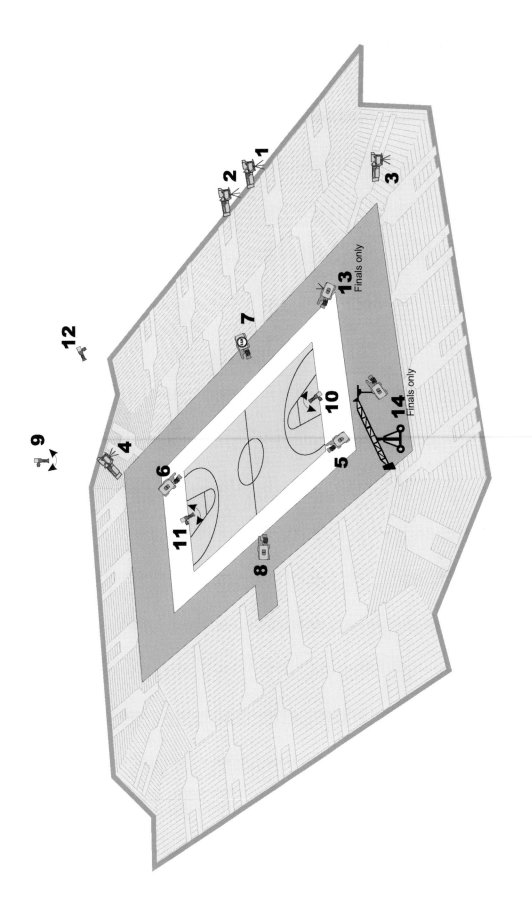

Production – Cameras

Bobsleigh & Skeleton

No.	Type	Mount	Location	Coverage
1	Hand-held	Sticks	Warm-up room	Athletes preparation
2	Hand-held (RF)	Sticks	Roving start house/running track	Athletes preparation
3	Specialty	Railcam	Sled right; lens 6 ft. high from track gully; extend appx. 50m	Leaving start
4	Fixed	Tripod	On scaffolding between bob and luge tracks (straight on to sled start)	Action
5	Hand-held	Sticks	Sled right; on luge course; at bobsleigh/luge merge	Action
6	Hand-held	Sticks	Sled left; level with existing concrete walkway; under existing pedestrian bridge	Action
7	Hand-held	Sticks	Sled right; entering Sunny corner; start of wood overhang (cameraman sits on top of overhang)	Action
8	Hand-held	Crane – specialty PBCS* (medium)	Sled left; inside Sunny (Turn 4)	Action
9	Mini	Fixed mount	Sled left; on roof of Cutthroat straightaway, 18 ft. in from start of wooden overhang	Action
10	Hand-held	Sticks	Sled left; entering Snowy (Turn 6) on top of roof; at start of wooden overhang	Action
11	Fixed	Tripod	Sled right; inside Snowy (Turn 6); lens height even w/existing speaker	Action
12	Hand-held	TBD	Sled left; start of Turn 7; platform ¼ in from start of wood overhang; 15 ft. before start of water spigot	Action
13	Mini	Fixed mount	Sled left; attached to end of wooden overhang in Turn 7; entrance of Albert's Alley (Turn 8)	Action
14	Hand-held	Sticks	Sled left; on top of roof entering Albert's Alley (Turn 8); at third support bracket from coolant.	Action
15	Hand-held	Sticks	Sled right; mid-Albert's Alley; just under yet-to-be-built pedestrian bridge; on 4-20 ft. platform	Action
16	Mini	Fixed mount	Sled right; attached to end of wooden overhang in Turn 9	Action
17	Mini	Fixed mount	Sled right; appx. 15 ft. from come camera (third fence post)	Action
18	Fixed (SSM)	Tripod	Sled right; entering Turn 11; platform behind track wall shooting straightaway	Action (replay)
19	Fixed	Tripod	Sled left; inside Turn 11; on scaffold	Action

* Pan Bar Control System

Production – Cameras

Bobsleigh & Skeleton

No.	Type	Mount	Location	Coverage
20	Hand-held	Sticks	Sled left; on top of roof entering Olympic (Turn 12); appx. 10ft. from start of wooden overhang	Action
21	Hand-held	Crane – specialty PBCS* (medium)	Sled right; mid-Olympic	Action
22	Hand-held	Sticks	Sled left; entrance to Turn 13; appx. 4ft. platform	Action
23	Hand-held (SSM)	Sticks	Sled left; entrance to Turn 14; at start of wooden overhang	Action (replay)
24	Hand-held	Sticks	Sled right; mid-Turn 14; even with water pole; platform 6ft. from track and 2 ft. high	Action
25	Hand-held	Sticks	Sled left; straightaway following Turn 14; at existing sled crash take-out/platform	Action
26	Hand-held	Crane – specialty PBCS* (medium)	Sled right; entering final turn (Turn 15)	Finish
27	Fixed	Tripod	Over track; after finish line; On (approx.) 4 ft. platform from track gully	Braking
28	Mini	Fixed mount	Sled right; mounted on yet-to-be built weigh station building; unmanned, front of building	Athlete reaction
29	Hand-held	Sticks	Sled right; at sled take out area	Athlete reaction
30	Mini	Fixed mount	Sled right; mounted on yet-to-be built weigh station building; unmanned, back of building	Athlete reaction
31	Hand-held	Sticks	Weigh-in; review of monitors; pre- and post-unilaterals	Athletes post-run
32	Fixed (Build up) (RF)	Type I	Valley cam	Scenic
33	Specialty (RF)	Stabilized in Helicopter	Above venue, in helicopter	Scenic
34(BS)	Specialty	Pop up	*Bobsleigh only*; middle of track; between existing pedestrian bridge, and turn 12	Action
35(BS) 34(SK)	Mini	Fixed mount	Mounted on start house, directly overhead	Athletes leaving start house
36(BS) 35 (SK)	Specialty	Cable cam	Albert's Alley	Action
37+(BS)	Lipstick (RF)	Specialty	Mounted on bobsleigh's (number of sleds has not yet been determined)	Athlete perspective

* Pan Bar Control System

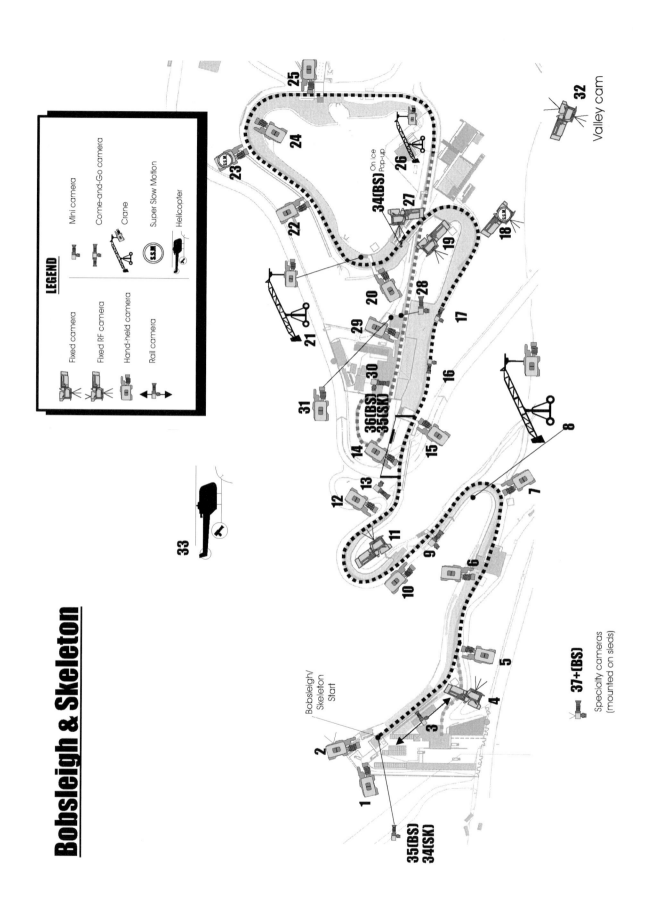

Bobsleigh & Skeleton

LEGEND

Fixed camera	Mini camera
Fixed RF camera	Come-and-Go camera
Hand-held camera	Crane
Rail camera	Super Slow Motion
	Helicopter

Valley cam

34[BS]
On Ice Pop-up

Bobsleigh/
Skeleton
Start

35[BS]
34[SK]

37+[BS]
Specialty cameras
(mounted on sleds)

Production – Cameras

Figure Skating

No.	Type	Mount	Location	Coverage
1	Fixed	Low boy	Ice level, northwest end, 12 ft. cutout in dasher	Action
2	Fixed	Tripod	Below lower bowl; cantilever built to hang over judges' table. Section 18.	Main follow
3	Fixed	Crane (medium) (counterbalance)	Southwest end corner, 12 ft. cutout in dasher	Action
4	Fixed	Tripod	Top of lower bowl, Northwest end	Action
5	Fixed (SSM)	Tripod	Southwest end zone	Action
6	Fixed (SSM)	Tripod	Ice level; opposite judges' table. Directly opposite main camera	Action
7	Fixed	Tripod	Below lower bowl; cantilever built to hang over judges' table. Section 18.	Tight follow
8	Hand-held	Sticks	Kiss & Cry	Athletes' faces; action
9	Hand-held	Sticks	Kiss & Cry	On deck in corral/ coach; in front of curtain
10	Hand-held	Crane (medium)	Section 4	Sweeping crowd shots; atmosphere
11	Mini	Fixed mount	Southwest ceiling truss	Beauty shot
12	Mini	Type III (robotic)	Backstage; waiting area	Athletes' preparation
13	Hand-held	Type II (robotic)	Over center ice	Atmosphere athletes on/off ice
14	Hand-held (RF)	Sticks	Roving in stands	Crowd response
15	Specialty (RF)	Mini cable cam	Length of ice, judges' side	Action (replay)

Figure Skating

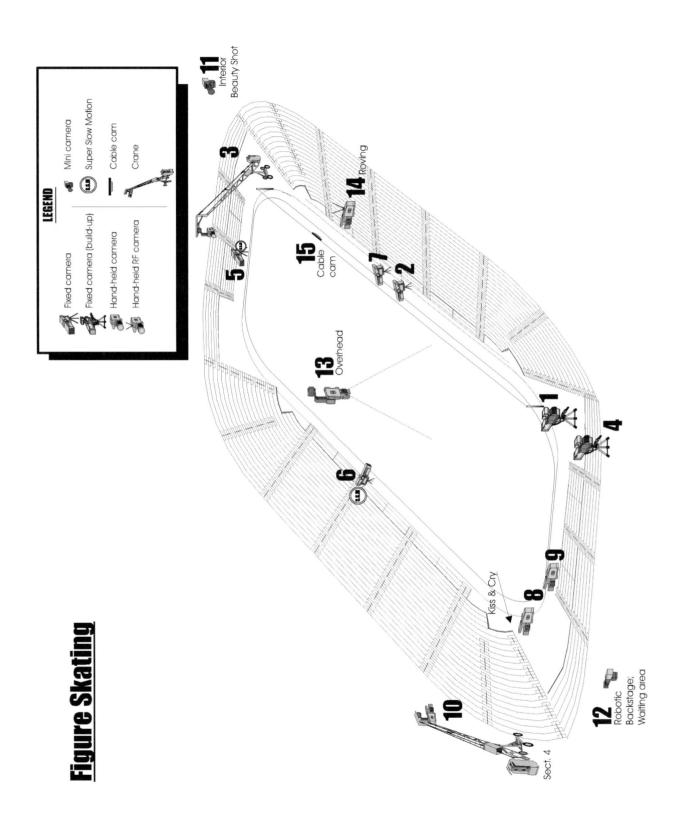

LEGEND

Fixed camera

Fixed camera (build-up)

Hand-held camera

Hand-held RF camera

Mini camera

Super Slow Motion

Cable cam

Crane

11 Interior Beauty Shot

3

14 Roving

5

15 Cable cam

7

2

13 Overhead

1

4

6

8

9

Kiss & Cry

10

Sect. 4

12 Robotic Backstage; Waiting area

Production – Cameras

Football

No.	Type	Mount	Location	Coverage
1	Fixed	Tripod	High 25-30yd line (left)	Game action when inside the 35yd line (left)
2	Fixed	Tripod	High 50yd line	Game action when at midfield
3	Fixed	Tripod	High 25-30yd line (right)	Game action when inside the 35yd line (right)
4	Fixed	Tripod	Mid-high 50yd line	Close ups on field and opposite sideline
5	Fixed	On dolly	Near sideline (left)	Close ups on field, replays
6	Hand-held (SSM)	Sticks	Near sideline	Replays of game action
7	Fixed	On dolly	Near sideline (right)	Close ups on field, replays
8	Fixed	Tripod	High end zone (left)	Game action, replays, field goals and PATs
9	Fixed	Tripod	Low end zone in stands (left)	Game action, replays
10	Fixed	Tripod	Low end zone in stands (right)	Game action, replays
11	Fixed	On dolly	Far sideline (left)	Close ups on field, reverse angle replays
12	Fixed	On dolly	Far sideline (right)	Close ups on field, reverse angle replays
13	Hand-held (RF)	Sticks	Goal post crossbar	Replays of field goals and PATs
14	Fixed	Tripod	Low end zone (right)	Close ups, replays
15	Hand-held (RF)	Sticks	Goal post crossbar	Replays of field goals and PATs
16	Hand-held (SSM)	Sticks	Far sideline	Replays of game action
17	Fixed	Tripod	Low end zone (left-far)	Close ups, replays
18	Fixed	Tripod	Low end zone (left-near)	Close ups, replays
19	Fixed	Tripod	High 50yd line	Wide field replay
20	Fixed	Tripod	High end zone (right)	Game action, replays, field goals and PATs
21	Fixed	Tripod	Mid-high 25-30yd line (left)	Close ups, replays

* A typical six-camera set-up for football would usually include cameras 2, 4, 9, 16, 20 and 30.

Production – Cameras

Football

No.	Type	Mount	Location	Coverage
22	Fixed	Tripod	High 50yd line (far)	Near sideline close ups, reverse angle replay
23	Fixed	Tripod	Mid-high 25-30yd line (right)	Close ups, replays
24	Fixed	Tripod	Mid-high 50yd line	Close ups, replays
25	Fixed	Tripod	Low end zone (left-far)	Close ups, replays
26	Fixed	Tripod	Low end zone (right-far)	Close ups, replays
27	Fixed	Tripod	High end zone (right-near)	Close ups, replays
28	Hand-held	Sticks	Under goal post (left)/ Left locker room exterior	Close ups, replays/ Player field entrance/exit, sideline reporter
29	Hand-held	Sticks	Under goal post (right)/ Left locker room exterior	Close ups, replays/ Player field entrance/exit, sideline reporter
30	Hand-held (SSM)	Sticks	Near sideline	Replays
31	Mini	Fixed mount	NFC coaches box	NFC coaching staff
32	Mini	Fixed mount	AFC coaches box	AFC coaching staff
33	Hand-held	On jib	Low end zone corner (left-far)	Beauty shot, halftime show
34	Hand-held (RF)	Sticks	Ceiling (above left end zone)	Replays
35	Hand-held (RF)	Sticks	Ceiling (above mid field)	Replays
36	Mini	Fixed mount	NFC tunnel	NFC locker room entrance/exit
37	Mini	Fixed mount	AFC tunnel	AFC locker room entrance/exit
38	Hand-held	Sticks	High 30yd line	Game clock
39	Hand-held	Sticks	High end zone (left)	40-second clock
40	Hand-held	Sticks	Announce booth	Talent on camera
41	Gyro/ Wescam	Mounted in blimp	Above venue	Exterior aerial scenics
42	Gyro/ Wescam	Mounted in helicopter	Above venue	Exterior aerial scenics

Football

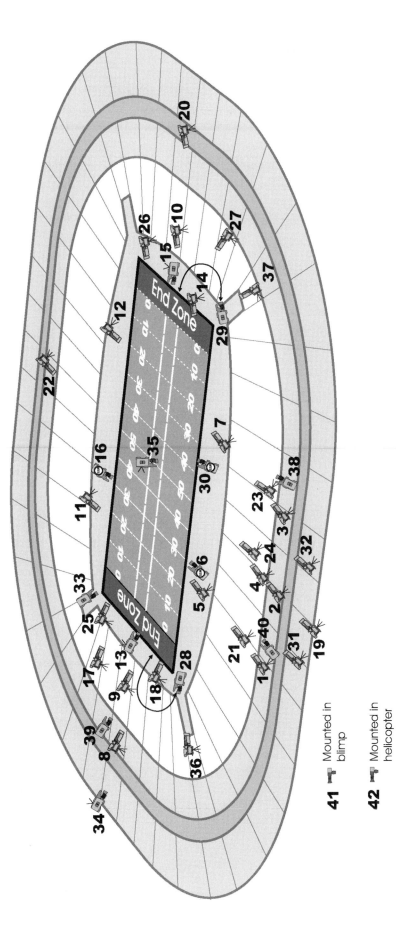

41  Mounted in blimp

42 Mounted in helicopter

Production – Cameras

Football (Soccer)

No.	Type	Mount	Location	Coverage
1	Fixed	Tripod	Center	Main follow
2	Fixed	Tripod	Center	Close ups, isolation
3	Fixed	Tripod	16m line left	Offside replays
4	Fixed	Tripod	16m line right	Offside replays
5	Fixed	Tripod	Field level near side, between benches	Midfield isolation, replays
6	Hand-held (RF)	Steadicam	Field level near side, length of benches	Isolation, bench reactions
7	Hand-held (RF)	Steadicam	Field level near side, length of benches	Isolation, bench reactions
8	Fixed	Tripod	High end zone	Shots on goal, replays, beauty shots
9	Hand-held	Crane	Behind left goal	Isolation, replays
10	Hand-held	Crane	Behind right goal	Isolation, replays
11	Fixed	Tripod	Field level near side, between benches	Midfield isolation replays
12	Mini	Type III	Top of stadium	Beauty shot

* A typical five-camera set-up for soccer would usually include cameras 1, 2, 5, 6 and 8.

Football

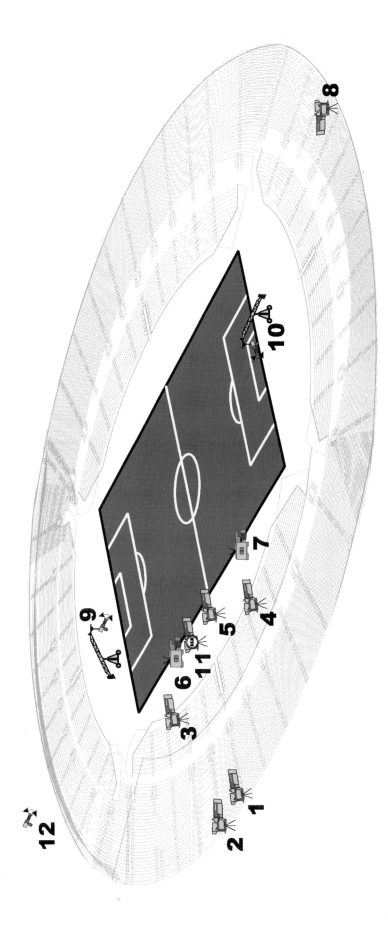

Production – Cameras

Motorcycle Road Race

No.	Type	Mount	Location	Coverage
1	Fixed	Tripod	VIP Tower	Wide shot
2	Fixed	Tripod	South corner of field of play	Approach and first turn
3	Fixed	Tripod	Corner near Gate 4	Second turn
4	Mini	Fixed mount	Straightaway between second and third turn	Speed shot
5	Fixed	Tripod	Near scoreboard	Third turn
6	Fixed	Tripod	Near bridge	Fourth turn and start of fifth turn
7	Fixed	Tripod	At sixth turn	Racers coming out of fifth turn and going into sixth
8	Fixed	Tripod	Top of hill	Carousel turn
9	Fixed	Tripod	Kettle Bottoms	Long stretch between Carousel and eighth turn
10	Fixed	Tripod	Canada Corner	Eighth turn
11	Fixed	Tripod	Corner near Gate 1	Final turn and finish
12	Hand-held (RF)	Sticks	Roving	Competition paddock area

Motorcycle Road Race

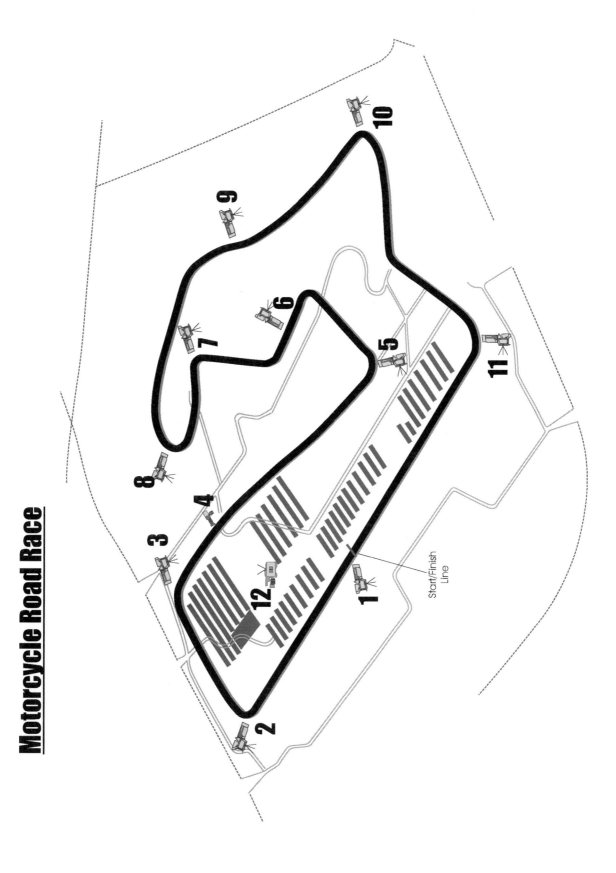

Start/Finish Line

Production – Cameras

Tennis

No.	Type	Mount	Location	Coverage
1	Fixed	Tripod	High centered	Wide shot
2	Fixed	Tripod	Mid centered	Main follow camera
3	Mini	Type III	Low, mounted top of court wall	Isolation
4	Hand-held	Sticks	Roving court level	Isolation, close ups
5	Fixed	Tripod w/wheels	Left of net, court level	Isolation, close ups
6	Fixed	Tripod w/wheels	Right of net, court level	Isolation, close ups
7	Fixed	Tripod	Low centered, reverse angle	Reverse angle replay
8	Hand-held	Type II	Suspended from roof edge in line with net	Isolation
9	Mini	Fixed mount	Mounted on top of building	Beauty shot
10	Fixed (SSM)	Tripod	Low centered, reverse angle	Low action replays
11	Fixed	Tripod	At net	Reverse angle

* A typical five-camera set-up for tennis would usually include cameras 1, 2, 4, 5 and 6.

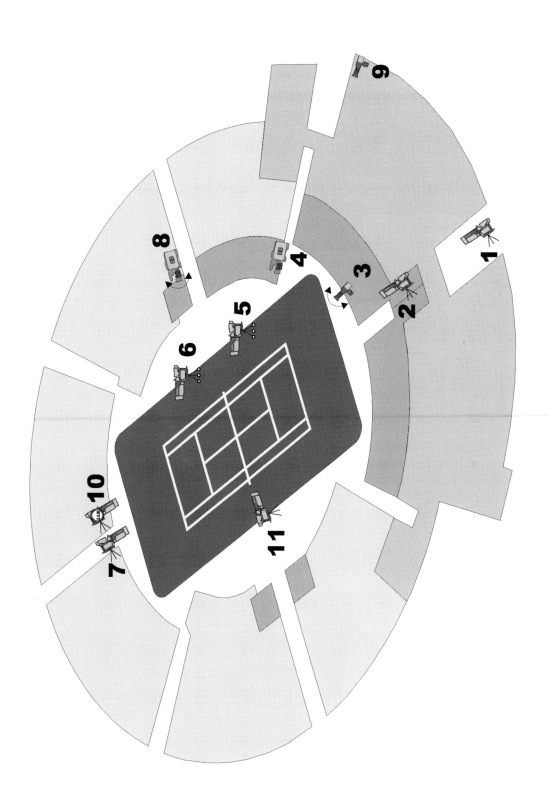

Tennis

APPENDIX IV:

Microphone Diagrams

The following microphone diagrams and descriptions are actual documents used by networks and production companies to produce television coverage of some of the Olympic Games. Since microphone descriptions are included, the microphone diagrams can be adapted to smaller events.

Production – Microphones

Baseball

No.	Microphone Type	Location	Coverage
1	Long shotgun on camera	On camera, low third	POV and close up of base runners
2	Long shotgun	Near camera behind home plate	Batter and umpire sound
3	Parabolic microphone	Near camera behind home plate	Batter and umpire sound
4	Long shotgun on camera	On camera, low first	POV and close up of base runners
5	Long shotgun on camera	On camera, left field	POV and close up
6	Boundary microphone	On camera, center field	Field ambiance
7	Boundary microphone	On wall in outfield	Pickup outfield sounds
8	Boundary microphone	On wall in outfield	Pickup outfield sounds
9	Boundary microphone	On wall in outfield	Pickup outfield sounds
10	Boundary microphone	On wall in outfield	Pickup outfield sounds
11	Boundary microphone	Behind home plate	Stereo image at home plate
12	Boundary microphone	Behind home plate	Stereo image at home plate
13	Lavaliere microphone	Visitors bullpen, on wall	Warm-up ambiance
14	Lavaliere microphone	Visitors bullpen, on wall	Warm-up ambiance
15	Lavaliere microphone	Home bullpen, on wall	Warm-up ambiance
16	Lavaliere microphone	Home bullpen, on wall	Warm-up ambiance
17	Shotgun microphone	Grandstands	Stereo crowd fill
18	Shotgun microphone	Grandstands	Stereo crowd fill
19	Shotgun microphone	Grandstands	Stereo crowd fill
20	Shotgun microphone	Grandstands	Stereo crowd fill
21	RF microphone	On home plate umpire	Umpire calls, tags
22	Parabolic microphone	Focused on first base	Umpire calls, tags
23	Parabolic microphone	Focused on first base	Umpire calls, tags

Baseball

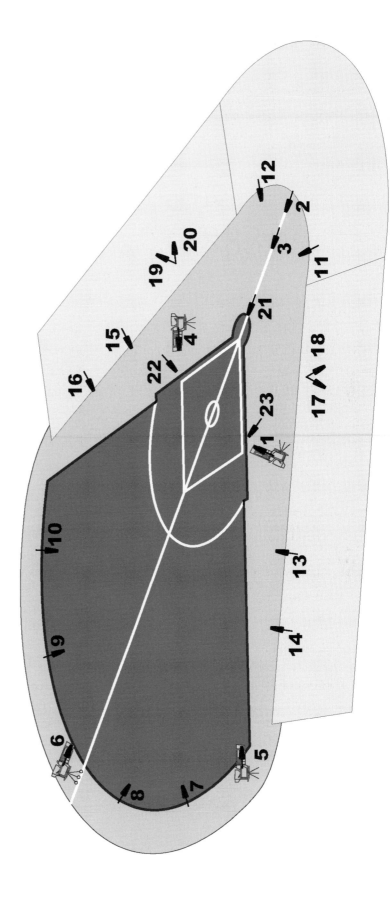

Production – Microphones

Basketball

No.	Microphone Type	Location	Coverage
1	Long shotgun with operator	Left side of court, under basket	Play action left
2	Long shotgun with operator	Rights side of court, under basket	Play action right
3	Long shotgun with operator	Near side, center court	Play action center
4	Short shotgun on 4" stand	Far side, center court, scorers table	Play action center
5	Lavaliere microphone	Left side under net	Close proximity of net
6	Lavaliere microphone	Right side under net	Close proximity of net
7	Long shotgun on camera	On camera, near court	POV and close ups
8	Long shotgun on camera	On camera, left court	POV and close ups
9	Long shotgun on camera	On camera, right court	POV and close ups
10	Long shotgun on camera	On camera, far court	POV and close ups
11	Lavaliere microphone	In the vicinity of bench	Team ambiance
12	Lavaliere microphone	In the vicinity of bench	Team ambiance
13	Short shotgun	On pole or stand in front of audience	Stereo crowd fill
14	Short shotgun	On pole or stand in front of audience	Stereo crowd fill
15	Short shotgun	On pole or stand in front of audience	Stereo crowd fill
16	Short shotgun	On pole or stand in front of audience	Stereo crowd fill
17	Short shotgun	On pole or stand in vicinity of non-competing athletes	Stereo crowd fill
18	Short shotgun	On pole or stand in vicinity of non-competing athletes	Stereo crowd fill
19	Short shotgun	On pole or stand in front of audience	Stereo crowd fill
20	Short shotgun	On pole or stand in front of audience	Stereo crowd fill

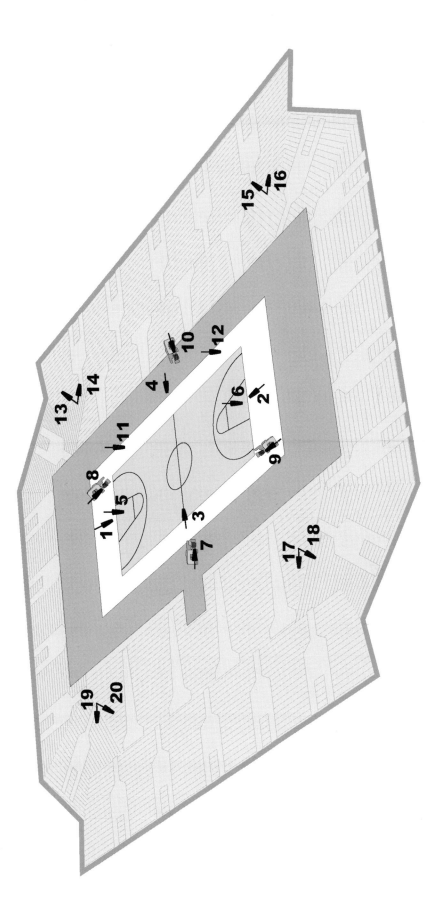

Production – Microphones

Football (Soccer)

No.	Microphone Type	Location	Coverage
1	Parabolic with operator	Far, left side of field	Play action far quadrant
2	Parabolic with operator	Far, right side of field	Play action far quadrant
3	Parabolic with operator	Near, left side of field	Play action near quadrant
4	Parabolic with operator	Near, right side of field	Play action near quadrant
5	Short shotgun	Behind goal, left	Play action goal area
6	Short shotgun	Behind goal, left	Play action goal area
7	Short shotgun	Behind goal, right	Play action goal area
8	Short shotgun	Behind goal, right	Play action goal area
9	Long shotgun	On camera	POV & close ups
10	Long shotgun	On camera	POV & close ups
11	Lavaliere microphone	Bench area	Coaches and athletes
12	Lavaliere microphone	Bench area	Coaches and athletes
13	Lavaliere microphone	Bench area	Coaches and athletes
14	Lavaliere microphone	Bench area	Coaches and athletes
15	Short shotgun	On pole or stand in front of audience	Stereo crowd fill
16	Short shotgun	On pole or stand in front of audience	Stereo crowd fill
17	Short shotgun	On pole or stand in front of audience	Stereo crowd fill
18	Short shotgun	On pole or stand in front of audience	Stereo crowd fill
19	Short shotgun	On pole or stand in front of audience	Stereo crowd fill
20	Short shotgun	On pole or stand in front of audience	Stereo crowd fill

Football

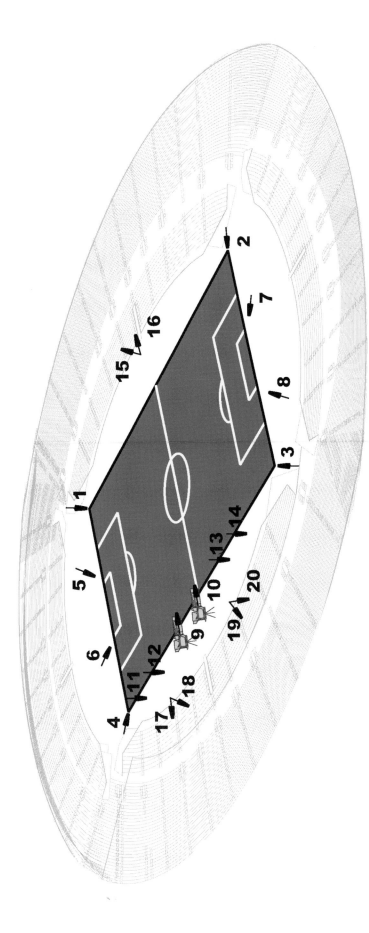

Production – Microphones

Tennis

No.	Microphone Type	Location	Coverage
1	Short shotgun	Mid-court, aiming at front left playing area	Athlete's close-up
2	Short shotgun	Mid-court, aiming at front right playing area	Athlete's close-up
3	Boundary microphone	Mid-court, aiming across playing area	Athlete's close-up
4	Boundary microphone	Mid-court, aiming across playing area	Athlete's close-up
5	Lavaliere microphone	Inseam of net, left side	Close proximity of net
6	Lavaliere microphone	Inseam of net, right side	Close proximity of net
7	Short shotgun	On pole or stand in front of audience	Stereo crowd fill
8	Short shotgun	On pole or stand in front of audience	Stereo crowd fill
9	Short shotgun	On pole or stand in front of audience	Stereo crowd fill
10	Short shotgun	On pole or stand in front of audience	Stereo crowd fill
11	Short shotgun	On pole or stand in front of audience	Stereo crowd fill
12	Short shotgun	On pole or stand in front of audience	Stereo crowd fill
13	Short shotgun	On pole or stand in vicinity of non-competing athletes	Stereo crowd fill
14	Short shotgun	On pole or stand in vicinity of non-competing athletes	Stereo crowd fill
15	Short shotgun	Back court, left in X/Y config.	Close up, back court sound
16	Short shotgun	Back court, left in X/Y config.	Close up, back court sound
17	Short shotgun	Back court, right in X/Y config.	Close up, back court sound
18	Short shotgun	Back court, right in X/Y config.	Close up, back court sound
19	Long shotgun on camera	On camera at mid-court	POV and close ups
20	Long shotgun on camera	On camera at mid-court	POV and close ups
21	Long shotgun on camera	Hand-held camera	POV and close ups
22	Long shotgun on camera	Roving hand-held	POV and close ups
23	Lavaliere microphone	In the vicinity of referee	Judges call
24	Lavaliere microphone	In the vicinity of referee	Judges call
25	Lavaliere microphone	Near scoreboard, celebrity area	Crowd mic

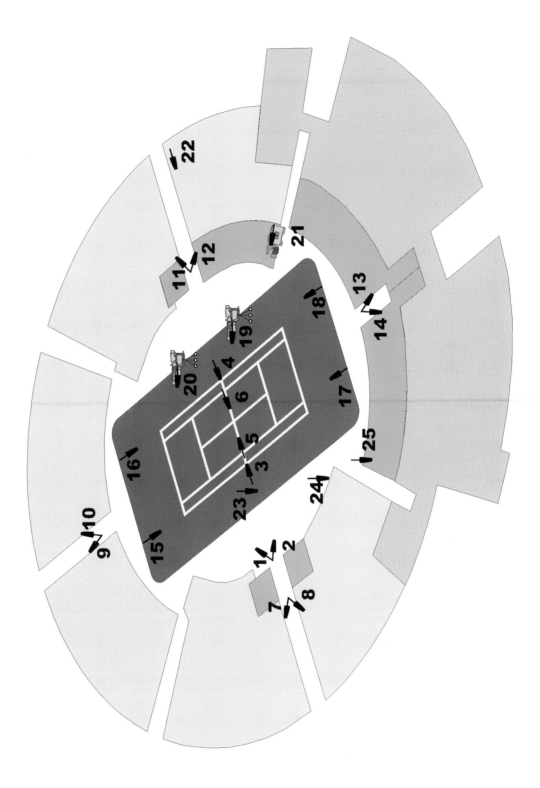

Tennis

APPENDIX V:
Event Storyboards

Two storyboard examples are included in this section:

-Runup storyboard from the Salt Lake Olympics

-Opening Ceremony of the Salt Lake 2002 Olympic Winter Games

      (a) Olympic Flag/Olympic Hymn

      (b) Olympic Flame enters and cauldron lighting

An additional production storyboard is available on page 95-96.

Figure 17: Runup Storyboards

:00 to :30 - Animation

:30 to :45 - Wide/Aerial of venue
GRAPHIC

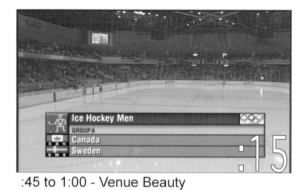

:45 to 1:00 - Venue Beauty
GRAPHIC

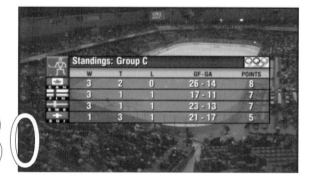

1:00 to 1:15 - Atmosphere at venue

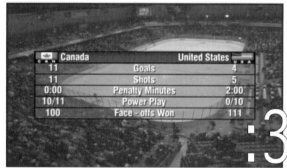

1:15 to 1:45 - Shots for **2 GRAPHICS**

1) Tournament Stats for Each Team

2) Group Standings

1:45 to 2:15 - Athletes enter ice

2:15 to 3:15 - Shots for **4 GRAPHICS**
(2 roster pages/team; Forward, Defense)

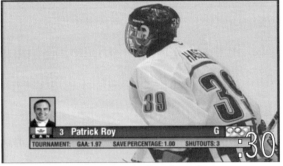

3:15 to 3:45 - ID Both Goaltenders
2 GRAPHICS

3:45 to 4:15 - ID both Coaches
2 GRAPHICS

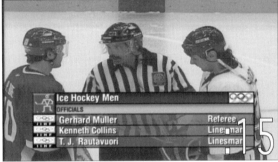

4:15 to 4:30 - Officials ID
GRAPHIC

4:30 to 5:00 - Athletes prepare for start / atmosphere at venue

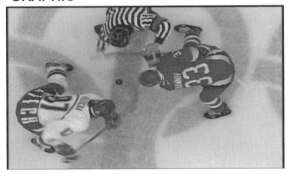

5:00 - Start of Competition

"Olympic Flag / Olympic Hymn"

Opening Ceremony * XIX Olympic Games * Salt Lake 2002   Page 1

Time	Length	Camera	Audio	Comm. Cue	Image
8:50:46	0:00:10	6		WIDE SHOT of flag carriers as they approach the flag pole.	**1** ANNOUNCE OLYMPIC FLAG
		2		People carry the flag.	**2** ENTRANCE OF OLYMPIC FLAG
8:53:46	0:03:00	mini come n go		Flag goes over camera.	**3** ENTRANCE OF OLYMPIC FLAG
8:55:46	0:02:00	24		Flag arrives. Music segues. Olymp Flag raised.	**4** OLYMPIC HYMN

"Olympic Flag / Olympic Hymn"

Opening Ceremony * XIX Olympic Games * Salt Lake 2002   Page 2

Time	Length	Camera	Audio	Comm. Cue	Image
		17		Olympic flag is raised.	**5** OLYMPIC HYMN
		9		CU of Olympic flag.	**6** OLYMPIC HYMN

"Olympic Flame Enters & Cauldron Lighting"

Opening Ceremony * XIX Olympic Games * Salt Lake 2002   Page 1

Time	Length	Camera	Audio	Comm. Cue	Image
9:08:56	0:03:00	NBC		Final runner approaches.	**1** OLYMPIC FLAME ENTERS
				WIDE SHOT of same action.	**2** OLYMPIC FLAME ENTERS
				Final runner enters hallway.	**3** OLYMPIC FLAME ENTERS
		6		Final runner hands the torch to a man and woman.	**4** OLYMPIC FLAME ENTERS

"Olympic Flame Enters & Cauldron Lighting"

Opening Ceremony * XIX Olympic Games * Salt Lake 2002   Page 2

Time	Length	Camera	Audio	Comm. Cue	Image
		9		Torch comes into stadium.	**5** OLYMPIC FLAME ENTERS
		3		WIDE SHOT of torch being passed around	**6** OLYMPIC FLAME ENTERS
					7 OLYMPIC FLAME ENTERS Deleted
		11		Torch skated around the stadium.	**8** OLYMPIC FLAME ENTERS

"Olympic Flame Enters & Cauldron Lighting"

Opening Ceremony * XIX Olympic Games * Salt Lake 2002   Page 3

Time	Length	Camera	Audio	Comm. Cue	Image
		23		The final runner lights the cauldron.	**9** CAULDRON LIGHTING
		MINI 24		Fire comes up to the cauldron.	**10** CAULDRON LIGHTING
		22		View from top of cauldron.	**11** CAULDRON LIGHTING
				WIDE SHOT of stadium with and pyro.	**12** CAULDRON LIGHTING

APPENDIX VI:
Intercom Diagrams

Three different types of sports production intercom system diagrams are included:

- Small
- Medium
- Large

Intercom diagram illustrations reprinted courtesy Telex Communications Inc.

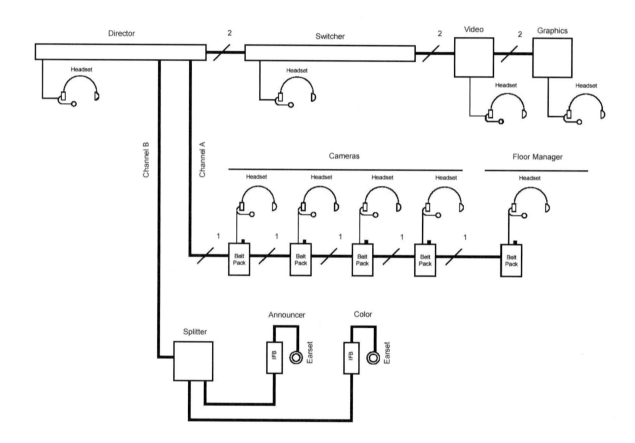

Small-scale production intercom system

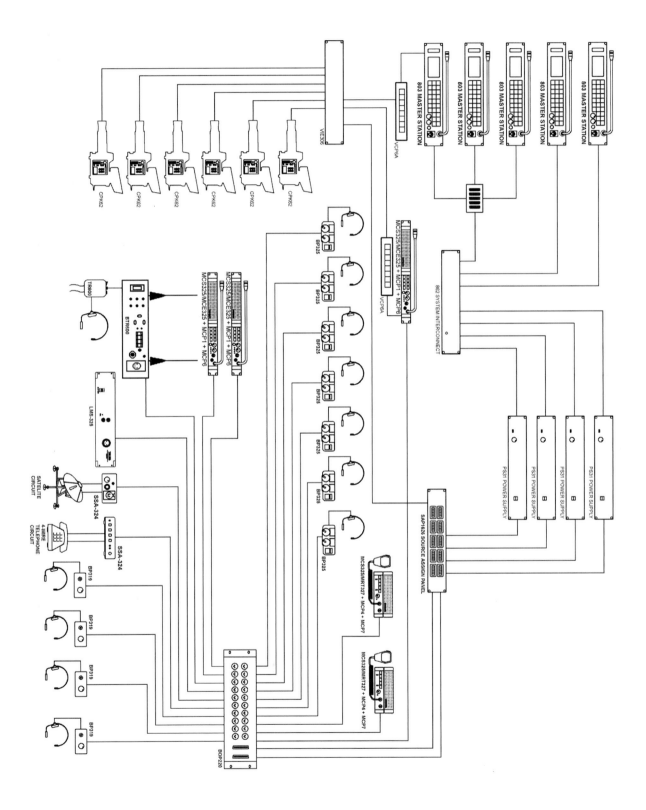

Medium-scale production intercom system

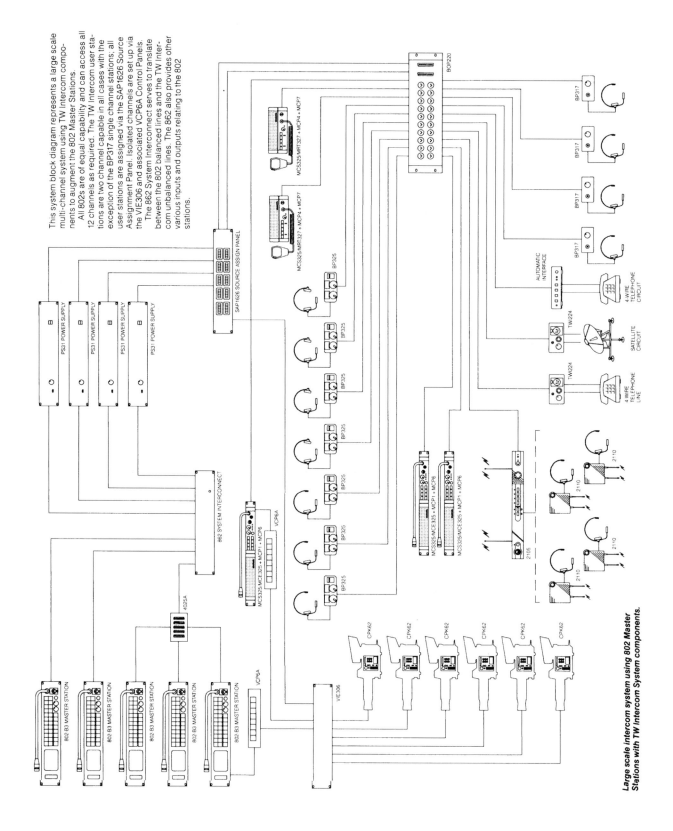

This system block diagram represents a large scale multi-channel system using TW Intercom components to augment the 802 Master Stations.

All 802s are of equal capability and can access all 12 channels as required. The TW Intercom user stations are two channel capable in all cases with the exception of the BP317 single channel stations; all user stations are assigned via the SAP1626 Source Assignment Panel. Isolated channels are set up via the VIE306 and associated VCP6A Control Panels.

The 862 System Interconnect serves to translate between the 802 balanced lines and the TW Intercom unbalanced lines. The 862 also provides other various inputs and outputs relating to the 802 stations.

Large scale intercom system using 802 Master Stations with TW Intercom System components.

Large-scale production intercom system

APPENDIX VII:
Lighting Plan

The following lighting diagram is an actual document used by networks and production companies to produce television coverage of an event.

Athens Olympic Broadcasting (AOB)

Sports Lighting for Television

Performance Specification

BASKETBALL

Issue V.00 : 17th May 2002
SUBJECT TO CHANGE

AOB Lighting for Television Specification SUBJECT TO CHANGE
Basketball

AOB Production Plan

Basketball is a game featuring lateral speed and vertical leaping ability. AOB's coverage philosophy dictates that both of these competition attributes be highlighted through the use of strategically placed courtside cameras, overhead and basket point of view perspectives and replay sources that will enable in-depth analysis and storytelling. AOB has positioned handheld cameras with the Field of Play (FOP) serving as a backdrop and are located on or adjacent to the FOP as individual competition circumstances dictate.

The AOB production style will concentrate on the 'theatricality' of basketball and the intention is to create dynamic images focusing on the athlete in contrast to the background.

Field Of Play (FOP)

The basketball FOP consists of the court area of 15m x 28m with a 2m perimeter area - a total FOP of 19m x 32m. A clear area of 25m x 40m is also defined bounded by the corral, which includes the FOP, the coaches and player seating and a photographer's moat – known as sport support.

Beyond the total FOP (outside the corral) is the run-off area which ends at the spectator barrier.

The exact location and dimensions of the court and corral shall be confirmed with ATHOC.

Multiple Venues

The basketball is played at two separate venues. The lighting of each shall be of the same performance quality. This is essential for the coordinated broadcast of the competition.

IMPORTANT

This specification covers the requirements for televised broadcast of the sport only. There may be other lighting and switching requirements for the venue – such lighting shall be arranged and switched so that there is no compromise to the specified sports lighting performance during a broadcast.

Camera locations are subject to change. The finalised location of cameras and their respective coverage shall be confirmed with AOB prior to lighting design approval, installation and commissioning.

All lighting performance criteria are minimums during the Games[1].

---

[1] In everyday non-Olympic use, usually a maintenance factor is specified. The Games are held over a short time scale and thus a maintenance factor is not an issue; however the specified minimum, or better, criteria shall be achieved during the Games.

AOB Lighting for Television Specification SUBJECT TO CHANGE
Basketball

TV Broadcast Lighting Performance Criteria

In this specification

- the court plus a 2m boundary zone is known as the **field of play** (FOP)
- the area between the FOP and the corral is known as **sport support**
- the total area within the corral is known as the **total FOP**.

The AOB lighting specifications use the term **Action Replay Zone**, ARZ, defined as an area of the FOP where critical action takes place and covered in televised 'highlights' or 'replays', also known as "the money shot". Typical examples are the apparatus and the "kiss & cry".

A camera allocated to be the principal camera for a part of the court is termed here as the relevant camera. For the purpose of this specification, cameras are referred to as either **'hard'** (located in a fixed position) or **'ERC'** (ENG roving camera). There are hard cameras on four sides of the court.

The lighting of the FOP shall meet the following requirements; see Table 1 on page 6 and Table 2 on page 7 for summary:

LIGHT SOURCE
The colour temperature within the venue covered by the broadcast shall be 5600K.
- All the lamps used during television broadcast shall
  - have a nominated colour temperature, Tk, of 5600K (or up to a maximum of 5900K) and be within the IEC[2] and manufacturer's tolerances
  - have a colour rendering index (CRI Ra8) of ≥ 90
  - be from the same manufacturer and from the same production batch.
- Low wattage lamps are preferred

CALCULATION & MEASUREMENT GRIDS, 2m grid interval; a horizontal plane at 1.5m above the competition surface:
- Vertical illuminance towards relevant cameras of
  - the FOP
  - the sport support area
  - ARZ_1: area bounded by the free-throw line and the end line; both ends
  - ARZ_2: 2m square area centred on the basket, 1m grid (9 points); both ends
- Horizontal illuminance:
  - on the FOP at the competition surface
  - the sport support area at the competition surface.

MINIMUM ILLUMINANCE
- The minimum vertical illuminance[3] at any point of the FOP shall be ≥ 1400 lux towards the relevant cameras
- The minimum vertical illuminance at any point of the total FOP shall be ≥ 1000 lux towards the relevant cameras.

UNIFORMITIES for FOP; with sport support shown in brackets:
- Vertical illuminance, for each relevant hard camera:
  - the minimum to maximum ratio (Ev-min/Ev-max), U_1, shall be ≥ 0.7 (0.4)
  - the minimum to average ratio (Ev-min/Ev-max), U_2, shall be ≥ 0.8 (0.6).

---

[2] IEC: International Electrotechnical Commission; e.g. IEC 61167 Metal Halide Lamps.
[3] International Olympic Committee (IOC) Broadcast Guide, minimum during the Olympic Games.

AOB Lighting for Television Specification SUBJECT TO CHANGE
Basketball

- Horizontal illuminance:
    - the minimum to maximum ratio (Eh-min/Eh-max), U_1, shall be ≥ 0.7 (0.6)
    - the minimum to average ratio (Eh-min/Eh-max), U_2, shall be ≥ 0.8 (0.7)
- The ratio of the average horizontal illuminance of the sport support to the average horizontal illuminance of the FOP shall be ≥ 0.6 and ≤ 0.7
- Action Replay Zones, both ends:
    - the maximum vertical illuminance within ARZ_1 shall be within ARZ_2; in principle, the maximum vertical illuminance should be at the basket
    - the minimum vertical illuminance within ARZ_1 shall be $\geq$ average vertical illuminance of the FOP
- the ratio of vertical illuminances at any point over the four vertical orthogonal planes facing the sides of the FOP shall be:
    - ≥ 0.6 for the FOP
    - ≥ 0.4 for the sport support
- the uniformity gradient[4], UG, for both horizontal and vertical illuminance (to cameras) shall be:
    - $\leq 10\%$ at 1m **and** 2m grid intervals for the FOP - both shall comply
    - $\leq 20\%$ at 4m grid intervals for the sport support
- the ratio of the average horizontal illuminance to average vertical illuminance shall be:
    - ≥ 0.75 and ≤ 1.5 for the relevant cameras for the FOP, preferably 1:1
    - ≥ 0.5 and ≤ 2.0 for the relevant cameras for the sport support

LENS FLARE and GLARE:
The Glare Rating, GR, shall be ≤ 40 for all hard cameras[5]. GRs may also be required for locations specified by FIBA and/or ATHOC.

LUMINAIRES and AIMING LOGIC:
- The lighting, whilst ensuring maximum visual comfort for the athletes, should recreate a television studio environment with an appropriate overall level of dramatic theming, natural modelling and creative effect
- The minimum mounting height of the luminaires shall be 8.5m
- No luminaire shall be located either over the marked court[6] or directly behind the baskets
- The luminaire aiming angle, in elevation[7], shall be $\leq 65°$
- No luminaire shall be aimed directly at a camera, and preferably not within a 50° cone centred on the camera
- Luminaires shall be located such that reflections off the court surface ("skip light") in the direction of the main cameras are to be eliminated
- The lighting shall limit shadows on the court from the basket and support apparatus
- If a hard camera is within a zone made by horizontal lines 25° either side of the horizontal aiming angle of the luminaire and either:
    - the vertical angle between a horizontal plane through the luminaire and the camera lens is <25°, **or**
    - the luminaire is aimed >40°,
      then the luminaire shall be constructed, or fitted with a glare-controlling device, such that the light-emitting area of the lamp is shielded from the camera's field of view or fitted with barn-doors[8]

---

[4] UG – percentage change at a single grid point from average illuminance in the 8 adjacent grid points.
[5] Although GR was not developed for TV, it has been found (in the absence of a suitable parameter) to provide a good indication as to the expectation of lens flare. GRs will also be required for locations specified by FIBA (Fédération International Basketball Amateur) or other authorised ATHOC body.
[6] FIBA requirement
[7] Elevation aiming angle away from downward vertical.
[8] Industry generic term.

AOB Lighting for Television Specification SUBJECT TO CHANGE
Basketball

- Light should reach any point within the total FOP from at least three directions where the third directional component should form a 'backlight' to one or both of the other two directions, with respect to the hard cameras
- The ratio of the total amount of light (luminous flux) projected from the main camera side to the opposite side should be ≥50% and ≤60%
- There shall be a clear path between any luminaire and any point of the total FOP – no structure or material (flags, banners, video-boards etc) shall obstruct the light path
- Every luminaire shall be clearly visible from any standing position on the FOP
- Noise – the lamp control gear shall be silent (no ballast "hum").

SLOW MOTION - flicker, stroboscopic effects and mains supply
- Gas discharge lamp luminaires should, preferably, be controlled by high frequency control gear
- Luminaires shall be single-phase supply type; mains supply shall be 3-phase
- Luminaires shall be mixed and spread equally over three phases
- Light reaching any point of the FOP shall be supplied from all three phases
- Flicker. Where luminaire control gear is **not** of the high frequency electronic type, a particular problem for SSM cameras is flicker due to phasing of the light. The flicker may not be apparent on the athlete (due to proper phase mixing) but if the luminaire is within camera shot, the luminaire itself may exhibit severe flicker. All attempts shall be made to eliminate flicker by screening, re-aiming or moving the luminaire.

SPECTATORS
- Lighting of the spectators, and the FOP, shall be capable of being switched such that the spectators are in a complete blackout (for gala[9] night)
- Spectators shall be illuminated so that the average illuminance level, towards the hard cameras, over the first 12 rows calculated at seated head height shall be ≥10% and ≤25% of the Ev-ave of the FOP
- The illuminance beyond the first 12 rows shall reduce uniformly
- Overshoot and flicker. Where luminaire control gear is **not** of the high frequency electronic type, a particular problem for SSM cameras is flicker due to phasing of 'spill' or 'overshoot' light primarily intended for the FOP. The flicker may not be apparent on the athlete (due to proper mixing of phases and aiming) but the background, the spectators, may exhibit severe flicker. All attempts shall be made to limit flicker over the background e.g. by mixing phases.

RUNOFF
- The gradation of light levels outside the FOP or corral is to reduce uniformly. The ratio of Eh-ave of the Run-off to the Eh-ave of the FOP shall be ≥0.1 and ≤0.3.

MIXED ZONE, PRE- and POST-UNILATERAL POSITIONS, MEDAL CEREMONIES, MEDAL CEREMONY FLAGS, FLAGS OF NATIONS, VENUE DRESSING
Separate lighting specifications are published by AOB for the (television) lighting requirements of these common applications within the Athens 2004 venues. The lighting of these areas, in performance terms, shall integrate with this specification.

VENUE
- The average surface illuminance of the underside of the venue roof shall be less than that of the spectators with a U_1 of ≥0.3; there shall be no 'hot spots'
- No direct or indirect (reflected) daylight shall enter the competition building interior during a broadcast including from adjacent noncompetition areas
- The illuminance of background eg walls, shall be <50% of the FOP vertical illuminance.

---

[9] Note: gala night lighting is not part of this specification

AOB Lighting for Television Specification SUBJECT TO CHANGE
Basketball

'SPORT PRESENTATION' and OTHER LIGHTING WITHIN THE VENUE

All other non-sports lighting that is required within the venue e.g. aisle lights, way-finding, concession lighting, press strobes including 'sport presentation', and that can influence a camera shot shall:

- not compromise the quality of the broadcast
- be integrated with, but without compromising, the sports lighting
- be subject to changes required by AOB to maintain the integrity of the broadcast image
- be screened if within camera shot
- as a general rule, not be the primary colours of light – red or green or blue (RGB) when used over large areas (wash)
- be of colours other than red or green or blue when used as a dominant source. RGB colour can be used in moderation and only as minor elements.

Note: FIBA rules require "The lighting over the playing court shall not be less than 1,500 lux. This level shall be measured 1.5 m above the playing court." The FIBA specified light level is not noted as being for television and is a 'horizontal' illuminance level. This is not an AOB requirement. FIBA also requires for "Olympic Tournaments" that "The lighting shall meet television requirements."

SUMMARY

See Table 1, p6 and Table 2, p7 for summary of performance criteria.

AOB

- The specification incorporates the requirements of the Rights Holding Broadcasters and the production philosophy of Athens Olympic Broadcasting; and is based on the guidelines and recommendations of the IOC, FIBA, GAISF[10], EBU[11] and CIE[12].

- The specification contains a level of detail necessary for high quality broadcast images. If any part of this specification and associated tables is unclear or requires further explanation, contact shall be made with AOB for clarification and confirmation of the intent.

- Subject to live camera tests during rehearsals, AOB reserves the right to instruct and approve final changes to the installed lighting under direction of the AOB Technical Manager, Lighting.

---

[10] GAISF: General Association of International Sports Federations
[11] European Broadcasting Union
[12] Commission Internationale d'Eclairage

AOB Lighting for Television Specification SUBJECT TO CHANGE
Basketball

Table 1 Lighting Performance Criteria

Lighting Levels and Uniformities	Illuminance (lux)		Uniformity (minimum)			
	Ev-Cam-min	Eh-ave	Horizontal		Vertical	
			Emin/Emax	Emin/Eave	Emin/Emax	Emin/Eave
	(see note 2)					
FOP (court) see note 7	1400	(see Ratios)	0.7	0.8	0.6	0.7
Sport support	1000	(see Ratios)	0.6	0.7	0.4	0.6
Runoff (outside corral)			0.4	0.6		
Spectators (to Cam#1)*	(see Ratios)	≤150			0.3	0.5

* first 12 rows; beyond first 12 rows, light level to reduce uniformly

Ratios

Eh-ave-FOP/Ev-ave-Cam-FOP:	≥0.75 and ≤1.5
Eh-ave-SS/Ev-ave-SS:	≥0.5 and ≤2.0
Eh-ave-SS/Eh-ave-FOP:	≥0.6 and ≤0.7
Ev-point-over 4 planes (see note 4)	≥0.6
Ev-ave-C#1-spec/Ev-ave-C#1-FOP	≥0.1 and ≤0.25
Ev-min-ARZ₁ (see also note 9)	≥ Ev-ave-C#1-FOP

Uniformity Gradients (maximum):

UG-FOP (2m AND 1m grids)	≤10%
UG-arena-floor (4m grid)	≤20%
UG-spectators (to C#1)	≤20%

Light Source:

CRI Ra:	≥90
Tk :	5600K

Lens Flare – glare rating	
GR to hard cams	≤ 40

NOTES:

1. For vertical Illuminance calculation planes (Ev) and Cameras, see table 2.
2. "Ev-min" is a minimum value at any point (not "minimum average").
3. Spectators - sloping calculation plane through seated head position, first 12 rows.
4. Ev-max and Ev-min at any point, within FOP, over four orthogonal vertical planes parallel to FOP sides, to be equal to or greater than 0.6 (0.4 for sport support).
5. All grids to be on 1.0m intervals, unless stated otherwise.
6. The illuminance levels are minimums during Olympic Games.
7. If all main cameras (i.e. other than ERC) meet Ev-min = 1400, then Ev-min to ERC can be 1000 lux.
8. No daylight, direct or indirect, during broadcast
9. Ev-max in ARZ₁ shall be within ARZ₂.

Abbreviations and Definitions:

Sport support = SS = outside FOP up to corral
Runoff = between corral and spectator barrier
Cam = Cameras (see table 2)
ARZ₁ = area within free throw line and endline; both ends
ARZ₂ = 2m square area centred on (each) basket
spec = spectators
ERC = ENG roving camera (see table 2)
C#1 = main camera

AOB specification based on IOC, FIBA, EBU and CIE recommendations plus Rights Holding Broadcasters requirements with additional emphasis on super slow motion & theatricality.

17 May 02

6

AOB Lighting for Television Specification SUBJECT TO CHANGE
Basketball

Table 2 Cameras and Calculation/Measurement Grids. SUBJECT TO CHANGE.

Cam #	Camera Location	Coverage	Notes
1	High/Midcourt	Wide	
3	Mid left ¾	Isolation	
4	Mid right ¾	Isolation	
7	Midcourt on floor/nearside	Low action + isolation	SSM**
8	Midcourt on floor/farside	Isolation + benches	
10	Behind left backboard	Isolation	
11	Behind right backboard	Isolation	
12	¾ high near right corner roof	Venue wide shot	
ERC*	4 orthogonal directions	FOP	

*ERC: ENG Roving Cameras - 4 vertical illuminance planes in orthogonal directions parallel to FOP sides.
** SSM: super slow motion camera

Camera location naming convention: relative to main camera #1 when facing FOP from C#1.

Compliance:
Calculation – all cameras
Measurement – cameras 1, 2, 7, 9; and ERCs.

17 May 02

AOB Lighting for Television Specification SUBJECT TO CHANGE
Basketball

OAKA - Indoor Hall - Basketball (Finals) - Camera Positions

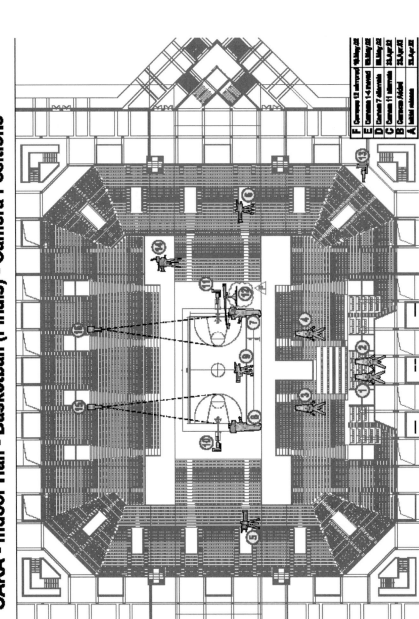

This specification covers the requirements for televised broadcast of the sport only. There may be other lighting and switching requirements for the venue – such lighting shall be arranged and switched so that there is no compromise to the specified sports lighting performance during a broadcast.

17 May 02

Sources and Recommended Readings

1st World Broadcaster Meeting, International Sports Broadcasting, 1999

360 Degrees in Motion, Cahners Business Information, rlrassociate.net/clients/kewingsa, 2001

1996 Atlanta Olympic Broadcasting Audio Plans, Atlanta Olympic Broadcasting, 1996

ABC Sports Broadcast Guide: Superbowl XIX 1985

Address, Eric, and Michael Muderick, And Now Live: More goes into a remote shoot than meets the eye, Video Systems, January 1996

AMA Road Racing Production Schedule/Elkhart Lake, Chet Burks Productions, 1999

Arledge, Roone, interview, Sportsline.com, 1976

Audio Production Plan, Athens 2004 Olympics, 2003

Bender, Gary, *Call of the Game*, Bonus Books 1994

Berman, Chris, biography, espn.sportszone.com, 2000

A Brief Guide to Microphones, Audio-Technica, 1996

Brilliant, Robert, NBC Blends Drama with Technology in NBC Playoff Coverage, *TV Technology*, June 2, 1999

Brilliant, Robert, Tips for Shooting in High Definition, *TV Technology*, February 9, 2000

Brilliant, Robert, Plenty of Horsepower for Daytona 500 Coverage, *TV Technology*, February 23, 2000

Brilliant, Robert, "March Madness" To Peak in HD: CBC Sports to Broadcast Final Four in High Definition, *TV Technology*, March 8, 2000

Brilliant, Robert, HD Hoops, *TV Technology*, March 2001

Broadcaster Handbook: Salt Lake 2002, International Sports Broadcasting 2002

Broadcasters Handbook, XV FIFA World Cup, EBU Sports International, 1994

Broadcast Information Manual, Sydney Olympic Broadcasting Organisation, 2000

Broadcasting the Olympics, Musee Olympique, 1999

Brown, Blain, *Cinematography: Theory and Practice*, Focal Press 2002

Burrows, Thomas D., Lynne S. Gross, and Donald N. Wood, *Video Production: Disciplines and Techniques*. McGraw-Hill, Inc., 1998

Campbell, Robert, *The Golden Year of Broadcasting: A Celebration of the First 50 Years of Radio and TV on NBC*, Rutledge Books, 1976

Carlson, Scott, Carnegie Mellon Provides Special Effects for Super Bowl Broadcast, Berkeley.edu/mhonarc/openmash-developers, January 2001

Catsis, John R., *Sports Broadcasting*, Nelson-Hall Publishers 1996

Chapple, Barton, The Thrill of a Televised Derby, *Television News*, September–October, 1931

Chapple, Barton, Televising a Horse Race, *Radio News*, March 1932

Church, Rachel, Current Trends in Sports Interactive Advertising, Media presentation, November 2001

Colborn, David, and Chuck Petch, Grass Valley Dictionary of Technical Terms, The Grass Valley Group, 1991

Coleman, Ken, *So You Want to Be a Sportscaster*, Hawthorn Books, 1973

Daudelin, Art, A Flurry of Innovative Events and Technologies Highlight Winter X-Games, *TV Technology*, February 7, 2001

Deer Valley Ski Resort Technical Operations Survey/Women's Super Series NorAm Cup, NBC Sports, 2000

Definitions and Assumptions (AOB Planning/IBC Personnel) Athens Olympic Broadcasting planning document 2003

Downing, Taylor, *Olympia*, BFI Classics, 1992

Dupuy, Judy, Television Show Business, General Electric Company, 1945

engsaftety.com (web site), March 2000

Epstein, Al, and Lou Riggs, Play-By-Play Sportscast Training, 1992

Foley, Mark, and Peteris Saltans: Makes It All Sound Good, *Sports TV Production*, April 2003

Games of the XXVI Olympiad, Research Manual Volume 1, NBC Sports, 1996

Gernsback, H., The Radiophot. Television by Radio; *Science and Invention*, July 1922

Grade, Michael, Opening Speech, Interactive TV Show Europe 2004, Barcelona, Spain, October 14, 2004

Grotticelli, Michael, Supply and HDemand, *Television Broadcast*, January 2000

Hallinger, Mark, Review of the Atlanta Olympic Broadcast, *TV Technology*, September 1996

Hallinger, Mark, TVNZ Chases America's Cup, *TV Technology*, February 2003

Handbook of Intercom Systems Engineering, Telex ® Communications Inc. 2002

Hay, James, Olympics Television Production (Getting to Know It Before You Do It), American Broadcasting Companies 1984

Henry, Lee, Director's Cut, Directing Basketball, *Sports TV Production*, May 2004

Hickman, Harold R., *Television Directing*, McGraw-Hill, Inc., 1991

Higgins, Jonathan, *Satellite Newsgathering*, Focal Press, 2000

Hodges, Peter, *Video Camera Operator's Handbook*, Focal Press, 1995

Hyde, Stuart W., *Television and Radio Announcing*, Houghton Mifflin Company, 1995

Interactive Broadcasters Handbook (France 98 World Cup), TVRS 98/France Telecom, 1998

International Amateur Athletic Federation Television Guidelines, IAAF, 1987

International Olympic Committee Marketing Fact File, IOC 2001

IOC Broadcasting Guide, International Olympic Committee, 1997

Lake Placid/Production Manual/Inaugural Winter Goodwill Games, Turner Sports, 2000

Lambton, D'arcy, and Matthew Glendinning, Virtual TV Becomes Reality

Liles, Bennett, Sports Production, *Broadcast Engineering*, October 2000

Lyons, Christopher, Shure Guide to Audio Systems for Video Production, Shure Incorporated 1998

Maar, Joseph, Strangers in the Night: The Challenge of Calling The Shots on-the-Road and Strangers in the Truck: Building Teamwork on a Sports Remote, *TV Broadcast*, December 1997

Maar, Joseph, Starting Here, Starting Now: What to Know Before You Do a High Definition Show, *Television Broadcast*, January 2000

Maar, Joseph, A Master of His Craft, *Television Broadcast*, February 2000

Maar, Joseph, How to Look Like a Network: The Art of Creating Backup Plans, *Television Broadcast*, March 2000

Maar, Joseph, Football and Television—a Perfect Match, *Television Broadcast*, November 2000

Maar, Joseph, and Ron Rosenblum, Working a Live Sports Remote, *Television Broadcast*, July 1998

Maar, Joseph, and Ron Rosenblum, Working a Live Sports Broadcast, *Digital TV*, July 2001

Manual of Information: International Broadcast Centre, Summer Olympic Games, American Broadcasting Company, 1984

Masters, Rachel and Alistair Jackson, Host Broadcast Training Manuals, Sydney Olympic Broadcasting Organisation, 1998

McKay, Jim, *My Wide World*, McMillan Publishing Co. 1973

McKay, Jim, *The Real McKay: My Wide World of Sports*, Plume/Penguin Group 1998

Millerson, Gerald, *Video Production*, Focal Press, 1999

Missett, William, Eye on the Game: Cameras in Sports, *TV Technology*, February 9, 2000

Morris, Andrew, People Are NBC's Greatest Olympic Asset, TV Technology.com, December 2001

Muller, Ray (Director), *The Wonderful, Horrible Life of Leni Reifenstahl* (film), A coproduction of Omega Film, Nomad Films, Channel Four, Zweites Deutsches Fernsehen, ARTE, 1993

NBC: The 2002 Olympic Winter Games IBC Technical Manual, NBC 2002

NBC's Coverage of the Games of the XXVI Olympiad, NBC 1996

New York '98 Goodwill Games Production Guide, Turner Sports, 1998

Olympic Broadcast Analysis Report, International Olympic Committee, 1997

Olympic Broadcast Marketing Handbook (The): Salt Lake 2002, International Olympic Committee 2001

Olympic Games and Television: Report on Athens 2004 and Outlook for Future Games, 15th International Symposium, Sportel, Monaco, October 12, 2004

Pegg, Jonathan R., Don't Aim for the Five-hole; Go Top Shelf!, *TV Technology*, February 9, 2000

Peters, Jean-Jacques (EBU), A History of Television, Digital Video Broadcasting web site, 1985

Pound, Dick, *The Sydney Morning Herald*, 1 June 2001

Production Guidelines, Sydney Olympic Broadcasting Organisation 2000

Real, Michael R., Is Television Corrupting the Olympics?, *Television Quarterly*, Volume XXX, Number 2, Fall 1999

Run-Ups: Introductory Sequences for Broadcasting of the Events, The Image of the XVIth Winter Olympic Games, ORTO 92, 1992

Sandberg, Phil, Van Out of Time: Technician from '56 Olympics Brings OB Unit Back to Life, *TV Technology*, 2000

Schultz, Brad, *Sports Broadcasting*, Focal Press 2002

Secor, Winfield, Strike One! Greets Japanese Visualists, *Television News*, November–December 1931.

Silbergleid, Michael, and Mark J. Pescatore, *The Guide to Digital Television*, 3rd ed., Miller Freeman PSN Inc. 2000

Smith, Mark, Adding a New Dimension to Broadcast Sports: POV Cameras Bring Viewers Close to the Action, *Videography,* January 2003

Spa, Miquel de Moragas, Nancy K. Rivenburgh, and James F. Larson, *Television in the Olympics*, John Libbey and Company Ltd., 1995

Spice, Byron, CMU Experts Helping CBS's 30 Robotic Cameras to Work as One, *Post Gazette*, January 24, 2001

Sport Needs a 21st Century Broadcast Technology, 2000 Spotted Eagle, Douglas, Mind Your Mics and Get Great Sound in the Field, *Studio Monthly*, September 2005.

Sydney Uplink, Issue Two, Sydney Olympic Broadcasting Organisation, 2000

Television in Germany: Olympic Games, Berlin 1936 (The official program distributed to television viewers during the Olympics), Berlin Olympics, 1936

Television in the Olympic Games, The New Era, International Symposium, Lausanne, 1998, International Olympic Committee, 1999

Ten Steps to Better Remote Switching, *Videography*, July 2001

Thorpe, Larry, Add Depth to HD Shoots with Canon HD Lenses, *Studio Monthly*, September 2005.

Tompkins, Al, Tips on Making Great TV Graphics, Poynteronline.org, May 24, 2000

U.S. Ski Team Women's Slalom Show/ Production Schedule #1,NBC Sports, 2000

Uusivouri, Kalevi, and Tapani Parm, TV Coverage of Major Athletic Events: The Basics, presented at the IAAF World Television Seminar, Athens, Greece, March 2004

Venue Technical Management, Sydney Olympic Broadcasting Organisation, 2000

Verna, Tony, *Live TV: An Inside Look at Directing and Producing*, Focal Press, 1987

Washington Opera Taped with 720p Panasonic HDTV Truck, *Videography*, January 2000

Webb, Jessica, Snow Daze: ESPN's Winter X Games Wows 'Em in Vermont, *Television Broadcast*, March 2000

Wells, Allan, Live HD: Designing the Grammys, Highdef, 2002

Whitaker, Jerry C., *DTV: The Revolution in Digital Video*, 2nd ed., McGraw-Hill, 1999

Whittaker, Ron, *Television Production*, Mayfield Publishing Company, 1993

Woodward, Steve, and Andy Bernstein, New Technology in Television, *Sports Business Journal*, October 2003

Zettl, Herbert, *Television Production Handbook*, Wadsworth, 1997

Zettl, Herbert, *Video Basics 2,* Wadsworth, 1998

Zipay, Steve, NBC to Make Heads Spin, Newsday.com, May 19, 2002

Zitter, Josh, Improving How Fans Watch Car Races, *TechTV*, May 2002

Glossary

2-Wire: A pair of wires that carry an audio circuit.

4-Wire: A four-wire communication circuit especially used for commentary or coordination.

4x3: Standardized aspect radio of standard television (SD).

16x9: Standardized aspect radio of HDTV and widescreen SD.

24p: Used to describe a video camera that shoots at 24 full frames per second. It may refer to SD or HD. It is thought to provide somewhat of a "film look."

60i: Used to describe a video signal where ½ of the total lines of the image are captured and displayed every 1/60th of a second.

720p: One of the internationally standardized HDTV formats. This format has 720 scan lines and utilizes progressive scanning. The 720p format is best for fast moving motion scenes.

1080i: One of the internationally standardized HDTV formats. This format has 1080 scan lines and uses an interlaced scanning system. The 1080i format has a sharper image than the 720p format.

Above-the-Line Personnel: Refers to all non-technical planning personnel such as producers, directors, chief engineer, and talent.

Active Device: Devices requiring operating power (battery or other) in addition to the signal. Examples are transistors, integrated circuits, amplifiers, and intercoms.

AD: Abbreviation for associate or assistant director.

Air Pack: See Flypack.

Ambiance: Background sound in the venue.

Aperture: The diaphragm opening of the lens that is usually measured in f-stops.

Aspect Ratio: The ratio of the proportions of the height to the width of the television image. NTSC, PAL, and SECAM televisions have an aspect ratio of 4:3 while HDTV has an aspect ratio of 16:9.

Attenuation: The amount of audio or video signal loss from point A to point B.

Attenuation Switch: An attenuation switch reduces the sensitivity of the input of a device and will generally eliminate overloading and distortion.

Audio Check: Commentator speaks into a microphone for audio technician to check the audio level.

Audio-Follow-Video: Refers to when a video special effects generator (SEG) or switcher is designed so that the audio automatically changes when the video is switched. This is helpful in remote events when the director needs audio from whatever camera is on.

Back Focus: Back focus is the distance between the rear of the lens and the camera target. When the back focus is properly adjusted, the camera operator should be able to zoom in, focus, then zoom out, maintaining accurate focus from the zoom in to the wide shot.

Balanced: A cable having two identical conductors that carry voltages opposite in polarity and equal in magnitude with respect to the ground.

Barrel: Also known as "turn around" or "gender bender." An adapter that is male to male or female to female, allowing identical cables to be connected together.

Bars: See Color Bars.

Beauty Camera: A fixed camera designed to shoot wide angle "beauty" shots. It is generally installed on a stadium roof or surrounding tall structure. This camera can also be called a panoramic camera.

Below-the-Line Personnel: Refers to all technical personnel, such as camera operators, technical director, tape operators, etc.

Belt pack: This portable headset intercom station box is designed to be worn on a user's belt but is also fastened to the underside of consoles, taped to a structure near the user or mounted on a piece of equipment. The intercom headset plugs into the belt pack as does the connection to the rest of the intercom.

Bib: A vest that identifies a crew member as someone who is allowed access to restricted areas. Generally worn at larger events by camera and audio personnel.

Binding Post: Converts a dry pair to XLR.

Biscuit: A portable speaker station

Blocking: Occurs when the director works through the process of establishing camera angles, positions, and movement as well as the talent's positions before a rehearsal.

BNC: The standard professional video connector.

Booth Monitor: The monitor that is located in the commentator's area. This monitor usually gets the program feed. Generally the commentators will also have a second monitor that will allow the director to show them a replay before it actually occurs on-air.

Broadcast Supply Panel (BSP): See I/O.

Cam: Abbreviation for camera.

Camera Control Unit (CCU): A remote unit that controls the color balance, registration, aperture, and other technical adjustments on a professional video camera. This unit is operated by a video operator to adjust the camera before and during a production. The operational controls for the CCU, when separate, is called a remote control unit (RCU).

Canon Connector: A three pin shielded audio connector used with most professional microphones. Also called XLR connector.

CCTV: Closed-circuit television.

Character Generator (CG): A special effects generator that electronically produces the words, numbers, and possibly logos that are seen on the TV.

Chip Chart: A test chart used by engineers to set up and adjust a video camera.

Clean feed: A video signal complete with camera and video sources without any graphics.

Coaxial Cable: A video cable that can be used for relatively short distances but is susceptible to outside interference.

Color Bars: The color standard used to align cameras and VTRs. Color bars are generated by professional video cameras, SEGs, or color bar generators.

Come and Go: Refers to two cameras situated back-to-back to capture a subject rapidly moving past them. An example would be of a skier coming down a mountain, the director would use the "come" camera as the skier moves toward the cameras and the "go" camera as the skier moves away from the two cameras. One camera could not adequately document the skier.

Commentary Booth: Location where commentators sit or stand to broadcast the event. Generally it is an enclosed booth that shields the talent from weather and unwanted sounds.

Component Signal: An RGB component system that separates the RGB signals through the recorder and keeps them separated on the tape or disk. A Y/C component system refers to the separation of the luminance "Y" (black and white) and chrominance "C" (color) signals inside the video recorder and then combines the signals when recorded onto the tape or disk.

Composite Signal: The video system where the luminance "Y" (black and white), chrominance "C," and sync are encoded together. Includes both NTSC and PAL.

Compound: The area at the venue designated for the parking of production trucks, office trailers, and other vehicles. Also referred to as a Broadcast Compound.

Crane: A camera crane is used to move a camera (and sometimes operator) to high, medium, and low shots. A crane movement is when the camera is moved up or down.

Crawl: The movement of text across the screen usually from the right.

Crosstalk: Unwanted interference caused by audio energy from one line coupling or leaking into adjacent or nearby lines.

CU: Refers to a camera's close-up shot.

Cue Cards: Cards that have the script, script outline or key words on them for the talent to view during a production. The cards are held up to the lens of the camera so that the talent looks as though they are looking at the camera.

Cut: A transition between two video images that is instantaneous, without any gradual change.

Cutaway: A shot that takes the viewer away from the main action briefly to clarify what is being said, or a shot used to combine two similar shots. If the program is showing a close-up of an athlete's interview and the editor wishes to shorten the athlete's lines, using the first and last few words only and eliminating the middle, a cutaway shot of the athlete on the field of play will allow the editor to create an edit that will be unnoticed by the viewer.

DDR: Abbreviation for digital disk recorder.

Depth of Field: The distance between the nearest and farthest objects in focus.

Digital Disk Recorder: A type of hard drive raided array that can be used to play back and record at the same time. It can be used to record super slow motion, split screen, or two inputs and two outputs. This unit is sometimes called an "EVS," which is the name of the original company that manufactured the digital disk recorders. Directors sometimes call them "Elvis" units, a term that comes from EVS.

Digital Television (DTV): Refers to the broadcast of a signal that consists of digital data.

Digital Video Effects (DVE): Working with the switcher (SEG), this equipment is used to create special effects between video images. A DVE could also refer to the actual effect instead of just the equipment.

Dissolve: The gradual transition from one video image to the next. The two images temporarily overlap.

Distorted Sound: Distortion occurs when the output signal from a piece of equipment is greater than the input capabilities of the receiving equipment. This occurs when the microphone output is too strong for the microphone pre-amplifier in the receiving equipment.

Distortion: Any undesired change in a wave form or signal.

Dolby AC-3: The audio standard for DTV broadcasting. This digital audio compression technique can support from 1 to 6 audio channels (5.1 surround). It was designed as a distribution format and is not directly editable.

Dolby E: Designed as a production and transportation format for discrete surround audio, it is editable and supports up to 8 channels of audio.

Dolby Pro-Logic: An advanced form of surround sound that provides a wider listening/viewing area and better channel seperation.

Dolby Surround: The first generation home theater format that outputs to three channels: left, right, and surround (which is usually split into 2 rear speakers).

Dolly: A camera support that allows a camera to move in different directions. It can also refer to the actual camera move (dolly in or dolly out).

Downlink: The segment of a satellite transmission from the satellite to an earth station.

Dropout: A momentary loss or deterioration of the audio or video signal when playing back on videotape. This is generally caused by recording head malfunctions or poor coating on the videotape.

Dry Pair: A pair of wires without any voltage.

Dub: A duplicate copy of a audio or videotape.

EFP: Electronic field production. Television production activity outside the studio usually shot for post-production (not live). See ENG for additional information.

Electronic Still-Store (ESS): Equipment used for the capture, storage, manipulation, if needed, and playback of still images from video. The ESS can capture a still from any video source, such as camera, videotape or computer and store it on a hard drive. A large ESS system can store thousands of these still images, allowing instant retrieval.

ENG: Electronic news gathering. The use of portable, lightweight cameras, VTRs, lighting and sound equipment for the production of news stories or short reports. Usually done for immediate post-production and editing although the pictures can also be transmitted live from the field.

ESS: Abbreviation for Electronic Still-Store.

F-Stops: The calibration markings on the lens that indicate the aperture or diaphragm opening. The larger the f-stop number, the smaller the aperture, which means the larger the depth of field.

Fade: The graduate dissolve of a video image to or from video black.

Fast Lens: A lens that can capture images in low light situations.

FAX: A facilities check to see that all equipment is working correctly.

FAX Sheet: A facilities request form that lists all technical needs for the production.

Feed: Audio or television electronic signal. Also a signal transmission from one program source to another.

Fiber Optics (F/O): Light transmission through optical fibers for communication and signalling. Fiber optic transmission is immune to most electromagnetic interference and common mode noise (hum).

Field Camera: Camera used outside of a studio on the field of play.

Fixed Camera: Same as hard camera.

Fluid Head: A tripod or other camera mount head that uses a type of hydraulic fluid so that the camera pans and tilts will be smooth.

Flypack or Fly Away Kit: At times it is not cost-effective to transport a mobile unit to the site of an event. One of the options is a flypack. Basically it has the majority of the equipment that a mobile unit would have. However, the equipment racks are built into shipping cases that can be assembled like building blocks and then wired together to make a portable production unit. These units can be shipped via standard air, making them a cost-effective alternative to the mobile unit. Flypacks do take more time to assemble on-site. Sometimes these are also referred to as air packs or grab-and-go packs.

Follow Focus: Follow focusing is when a camera operator keeps the subject in focus as the camera or subject moves around.

Font: A specific size and typeface of lettering or numbers.

Font Operator: Operates the character generator to place text and graphics on the television image.

Format: This term can mean a number of different things in television. It could refer to the medium used to record the event, such as Betacam SP or D-5. It could also refer to the show format or the script of the production.

Frame Synchronizer: A digital device that "locks" a video signal to a known timing reference (for example, black burst). Usually used for incoming video signals from a venue or remote that is not synchronised.

Freeze-Frame: A video frame that is continuously replayed, making the image look as though it is a still shot.

FX: Abbreviation for effects.

Gain: The level of amplification for audio/video signals. Operators may need to periodically adjust these levels during a production.

GFX: Abbreviation for graphics.

Grab-and-Go Pack: See Flypack.

Ground Loop: A completed circuit between shielded pairs of a multiple pair created by random contact between shields. An undesirable circuit condition in which interference is created by ground currents when grounds are connected at more than one point.

Hard Camera: Camera mounted in a stationary or fixed position.

Hard Disk Recorder: A computer-type hard drive unit that is used to digitally record audio and video.

HDTV: A superior production format that touts 720 to 1250 scan lines as compared to an analog format of 525 to 625 lines.

HH: Abbreviation for hand-held camera.

High Impedance: The type of microphone's sound generally becomes distorted when used with an audio cable that is longer than 20 feet. These microphones are generally not used in professional applications. A matching transformer must be used if they are connected to low impedance inputs. Also known as high-z.

High-Z: See High Impedance.

HMI Light: A source that emits light that is the same color temperature as the sun.

Hot Head: Robotic controlled camera mount.

Hum: A term used to describe the 60 or 120 cycle per second noise present in the sound of some communications equipment. Usually hum is the result of undesired coupling to a 60-cycle source or the defective filtering of 120-cycle ripple output rectifier.

IFB: Interrupted fold back (or feedback). Communication system used by production personnel to give directions to on-air talent. Program audio is fed on this circuit.

Impedance: Resistance to the flow in an audio signal in a microphone and its cable.

I/O: The panel, generally located on the outside of the mobile unit, where audio and video are patched for inputs and outputs. The I/O panel is sometimes called the broadcast supply panel.

Interactive television: A television program with interactive content and enhancements. It actually combines traditional television viewing with the interactivity that is enjoyed by those communicating through a network like the Internet.

Interlaced scanning: A type of HDTV system that the beam scans every other line from top to bottom.

Isolated Camera (iso): A camera image that is sent to its own recorder, even when used in a multiple camera production. These iso images are usually used for replay shots.

Jib or Jib Arm: This camera mount allows the camera to move up and down and allows the operator to adjust tilt and pan. The jib arm is similar to a camera crane.

Jog or Jogging: The process of moving the videotape forward or backward one frame at a time with a VTR.

Jump Cut: Cutting between two shots that are so similar that the subject appears to jump on screen. The use of a cutaway in between the two shots helps to avoid the jump.

Lavaliere Microphone: A small microphone that can be clipped to a jacket, collar or other piece of clothing. Sometimes it is called a lapel microphone.

Level: The measurement of the strength of a video or audio signal.

Limiter: An effective communications system needs to limit dynamic range to ensure adequate intelligibility to the listener. The limiter/compressor has the following functions: (1) helps loud talkers and soft talkers be heard equally well; (2) prevents loud noises from being severely distorted; and (3) keeps the voltage levels from exceeding system limits.

Line Level: The audio level generally created by a VTR or line mixer output.

Line Monitor: The monitor that shows the video image going to air or video. This is also sometimes called the on-air monitor or program monitor.

Linear Editing: Linear editing systems assemble the edited program in a sequential fashion. Selected shots are copied from the raw footage tape in the source videotape machine to a master tape in the record videotape machine.

Live: Broadcasting an event as it takes place. As compared to live-to-tape or tape for later replay.

Live-on-Tape: The uninterrupted video recording of an event as though it was being broadcast live.

Location Sketch: A rough drawing that includes important dimensions, location of props and buildings, trucks, power source, camera locations, and sun during time of telecast.

Location Survey: A survey done of the production site during the planning stage. This would include reviewing access, lighting, electrical power, possible camera placement, and potential audio problems. Also referred to as a remote survey.

Loosen Shot: Refers to a zoom out or dolly out away from the subject.

Low Impedance: A low impedance microphone over very long cable (more than 1000 feet) loses little sound quality. These microphones are used in professional applications. A matching transformer should be used if they are connected to high impedance inputs. Also known as low-z.

Low-Z: See Low Impedance.

LS: Refers to a camera's long shot.

Master: The original video recording of an event. A dub master is generally a copy of the master that is used to make duplicates so that there is no risk of damaging the master copy.

Master Shot: The main coverage camera.

Master Station: An intercom user station and an intercom system power supply are combined into one package.

Memory Stick: A removable digital media card that is used to transfer camera setup information and scene files for specific video cameras.

Mic Level: The audio level generated by a microphone.

Microwave Relay: A transmission method from remote locations to the transmitter involving the use of several microwave units.

Minicam: A small remote-controlled camera that is generally used for POV shots.

Mixed Zone: An interview area at the venue located between the competition area and the athlete locker rooms where athletes and media, both electronic and written press, "mix" to conduct post-competition interviews.

Mobile Unit: A large truck housing production and technical facilities at a venue, usually parked in the broadcast compound. Also called an OB van.

Monitor: Professional standard television set, generally does not have audio. This could also refer to an audio speaker that monitors the quality of the audio.

Monochrome: Refers to a black-and-white monitor.

MS: Refers to a camera's medium shot.

Neutral Density Filter (ND): A filter that reduces the amount of light coming into the camera without changing the color of the image.

Non-linear Editing: Non-linear editing takes the video footage shot in the field, usually shot on videotape, and digitizes it onto a computer's hard drive. Digitizing means converting the video and audio signals into data files on a computer. The program is then edited using the computer editing software. When the project is complete, the final product may be output back to videotape or distributed using another medium.

NTSC: The television system used by the United States and Japan. It has 525 scan lines.

OB Van: Outside broadcast mobile unit. See Mobile Unit.

Off-line Editing: Shots are assembled to obtain a rough cut to approximate the edited program. typically, the off-line edit has rough audio, graphics are often not included, and special effects are missing. The final production of an off-line edit may be a videotape that approximates the final product and an edit decision list (EDL) that can be used to expedite the on-line edit.

Omnidirectional Microphone: A microphone that is able to pick up audio equally well from all directions.

On-line Editing: In on-line editing, the program is assembled in its final form, complete with music, effects, and titles in a ready to air version.

Out boarded Equipment: This refers to when equipment is taken out of the mobile unit (such as graphics equipment or VTRs) and put in a temporary trailer or building in order to provide more space for personnel or more units for the production.

PA: Abbreviation for production assistant.

PA System: The public address loudspeaker system at the venue.

PAL: Abbreviation for phase alternating line, which is the color television system widely used in Europe and throughout the world. It was derived from the NTSC system but avoids the hue shift caused by phase errors in the transmission path by reversing the phase of the reference color burst on alternate lines. It has 625 lines of resolution.

PAN: Moving the camera from left to right on a stationary camera mount.

Parabolic Microphone: A parabolic dish with a microphone used to capture faraway sound, especially on the field of play.

Patch Field: See I/O.

Personalized Multiple-Camera Angles: When the content provider (cable, satellite, Internet, network) makes it possible for the viewers to choose what camera angles they want to see a particular event in.

Phantom Power: Voltage sent from the audio console to power a condenser mic.

PL: Abbreviation for any type of communication circuit used as an intercom system. PL was derived from the telephone term "party line."

POV Camera: Point-of-view. Usually a mini-camera placed in an unusual position to give the effect of being part of the action or competition.

Preview Monitor: A monitor generally used to show the director what the next shot will look like. A director can also use the preview monitor to review other camera shots before taking them.

Production Switcher: A switching device used to move from one image to another during a production. This is considered to be live editing. This is also referred to as a switcher or special effects generator.

Program Monitor: See Line Monitor.

Progressive Scanning: A type of HDTV system that uses a beam to scan every line from top to bottom.

Punch Block: A panel used to connect or separate audio/telephone cable. This block is also referred to as a "telco block" or a "66 block."

Quick-Release Plate: The plate allows the camera to rapidly remove a camera or place a camera on a tripod or other camera mount.

Rack Focus: This occurs when a camera operator changes the focus, while on-air, from one subject to another subject. This focus change directs the audience where to look in the image.

Rail Camera: See Tracking Camera.

Record VTR: The VTR used to record the program.

Remote Control Unit (RCU): The RCU is the operational control panel for a camera control unit. The RCU is separate from the CCU.

Remote Survey: See Location Survey.

RF: A camera that uses radio frequency to transmit the video signal.

RGB: The three primary colors used in video processing: red, green, and blue.

Roll: The movement of text up or down the video screen. The director would tell the graphics operator to "roll credits."

Run-ups: Introductory sequences before the broadcast.

Safe Area/Safe Title Area: Roughly the center 80% of the scanning area, where all graphics or important video information should be placed in order to make sure that it is seen by the viewer. The term safe title area is used when referring specifically to the graphic area.

Satellite News Gathering (SNG): The use of a satellite system to transmit the video program from the remote site to the receiver (station, network, or home production facility).

Scaffold Mount: These mounts are primarily used with hard cameras and are mounted on the front rail of scaffolding. The advantage is that it allows the camera to tilt through its entire range. Scaffold mounting also gives the operator more space behind the camera for maximum freedom of movement.

Scanning Area: The area of the video image that is seen on the camera or in the graphics or on-air monitor.

SECAM: The video system used by France and many countries of the former USSR.

Segment Rundown: A list of the order of what will appear on the production within a specific segment.

Selective Focus: Shooting the subject with a shallow depth of field so that the primary subject is sharply in focus while everything else is out of focus.

Shader: The video operator is sometimes called a shader.

Shading: The video operator shades the cameras by adjusting the image contrast, color and black-and-white levels of the incoming video. The shading generally occurs at the camera control unit (CCU).

Shore Power: Electrical power sufficient to power production needs located at the venue.

Shot Sheet: A list of every camera shot that the director wants the camera operator to get with their specific camera.

Show Format: See Format.

Shuttle: The fast-forward and fast-rewind movement of the videotape as a VTR operator looks for a specific segment of the tape.

Signal: Any visible or audible indication that can convey information. Also the information conveyed through a communication system.

Signal-to-Noise Ratio: The ratio of noise to good picture information within a video signal, usually expressed in dB. Digital source equipment is theoretically capable of producing pure noise-free images that have an infinite signal-to-noise ratio.

Slo-mo: A VTR that can replay a videotape in slow motion.

Source VTR: The VTR that is sending the video images to the switcher.

Special Effects Generator (SEG): A switching device used to move from one image to another during a production. This is considered to be live editing. This is also referred to as a switcher or production switcher.

Spreader: A base for a tripod that stabilizes the legs and prevents them from spreading.

SSM: Abbreviation for super slow motion camera.

Stand-by: This refers to two different areas of television production. It could refer to a cue by the director, producer or stage manager to stop what you are doing and wait for instructions concerning an action that is about to happen. It could also refer to a button on a VTR that allows the tape heads to go up to speed before the video-tape is started.

Stand-up: On-camera commentator speaking directly to a camera.

Standard Definition (SD): SD generally refers to an NTSC or PAL analog image of interlaced video.

Steadicam: A device designed to stabilize a camera. The camera is attached to a special vest that is worn by the camera operator. An accomplished Steadicam operator has the freedom to walk or run, providing fluid shots.

Stick Mic: A slang term for a handheld microphone.

Still-store: See Electronic Still-Store.

Storyboard: A sheet that shows audio, any special audio or video effects, and the scene the camera will be capturing. It may also be marked for special camera or talent moves.

Strike: Refers to the tear down of all equipment at the end of a production.

Switcher: See Production Switcher.

Talent: A name for all performers who appear on television.

Tally Light: A light on technical equipment indicating a camera or other device is on line as the output of the video mixer.

Tape Format: Refers to the type of videotape that is used to record the event. Examples would include: Digital Betacam, DVC PRO 50, and D-5.

Tapeless Recording: Refers to audio and/or video recording of the event on a hard drive or disc.

TD: Abbreviation for technical director.

Teleprompter: A device that projects computer-generated text on a piece of reflective glass over the lens of the camera. It is designed to allow talent to read a script while looking directly at the camera.

Termination: When there are looping video inputs on equipment, all unused looping inputs must be terminated in 75 ohms to ensure proper signal levels and to minimize reflections. A male BNC connector that contains a 75 ohms resister load is typically used. Balanced audio requires termination at 600 ohms. If devices are designed to loop, like distribution amplifiers, it is sometimes necessary to use a 600 ohm resistor to terminate the path.

Tighten-up: Refers to a zoom in or dolly in to the subject.

Tilt: Whenever the camera moves up or down on a stationary camera mount.

Time Base Corrector: A device that processes a video signal and generally allows for stable playback of an unstable video image.

Time Code: A code that is laid down on video-tape to give each frame a unique number. This code is then used for logging, editing, and playback to find the correct image on the tape.

Tone: An audio signal that is consistently zero dB and generally recorded onto videotapes at the beginning of a production in order to properly set up the playback equipment. Generally the tone is recorded at the same time as the color bars.

Tracking: Tracking has multiple definitions in television. It can be an alignment adjustment of the video head to allow for proper play-back of the video and audio on a videotape. Tracking can also identify a camera/mount movement from left to right.

Tracking Camera: This automated or manually controlled television camera follows the motion of the object it is shooting. This camera can be mounted on rails, cables or other devices that allow it to move with the object it is shooting.

Transponder: A satellite's own receiver and transmitter.

Triax: A coax-type camera cable that includes three conductors.

Tripod: A three-legged camera support that is available in a variety of sizes. They have telescoping legs and may have multiple sections for height adjustment. A pan and tilt head is mounted on the top of these tripods.

Truck: A camera and mount movement to the left or right.

Two-shot: Framing two people within one shot.

Unbalanced Line: A transmission line in which voltage on the two conductors are unequal with respect to ground—for example, a coaxial cable.

Unidirectional Microphone: A microphone that is sensitive to sound coming from one direction. The most popular unidirectional is the shotgun microphone.

Uplink: Earth station transmitter used to send video and audio signals from the earth to a satellite.

Uplink Truck: A truck that is equipped with uplink capabilities that can send both video and audio signals to a receiver via a satellite.

VandA: Literally, video and audio circuit from one site to another. A VandA is comprised of one video circuit along with a minimum of two audio channels.

Vector Scope: Used by engineers to monitor adjustments made to decks, cameras, and frame synchronizers.

Venue: A specific location where an event is to take place.

Video Noise: Unwanted interference within the electrical system that causes "snow" on the video image.

Video Operator: Responsible for adjusting the cameras for optimal image quality before and during a production.

Voice-Over (VO): Refers to when the talent is speaking over related video but not seen in the image.

VTR: Videotape recorder.

VTR Log: A record of every shot on the tape. This lists all shots, whether good or bad, using time code as a reference. The list generally includes space to make comments about the shots stating what the quality is and relevant details. This log can be created on-the-fly (live) or compiled after the shoot.

Wave Form Monitor: A device used to monitor the video signal and its synchronizing pulses.

Wet Pair: A standard telephone cable that has a twisted pair with roughly 70 volts on it.

Whip-Pan: A fast pan that keeps the subject in the viewfinder. Generally the subject is blurred.

Wipe: A transition between two video images that takes the shape of a specified pattern. Wipes are made by special effect generators.

WS: Refers to a wide shot and is the same thing as an LS (long shot).

XCU: Abbreviation for extreme close-up. Can also be abbreviated as ECU.

XLR: The most commonly used XLR is a three pin shielded audio connector used with most professional microphones. Also called canon connector. However, the same type of connector is available with two to five pins, depending on the application.

XLS: Abbreviation for extreme long shot. Can also be abbreviated as ELS.

XY Pairs: A matched pair of microphones used for recording audio at a venue.

Zebra Stripes: Black lines that are seen in a zebra-equipped television camera that aid the camera operator in making video level adjustments.

Index